THE DEVELOPMENT OF
MODERN RIDING

OTHER BOOKS BY THE AUTHOR

. . . .

TEN TALKS ON HORSEMANSHIP
(in collaboration with Captain S. Kournakoff)

JUMPING THE HORSE

THE DEFENSE OF THE FORWARD SEAT
(in collaboration with Captain S. Kournakoff)

THE FORWARD SEAT

RIDING FORWARD

MORE ABOUT THE FORWARD SEAT

MORE ABOUT RIDING FORWARD

BE A BETTER HORSEMAN

COMMON SENSE HORSEMANSHIP

SCHOOLING YOUR HORSE

RUSSIAN HUSSAR

HOW A HORSE JUMPS

The
DEVELOPMENT OF
MODERN
RIDING

. . . .

Vladimir S. Littauer

HOWELL
BOOK HOUSE
New York

COLLIER MACMILLAN CANADA
Toronto

MAXWELL MACMILLAN INTERNATIONAL
New York   Oxford   Singapore   Sydney

Howell Book House
Macmillan Publishing Company
866 Third Avenue, New York, NY 10022

Collier Macmillan Canada, Inc.
1200 Eglinton Avenue East, Suite 200
Don Mills, Ontario M3C 3N1

Library of Congress Cataloging-in-Publication Data
Littauer, Vladimir S.
The development of modern riding / Vladimir S. Littauer.
p.   cm.
Includes bibliographical references and index.
ISBN 0-87605-897-7
1. Horsemanship.   I. Title.
SF309.L512   1991
798.2—dc20   90-48828   CIP

Macmillan books are available at special discounts for bulk purchases for sales promotions, premiums, fund-raising, or educational use. For details, contact:

Special Sales Director
Macmillan Publishing Company
866 Third Avenue
New York, NY 10022

10   9   8   7   6   5   4   3   2   1

Printed in the United States of America

To the Horse—
Who Took the Rap

Contents

. . . .

Illustrations ix
Foreword xiii
Preface to the First Edition xvii

BY WAY OF INTRODUCTION
1. Jumping Is a New Game 3
2. In Retrospect 12

THE ARISTOCRATIC PERIOD
3. Early Dressage Riders 25
4. Early Dressage Teachers 37
5. Early Dressage's Place in Life 50
6. The Substance of Early Dressage 71
7. The Last of the Old Regime ˙89

THE MILITARY PERIOD
8. Baucher versus d'Aure 107
9. Lesser Lights 128
10. James Fillis 155
11. Federico Caprilli 175

THE DEMOCRATIC PERIOD
12. Since Caprilli 197
13. The 20th Century in Print in America 227

Contents

14. International Competitions in the 20th Century   251
15. Modern European Literaure   267
16. The Long Arm of the Cavalry   287

     Bibliography   295
     Index   299

Illustrations

. . . .

The Polish Rider by Rembrandt   2
Cover of the program of a London Horse Show in 1876   7
Medieval animal trainers' horses   27
18th century "airs above the ground"   29
A 17th century fancy-dress hunt   30
The hunting lodge of the Duke of Savoy   31
Showing horses in hand in the 18th century   34
Work in double pillars   41
Courbettes on a circle   42
Work around a single pillar   43
The Duke of Newcastle executing a ballotade   46
Apotheosis of the Duke of Newcastle   48
Mid-16th century German armor   51
Jousting armor   52
15th century spurs   53
A bit by Pignatelli   54
A severe 17th century bit   54
Horses caparisoned for jousting in the 17th century   57
Jousting in Paris in the 17th century   59
Louis XIII riding at the Quintain   62
Horses pulling baroque sleighs   64
Horses caparisoned for the carousel's parade   66
The horse ballet of a carousel   67

Schooling in the 16th century 75
Some Dressage movements of the 18th century 80
An aristocratic rider in the 18th century 84
English foxhunters of the 18th century 86
An 18th century study of the horse's anatomy 98
Astley's circus in 1810 101
Baucher on Capitaine making an abrupt halt 110
Baucher on Capitaine making a Pesade 110
Flexions in hand 117
A 19th century hussar's uniform 125
Executives and instructors of the Officers' Cavalry School,
    St. Petersburg, 1906 126
Entry of the allied armies into Paris, 1814 130
British uniforms of 1856 131
A gentleman's stable in 1820 132
Early instantaneous photographs of the horse jumping 133
Early instantaneous photographs of the horse galloping 136
A Victorian riding school 139
A geometrical approach to the horse's conformation 140
Instantaneous photography by Muybridge 142
A 19th century attempt at analyzing the horse's locomotion ... 143
Changing fashions in English foxhunters 151
Cantering on three legs 157
The "gallop to the rearward" 159
Fillis' "ordinary trot" 161
The Russian army regulation seat at the end of
    the 19th century 162
High School in the 19th century 166
Work in hand under Fillis 167
A Russian Cossack at the end of the 19th century 172
A Russian mounted policeman at the end of
    the 19th century 172
Tartars racing, 1800 173
Caprilli jumping 182
Italian cavalryman jumping before 1906 182
A later Italian officer exhibiting the perfected Forward Seat ... 183

. . . .

The successive phases of the jump as revealed by the motion
  picture camera   204–209
Transition from a trot to a canter as revealed by the motion
  picture camera   210
Children grooming horses   214
Modern junior jumping   215
The Forward Seat on postage stamps   224
"Travail à la Longe"   231
Colonel Chamberlin at a posting trot   240
Colonel Chamberlin at a canter, sitting in the saddle   240
Colonel Chamberlin at a gallop, riding in stirrups   241
Junior Riding at Madison Square Garden   262
The Forward Seat in the United States in the
  middle thirties   280

Foreword

. . . .

VLADIMIR S. LITTAUER, author of *The Development of Modern Riding*, was a very interesting and very unusual man. Since his book speaks for itself, I would like to devote these prefatory comments mainly to the man himself, whose earlier writings I devoured as a child, and whom I was later privileged to know personally for many years. It has always seemed to me that Littauer's life and personality both encompassed a fascinating range of contrasts and even paradoxes. It was entirely characteristic that although he lived to an age at which many are overcome by cynicism and withdraw from life, he retained his interests and especially his youthfully ardent passion for horses, right to the end.

Littauer was born in Russia's Ural Mountains, traditionally the border between Europe and Asia, in 1892. He grew up in St. Petersburg and after graduating as an officer from the Nicholas Cavalry School, he entered the 1st Sumski Hussar Regiment of the Imperial Russian Cavalry. (His absorbing reminiscences of these military years were published in 1965 under the title *Russian Hussar*.)

His formal equestrian training was based on traditional French Dressage doctrines as codified by James Fillis. (He later turned away from these methods, but always respected what gifted horsemen could accomplish with them.) Even then he must have been aware, however, that notable competitive results were being achieved in Europe by a handful of Russian officers who rode in a radically different style. And he would rightly have attributed their successes, which included consecutive victories in London's Nations' Cup in 1912 and 1913, to the fact that they had been permitted to study Captain Federico Caprilli's new *systema* of forward riding in Pinerolo, Italy.

Following the Revolution and its harrowing aftermath, Littauer escaped from Siberia with his father and sister, and eventually found his way via Canada to the United States. A period of manual labor followed, during which he learned his new language, and then in 1927 a chance encounter with two other former officers led to the establishment of a riding school in New York City, Boots and Saddles.

At first the three émigré officers taught the methods they had learned in the Imperial Cavalry. However, given at last the chance to experiment with the still-revolutionary precepts of Caprilli, they soon became persuasive exponents and advocates of forward riding. Despite the Great Depression the school prospered, and before long there were branches in Westchester and Connecticut and on Long Island. Historically American equitation had always looked to English and Irish models, but now a keen interest in the "forward seat" was developing, and Boots and Saddles was the most accessible place for the progressive horseman to learn about it.

In the midst of a busy teaching schedule Littauer somehow found time to start writing about these new ideas, and within the next few years produced *Jumping the Horse* (1931), *The Defense of the Forward Seat* (with Sergei Kournakoff, 1934), *Riding Forward* (1936), and *More About Riding Forward* (1938). By the time he left the school in the late 1930s, Littauer was recognized as one of the most influential teachers, lecturers, and equestrian authors in the country.

For the next thirty-odd years he remained much in demand as a teacher and clinician at schools, hunt clubs, and colleges (including a long relationship with Sweet Briar College in Virginia) and also taught privately from his home base on Long Island. His literary productivity continued unabated: *Be a Better Horseman* (1941) was followed by his most comprehensive book of riding technique, *Common Sense Horsemanship* (1951), and *Schooling Your Horse* (1956). The present volume, his personal favorite, was originally published under the title *Horseman's Progress* in 1962, followed by *Russian Hussar* (1965), and finally, *How a Horse Jumps*, the last two being published in England. Littauer retired in the late 1970s, but retained an active interest in equestrian matters—from the earliest origins of riding through the present era—until his death.

One might expect that the man whose life has been so briefly recounted would be an interesting person, but Volodya (as he permitted his friends to call him) was truly unforgettable. Though a self-confessed realist, he was in fact extremely idealistic, and loved theoretical ideas even if the facts didn't work out. He was a born bibliophile, with a private equestrian library that would admit few peers. (The reason why the excellent bibliography for the present work notes only the editions actually consulted, and not necessarily the first editions in every case, is because these were the editions on Littauer's shelves.) Not particularly interested in competitive riding per se, he was far more concerned with the needs of the average rider and the average horse. Even so, his influence extended, both directly and through such disciples as Jane Marshall Dillon, to many competitive riders, among them Bernie Traurig, Kathy Kusner, and Olympic Gold Medalist Joe Fargis.

Though Littauer's personal manner never lost a faintly military, distinctly patrician fastidiousness, his teaching style was serious but often enlivened by a sense of humor, though he could at times be quite severe. He was an extraordinarily stimulating person with whom to discuss equestrian techniques, for while his knowledge was profound and he often expressed himself strongly, he was basically very tolerant of dissent. He used to say, "One learns through argument."

All of these qualities are clearly reflected on the following pages which are not only "scholarly, but by no means dull," as a noted bibliographer has written, but something even rarer: wise without being pontifical. An evening with the Littauers in their charming old Syosset home, surrounded by dogs, cats, books, and memorabilia, was always a great treat, especially since Vladimir's wife (and sometime collaborator) Mary fully equaled his breadth of interest and erudition. I find it quite impossible to think of him without seeing the twinkle in his eyes and remembering his warmth, his humor, and his enormous generosity of spirit, and I am sure this is true of the whole army of riders whose lives he touched.

Vladimir S. Littauer, formerly Captain, 1st (Sumski) Hussars, died peacefully at home in August 1989. He was in his ninety-seventh year.

WILLIAM C. STEINKRAUS

Preface to the First Edition

. . . .

ALTHOUGH my name appears as author on the title page of this book, I have my doubts whether I have a full claim to this. In order to "render unto Caesar the things which are Caesar's" it is perhaps fair to tell how this book was really written.

After the first tentative draft of a chapter had been read aloud to my wife, its substance discussed and often argued, altered, augmented or reduced, she would attempt to turn the second re-typed version into some sort of respectable English. In this state it would be passed on to my old pupil and friend, Mrs. Nancy M. Graham, only to be promptly returned, almost invisible beneath the red pencilling. To my no small satisfaction I found that people could disagree about the proper use of their mother tongue. When Mrs. Graham's corrections and suggestions had been incorporated or (occasionally) discarded, the newest version of the chapter would be mailed for similar treatment to New Mexico, to my old friends Mr. and Mrs. David H. Munroe. Since they are most knowledgeable in matters of history, equitation and languages, their comments and criticisms were invaluable.

A copy of this supposedly finished cooperative effort would finally reach my publishers' sporting book editor, Eugene V.

. . . .

Connett, who, in the past, edited four of my books, two of which he published when he had the Derrydale Press. His red pencil still found constructive work to do.

I am profoundly grateful to all these people who gave their time and effort so generously, and I particularly appreciate the fact that we are all still friends. I would also like to thank the many others, too numerous to list, who had to sit and listen to different versions of various chapters, and whose verbal comments were often helpful.

I am also indebted to Mrs. Graham for the translation of Federico Caprilli's writings from the Italian, and to my wife for helping me with many translations from the French.

My thanks go as well to Mr. Stephen V. Grancsay of the Metropolitan Museum of Art, who very kindly discussed the medieval material with me and furnished pertinent information.

VLADIMIR S. LITTAUER

Syosset, New York
December 1961

BY WAY OF INTRODUCTION

The Polish Rider

At a time when Western aristocracy was playing the elaborate game of Dressage, the distance-covering horsemen of Eastern Europe continued to go their traditional, relaxed and practical way, using a position which foreshadowed the modern Forward Seat. *(Copyright The Frick Collection, New York)*

CHAPTER 1

Jumping Is a New Game

. . . .

S OMETHING new and important has happened in the riding world in the course of our century—that is, the sudden rise of interest in competitive jumping. This new sport, which first started in a small way less than one hundred years ago, is fast becoming the most popular game of the time.

Why? Why didn't it attract people earlier? Why didn't horsemen of two hundred years ago think of it? What are the reasons for its overwhelming success today? Why are present methods of schooling and riding jumpers so different from those practiced sixty years ago?

For years these and similar questions have made me curious. Although from time to time I have guessed at the answers, I always realized that only equestrian history could fully explain our present attitudes.

It is obvious that the history of riding is merely a small segment of larger human history; the former has thus naturally reflected the trends of the latter. The aims which riding pursues today, and the forms it has consequently taken, result from a combination of social evolution and revolution. But revolution itself is inevitably shaped by that against which it revolts.

So for some time I have been trying to trace the history of

educated (reasoned) riding in the Western world, particularly the development of equestrian thought. This book is the result. I have written it mainly to help today's horseman find the place of riding in today's world, and his place in today's riding. If it seems sometimes written with a personal slant, this is because evaluations of circumstances are almost always personal, and yet without them it is difficult to stimulate that thought which, whether it agrees or violently disagrees, is the basis of an intelligent approach to any subject. The bulk of the book will consist of an historical sketch; later on I shall discuss the present, with all its varying tendencies, and the gradual ascendency of the new type of riding, in the development of which I have actively participated.

I became a professional riding teacher in the fall of 1927, and am still teaching. One might be expected to have become bored saying the same things over and over again for thirty-five years, and I imagine that if one were merely to repeat the same old formula day in and day out at every lesson, it would be rather tiresome. But there has been no necessity for this in a century that has offered so many opportunities for original and creative work. The latter, in the case of many professionals, has more than compensated for the hours monopolized by such routine remarks as "heels down," or "look straight ahead."

Unquestionably there have been stagnant periods in the history of riding, corresponding to placid epochs of human life, but the century in which we live has not been one of them. Life has changed drastically all over the world in the course of the last fifty years. Since the First World War people have developed new interests and new ambitions, in the saddle as well as out of it. At the same time that riding began to take a new road, the proportion of people of moderate means indulging in the sport was greatly increased, while the number of big private stables diminished; the competitive spirit, so typical of our century, started to play a big role in amateur equestrian games; the

4

. . . .

improvement of horseflesh provided even the average horseman with a better mount; and no one had as much time as before to spend on actual riding. These and many other factors, taken together, necessitated a revaluation of old principles in riding and schooling horses, as well as in methods of teaching.

After all, a realistic point of view focussed on practical results, rather than devotion to the doctrines of the past, is what advances skills or sports and adjusts them to contemporary conditions. Anyone with the imagination of a horseman, with sympathy for the horse, who has been in touch with contemporary life, and who has been able to think independently, has had the opportunity in our century of leading a very interesting equestrian life.

I imagine that many young riders of today don't even realize that the origin of their favorite type of riding, competitive jumping in any of its various forms, is rather recent, and that jumping fences, even in the hunting field, does not go back to a very remote past. Today in many countries fields still are not enclosed. Fashionable stag hunting in France is still traditionally practiced (at least in many cases) along the well-kept avenues of great forests, and in England, the homeland of foxhunting, the fields were not enclosed to any great degree by hedges or fences before the 18th century. To be more precise, the slow process of enclosure began at the time of Queen Elizabeth and was completed only around the year 1850 in Queen Victoria's reign.

"Before the days of enclosures, it is probable that no hunting man was ever called upon to ride over any obstacle more formidable than a ditch or narrow stream; there were no hedges, no stake-and-binders, and post-and-rail were a pleasure—or downfall, as the case might be—which awaited later generations; so that jumping, as we know it now, did not come into the argument with regard to hunting." (*Steeplechasing*, by John Hislop, E. P. Dutton & Co. Inc., New York.)

The first recorded example of competitive jumping—and it was in the form of a steeplechase—took place in Ireland in 1752; it was a match between two gentlemen. "In due course matches developed into races with three or more runners, the earliest of this description being held in 1792. . . . It was only by the middle of the 19th century that steeplechasing had become firmly established." (J. Hislop) The first Grand National was run at Aintree in 1839. And yet steeplechasing (always a sport of the few) preceded arena jumping by many years. As a matter of fact, I can find no reference to the latter (that is, in a form familiar to us today) before the last quarter of the 19th century.

The earliest document I have come across relating to arena jumping is a program of a London horse show in 1876; the cover of this "catalogue" is among the illustrations for this book. It was a big five-day show, in which over four hundred horses participated, in hunter (on the flat), pony, cob and other divisions. Horses entered in the show had the right to take part without additional fee in a "competition for leaping horses." There were four leaping classes for horses of different sizes, with a total of about seventy entries. The catalogue stated that every day after the conclusion of the afternoon program "the hurdles will be put up, that the competitors for the Leaping Prizes may practice."

The rules for the "leaping competition" clearly indicate that it was still in the cradle. Here are some:

> The fences will be such as the Judges select.
>
> Every rider may, if he pleases, take two turns round the ring to warm up his horse before commencing the competition.
>
> In case of a horse going through, or breaking down a fence the fence shall be made up again, and (if Judges think fit) one more trial shall be allowed. . . .

6

. . . .

All eight judges of these competitions were M's.F.H. Many of the riders were grooms, for the catalogue states that "The Manager will reward grooms who ride well, whether they win or not. A Gentleman in the same circumstances will have the offer of a Whip or pair of Spurs for superior horsemanship."

In the previous year (1875) officers of the Cavalry School of Saumur were demonstrating High School at a show at Nantes, France. A few of them also jumped obstacles, riding without

AGRICULTURAL HALL,
1876.

CATALOGUE

OF THE

THIRTEENTH ANNUAL

HORSE SHOW

LONDON.

PUBLISHED BY THE AGRICULTURAL HALL COMPANY (LIMITED).

M'Orquodale & Co., Printers, London, N.W.

PRICE ONE SHILLING.

This was then a rich man's sport. Entry fees in hunter classes were £2/2/-, while the price of a "superior hunting saddle," advertised in the catalogue, was £5/5/-. The first prize (cash) was £60/-/-.

A social slant on the period is given by the stipulation in the program that "from 1 to 2 o'clock horses fed and grooms dine."

stirrups—a High School rider's, rather than a hunting man's practice.

Unquestionably there must have been other isolated competitions in jumping even a few years earlier, but in any case this sport was developing very slowly and was of no great importance even in the nineties of the century.

James Fillis, in his book, *Principes de Dressage et d'Equitation*, first published in 1890, in his Conclusion says:

> To be an accomplished rider, or at least to approach as close to perfection as possible, one should be able to pass the five following tests:
>
>   1. To ride a bad actor;
>   2. To ride a steeplechase;
>   3. To ride a trotting match;
>   4. To ride a flat race;
>   5. To know how to school and ride a school [High School] horse.

As you see, horse-show jumping is not mentioned. Later I shall tell you at length how ridiculously and briefly jumping was usually treated in books of the 19th century, while a few paragraphs normally sufficed for it in earlier works.

But once established, horse-show jumping progressed swiftly, and the first international competition in riding over obstacles took place in London in 1907. The last comer to the field of today's competitive jumping was the "Three-Day Event," which had its start as an all-around test for an officer's charger, and was held as a military event in the first equestrian Olympic Games in 1912.

For many present day young riders, both in England and on the continent, and in many parts of the United States, riding devoid of jumping has little attraction. But this was not the case with our great-grandfathers and their predecessors, for most of them enjoyed horses without riding over obstacles (except possibly when foxhunting). This was true since the horse was first backed. And after the middle of the 16th century when riding on the flat was first given a scholastic background, the possibility of obtaining from the horse a variety of intricate movements at slow collected gaits seems to have fascinated especially continental horsemen much more than fast but uneducated riding to hounds.

In 1550 there appeared in Italy a book written by a Neapolitan gentleman named Federico Grisone; this may be considered as the work on equitation that officially inaugurated a new educated type of riding and established a pattern for the next three hundred and fifty years. As a matter of fact, this form of riding, which today we call Dressage, is to some extent still with us.

Here and now is probably the place to clarify the use and meaning of the word *dressage*. This is a French word, and in its native tongue it originally meant simply *schooling*. But since during several centuries the only horses that were really schooled were those being prepared for manege riding, and since for so long the chief source and inspiration of this type of riding was France, the word came to be generally and often far from accurately adopted to signify manege riding, including the modern program of High School. I shall use the term in this modern interpretation. But today Dressage is no longer, as it was until around 1900, the only educated type of riding in existence; good modern Forward Riding is educated too.

The modern method for cross-country riding and jumping originated in Italy. Although clumsy and isolated attempts to base cross-country riding on other principles than those of Dressage can be traced back one hundred and fifty years, these ideas were presented in a well-rounded, logical form for the first time only at the turn of this century. This new type of riding, based on the proposition that "there is little in common between ring

9

riding and cross-country riding" was initiated by an Italian cavalry officer, Captain Federico Caprilli, around the year 1900. Today we call it "the Italian Method," "the Natural Method," or "Forward Riding."

This method appeared on the threshold of a century which was to be oriented toward speed, sport and efficiency. Had it been devised earlier it might well have died still-born. As it was, it took a good score of years before its significance was generally recognized. Then it brought with it many innovations in methods both of riding and of schooling horses.

We live today at a time of development of the principles proposed by Caprilli and of adjustment of them to the new forms that equestrian sport has taken. On the other hand, Dressage goes on, practiced by a few for its own sake and adapted by some as a preparation for cross-country riding and jumping. The attempts to combine it with fast riding across uneven terrain and over obstacles have led to much controversy. There had been arguments, some of them leading to duels, even at a time when fundamentally only one school of thought existed. As a matter of fact, the manege riding of former days developed and grew to be an art as the result of innovations and hence arguments. Today when we have side by side two equally educated, although in aims and techniques drastically different forms of riding, variances of opinion are bound to be yet more prevalent.

But in addition to the argument between these two schools of thought there is still much work to be done within Forward Riding itself. It has developed tremendously during the last quarter century, and yet many details of its present state surely can be further improved.

Through my formal equestrian education and through the manner in which I was officially required to ride in the Russian army in my youth, I was once upon a time a Dressage rider. Later on, when faced with teaching civilians in this country, I began to think more seriously about the possibilities opened up by Caprilli, and I found that they would require practical adaptation for conditions rather different from those obtaining in the Italian cavalry at the beginning of the century. Not only were civilian amateurs, old, young, plump, slender, timid or foolhardy, weak or strong, indifferent or "mad about riding," with a variety of aims, very different pupils from the members of an officers' corps, but much of Caprilli's writing even for the latter had been no more than mere outlines. It became imperative to fill in these outlines and to adapt them to the schooling of horses in modern civilian life and the teaching of modern amateur riders. Many of us have worked toward it. The past twenty-five years have witnessed the blossoming of a totally new form of educated riding. This is the first time in three hundred and fifty years that anything comparable has happened in the field of equitation; the opportunities for imaginative work have been exceptional, as have been the corresponding satisfactions. It is hard to see how any horseman could have been bored working in such dynamic times.

CHAPTER 2

In Retrospect

. . . .

WHAT proportion of the alterations in social conditions over the centuries is brought about by popular reaction against tradition or privilege, by the imposition of the will of a single powerful individual, as the result of wars, plagues or famines, of new ideas and inventions, or discoveries of new gold mines or new continents, is for the historian to decide.

Whatever has caused changes through the ages in the social order, the mode of riding has always changed with them. The past shows that altered circumstances of life alter human points of view, interests, behavior and ideals. This is true not only of what we do but of how we do it. People in different periods have spoken, danced, sung, dressed, fought, eaten and even greeted each other differently. Riding as a part of life has never been practiced in a vacuum; it has been as subject to changing modes of living as anything else. But this is a fact of which some of us need to be reminded.

Throughout the three thousand odd years of its history in different parts of the world, riding has pursued different aims and assumed different forms. For instance, riding today in Mongolia has little in common with that in an American hunter show. Riding will also vary in varying parts of the same country, at the same time. For example, not so long ago riding in the United States was rather sharply divided along geographical lines into Eastern, Western and Southern types, each with its intrinsic style. The type of riding in any one locality also changes with the times. Look at the photographs of American foxhunters jumping in the early days of this century, and then at those of our young people jumping in today's shows. What a striking difference there is between both the form of the riders and the manner in which the horses jump. Obviously the method of riding over obstacles has changed.

While the picture of riding in the past is usually presented in a simplified form which gives an aspect of uniformity to the period, it is well to remember that riding was never more homogeneous than any other human activity. Far from it—at least in civilized communities and in recent centuries. Along with the major sport of the moment there have usually existed other minor games. So today in this country, besides the thousands whose sport is jumping, there are the comparatively few who play polo, the many who fancy gaited horses, and those who may ride Western even in New York State. It is possible that in the future, if today's tendency to standardize all forms of human activities continues, the time will come when the world's taste will agree not merely on Coca-Cola but on riding as well. If this should happen, my guess is that the first form it will take will be jumping.

Whenever in this and the following chapters I state that the popular riding of today is jumping, or that in the 18th century it was Dressage, this will merely signify that each of these attracted in its time many more serious horsemen and stimulated more interest than any other form of riding, to the point where many efforts were made to improve that particular type of equitation. Thus in our century many more original books, representing research on the subject, have been written about jumping than about any other equestrian game. This search for better methods, rather than the number of people involved in a type of riding, is what makes history as far as educated horsemanship goes. Dressage in its time had as many innovations as the art of jumping has today.

There is nothing black or white in the history of riding. Every period since the Renaissance, when man for the first time since antiquity began to theorize on practical things, has had its own original ideas, its opposition to them, as well as points of view outside the main stream of thought. Thus, in the century that could be called the Dressage Century, there existed, side by side with an enlightened attitude toward the newest in manege riding, a traditionalism that clung stubbornly to the good old ways, as well as the completely pragmatic and quite uninterested approach of those people who simply rode to get places. Although the latter were certainly in the vast majority, it is to be noted that not then, nor at any other period, were they the ones to write the history of educated equitation. Improved techniques of equitation have come about almost always as the result of original thinking on the part of a few people in the field.

Although, as far as we can tell, people may have been writing about horses for three thousand years before the 16th century, when the Dressage type of equitation first made its appearance, we have no trace of anyone having previously formulated a complete, reasoned method of riding.

Indeed, the earliest extant work on horses seems to have been written some 500 years before the *ridden* horse began to take over seriously from the *driven* horse. It was composed in the 15th century B.C. by one Kikkulis, a Mitannian in the service of the Hittites, then overlords of eastern Asia Minor. It does a very exhaustive job of a day by day schedule for conditioning chariot horses over a period of several months.

Some thousand years later (at the beginning of the 4th century B.C.) a Greek, Xenophon, wrote a booklet for a cavalry officer on the selection, management and riding of horses. Less than twenty pages (out of a total of fifty) printed in large type and with extra-large margins (in my English edition of 1802) are devoted to riding proper—not sufficient to describe the seat alone in modern books.

The briefness of Xenophon's writing and the primitiveness of his techniques preclude the text being considered an important work on horsemanship. But many of his suggestions are immortal simply because they are based on an understanding of the horse's psychology, which has probably changed little since his days. His quite elementary advice is given with such engaging common sense that it is easy to forget that it all pertains to riding on a blanket, the saddle not yet having been invented. But even so, this can be considered as the first attempt to *reason* about riding that has come down to us.

Were I to write on the history of riding in general, and not merely on its educated manifestation, I would find Xenophon invaluable, for he throws much interesting light on equestrian life and habits of the time. For example:

> The groom ought to know too, that a muzzle should be put on the horse, both when he takes him out to be dressed, or to stretch his legs; and indeed he should at all times when taken out without a bridle, have a muzzle. . . .
>
> But when a horse is to be led, we do not approve his being led from behind. . . . [This was an inheritance from the days when the horse was primarily driven, not ridden.]
>
> . . . it is proper that the stable should be in such a part of the dwelling, where the master can see the horse oftenest . . .
>
> . . . the manger should be constructed so that it would be no more possible to steal the horse's food out of the manger . . .
>
> . . . one advanced in years should occupy himself with his family, his friends, and with state or military affairs, rather than with the breaking of colts . . . and whoever knows as

much as I do about the breaking of colts, will unquestionably
send his colt out to be broke.

Besides the fact that many riding enthusiasts are unaware of
the real components of educated riding, there are probably two
reasons why this conspicuously incomplete book has frequently
been hailed as one that established the basis for equitation in
the centuries to follow. The first is the circumstance that it did
mention collection! The second is that many people, unfamiliar
with what the Greece of Xenophon's time had achieved in other
fields, are impressed by the fact that someone wrote about riding
as far back as twenty-three hundred years ago.

As you will read in my later chapters, it is during the past
fifty years only (out of the four centuries of its actual existence)
that educated riding has taken a form not based on collection.
To our great-grandfathers, paragraphs such as those I am about
to quote meant that their principles were already established by
Xenophon:

> . . . when he [the horse] goes towards other horses, espe-
> cially if they are mares, then he raises his neck, bends his
> head with quickness, lifts his legs high, and throws up his
> tail.
> . . . when therefore any one can prevail on him to do these
> things which he has done of his own accord, when he wishes
> to appear beautiful; he will then exhibit his horse pleased
> with being rode, and having a magnificent, stately and beau-
> tiful appearance.

Those who practiced High School, and particularly the *airs
above the ground*—movements during which two front or two
hind legs, or even all four are off the ground—were unquestionably pleased to find such a venerable ancestor. This is what
Xenophon says about teaching the horse to rear:

16

. . . a horse who raises himself well, is a sight so beautiful, so astonishing, and so delightful to behold; that it attracts the eyes of all those who see him, both young and old. And no one leaves him, or ceases looking at him, so long as he displays himself in his splendor.

But if the person who happens to be possessed of such a horse is an officer, he ought not to be satisfied with enjoying this distinction alone, but should rather endeavor to make the whole of the cavalry under his command, like-wise worthy of being beheld.

When I first read Xenophon the question of why he wrote so little on the subject immediately arose in my mind. After all, the Greeks of those days, besides establishing the fundamental orders of architecture and producing enough pottery to adorn all the museums of the world, left us a formidable library of works of history, travel, philosophy, drama and poetry. Among those many volumes which have survived to modern times, but which represent merely a fraction of the original production, we can count only one book on riding; that there was another earlier book written by one Simon we know from Xenophon's reference to it. (A small fragment remains.) Why so much on so many subjects, and so little on riding?

As a matter of fact, Xenophon himself wrote several longer books and many pamphlets, among the latter being the text on horses. His most popular work today is the *Anabasis*—an account of a retreat of ten thousand Greek soldiers from an unsuccessful campaign in Persia; it is 300 pages long in the paperback edition. His longer books deal with history, philosophy, economics, politics, etc. So again the question poses itself—why so much on other subjects and so little on riding?

It is, of course, little wonder that natives of a country where the belief was prevalent that a man spent more than six hours daily on practical things only to the detriment of his mind and spirit, should produce more works of philosophy or history or poetry than treatises on simple technical matters. Yet the fact remains that classical Greece was not horse country. Made up of islands and a rocky mountainous mainland, lacking good pastures, its main military strength consisted in its navy and in its foot soldiers. In many important battles the Greeks were without cavalry, and they had next to none in the famous retreat from Persia. In Greece the horse was a luxury article; only the rich could afford it. The natural horsemen of the day were the Persians to the east, and the various semi-barbarous tribesmen of the Pontic steppes to the north. Xenophon implies this when he says:

"But what some persons fear, lest the shoulders of their horses should be broken in riding swiftly down steep places, let them be under no apprehensions about; knowing that all the Persians and Odrysians ride races down steep hills, who have horses not less sound than those of the Greeks."

It was only under Alexander the Great that cavalry became an important arm of the Greek military forces and, after all, Alexander came from the wide pastures of Macedonia, not from Greece proper—and he had a great deal of ground to cover in a short time.

Although Xenophon addressed the booklet on horses and riding to the cavalryman, he himself does not seem always to have had the greatest confidence in that branch of the service. When the ten thousand are left without the cavalry of their allies and are facing a far greater Persian force which had cavalry, he tells them:

... but if any of you is disheartened because we have no cavalry while the enemy has a great deal, remember that ten thousand cavalry are nothing more than ten thousand men. For no one yet died in battle from having been bitten or kicked by a horse; it is men who do what is done in battle.

We are on a far safer basis than the cavalry; for they cling to their horses in fear not only of us but of falling off, while we, marching along on the ground, shall strike much more strongly if anyone comes against us, and we can more easily hit whatever we want to. Cavalry is superior in one thing only; it is safer for them to run away than it is for us.

Our knowledge of riding in ancient Rome is very spotty. We know, for instance, that the trot was not a generally used gait —obviously, before the invention of stirrups, an amble would be considerably more comfortable. Then we know that after the conquest of Gaul by Julius Caesar, the Roman army no longer had its own cavalry but employed auxiliary cavalry drawn from different barbarian peoples. While mounted racing existed, chariot racing was by far the more popular. Acrobatics on horseback were also in favor; it is from these days that the term "Roman Riding" has come down to us. The Romans also had exhibitions of horses dancing to music and performing a movement called "Tripudium." From this term comes the French word for stamping with the feet, *Trépigner*. So Tripudium was evidently a sort of Piaffe. The Piaffe and other high-action movements were obtained at that time by attaching rattles to the pasterns. We know much more about mounted exercises in the cavalry but again, little about the techniques of riding.

In the Middle Ages (circa A.D. 400–1450) as little thinking was done about riding as about anything else "of this world," and no books on equitation proper have reached us from this period.

People often say that books on riding surely must have been written in the Western world between the fall of Rome and the 16th century. True enough, books on horses were written before 1550, but they were concerned with stable management, bitting, diseases of horses, and such matters of interest to horse owners; they barely touched on riding. Most of these works, written before the invention of printing in 1453, could obviously never have had a wide distribution in manuscript form; but a few of them were put into print much later. It is interesting to note that many of their authors were not even professional horsemen. For instance, Leone Battista Alberti (died 1472) was a painter and a distinguished architect. In equestrian literature he is known for a forty-page pamphlet, first printed some eighty years after his death, on the horse's conformation, on breeding, bits, etc., with a few pages on riding. A still earlier writer was Petrus Crescenzi (died 1320) who, as an agriculturist, wrote a twelve-volume work on his subject. In it there are fifty-seven pages concerning care, feeding, and diseases of the horse, and a little about riding. This work first saw print in 1471.

A very famous book on such matters was written by Lorenzo Rusio (died 1350), who was a professional stable manager, not a rider. As in the previous books, only a few pages deal with riding, and these are entirely from the point of view of a stable manager. Accordingly, Rusio describes how one should prepare the horse for riding, what is the best time of the year to work the horse, how to take care of the horse after riding, etc. This book, known in manuscript form for about one hundred and fifty years, was first printed around 1486, and was reprinted many times thereafter. I happen to have a copy of the last edition, printed in Paris in 1610. Thus the book endured for over two hundred and fifty years. This indicates the static condition of knowledge about horses over a long period of time.

Besides these, there were manuscripts on hunting, such as *The Master of Game*, by Edward, second Duke of York, the oldest English book on hunting, written between 1406 and 1413. The greater part of this book is not original but a translation from the French of Gaston, Count de Foix's *Livre de la Chasse*, which was begun on May 1, 1387. These two books, describing in detail the mounted hunting of different quarry, do not even mention riding; it was taken for granted as something every nobleman learned to do in childhood.

Another beautifully illuminated manuscript has come down to us (available today in reproductions) on the proper manner of holding tournaments; it was written by King René of Anjou, around the year 1465—that is, soon after the generally accepted end of the Middle Ages. The manuscript gives all the rules for holding such contests but, again, methods of riding are not discussed.

Since the theme of the present book is the evolution of *educated riding* in the Western world it must begin with the first record of a complete and reasoned method of equitation. It is generally considered that Federico Grisone's book, published in Italy in 1550, is the starting point. After this the story of the development of the art of riding may be divided approximately into three periods, the first and the longest of which lasted almost two hundred and fifty years, until the French revolution of 1789.

It was the period of the birth and development of complicated manege riding and of slow, dramatic, highly collected gaits. This manege riding, with "High School" as the ultimate aim, became progressively more sophisticated as the privileged class, which particularly practiced it, became more cultivated, and as techniques of riding advanced through innovation. As what was left of the illiterate knight of the Middle Ages was gradually replaced by the cultivated gentleman of the Renaissance, and as this new culture grew and became a habit, riding moved from the frequent brutality of the 16th century to the refinements of the 18th. All the important books of the period are concerned with "High School," and it is quite obvious from the texts that the authors themselves practiced this and nothing else. But this art-for-art's-sake approach evidently did not always satisfy less artistic natures, and so every one of these books ends by claiming that the proposed method has practical applications.

The second period begins after the Napoleonic wars and, embracing the rest of the 19th century, lasts until the First World War. It may be considered as the period of the predominance of military riding, which has survived into our times in the form of international military teams, and riding teachers who are former cavalry officers—I being one of them. The important point to consider concerning the 19th century is the fact that even outstanding High School riders, such as François Baucher in the first half of the century, and James Fillis at the end of it, made every effort to sell their methods to the army.

The majority of writing horsemen of the time worked on the same problem—how to adjust 18th century classical manege riding to modern military purposes. But to call the 19th century "military" only, is to disregard the vast amount of general uneducated riding practiced by, for example, the English fox-hunter, the gentleman who hacked over to see his neighbor, the fast-riding postillion, or the cook ambling to market. And we must not forget that English sportsmen were imitated by some of their continental counterparts, nor that the circus (which then reached its peak), by introducing new High School movements, considerably extended the repertory of the latter form of riding. But despite all this, the term "military" describes it better than any other.

The third period, the period in which jumping for sport in various forms has become the main subject of educated riding, is still going on. Later you will find out that it differs greatly from the two preceding periods in its aims, its techniques, the nature of its horsemen, and its organization.

THE ARISTOCRATIC
PERIOD

. . . .

CHAPTER 3

—

Early Dressage Riders

. . . .

W HEN attempting to recon-
struct the picture of educated riding during a certain period,
we must know more than merely how men then looked in the
saddle. We must also know how pleasure horses were used,
who used them, who were the individuals who promoted a
certain method of riding by teaching and writing about it and,
finally, of what this method consisted. I may not always take
these things up in this specific order but I shall attempt to cover
all these aspects of every period. In this chapter I shall discuss
the people who practiced High School in its early days.

I have already mentioned that the first book presenting a full
description of a special method was Federico Grisone's *Gli Ordini
di Cavalcare*, published in Italy in 1550. The ideas it contained
had perhaps been in circulation for some time. Undoubtedly
Grisone himself had practiced his method for many years before
formulating it. Even in earlier books on stable management one
finds here and there disconnected glimmerings of what was later
to become part of a riding system. It is also possible that similar
methods had already been used by a few individuals but had
never been set down on paper.

The fact that the exceptionally severe bits used by the medieval
knights were not only preserved, but their variety and severity

·   ·   ·   ·   ·   ·   ·   ·   ·   ·   ·   ·   ·   ·   ·   ·

increased by the early Dressage riders, indicates that highly collected gaits were also an elaboration upon an inheritance. They could have evolved quite naturally from the unregulated prancings of the nobleman's over-fed, under-worked animal when held back by a strong bit—a sight that was the admiration of the crowd at every parade and procession. Grisone must have observed this disorganized gait many times, and perhaps saw in it the possibilities of a regular cadence. This could certainly have been one of the inspirations of rhythmic movements such as the Passage. Another would have been circus movements. Since circus acts of various kinds can be traced back to very ancient times indeed, and since there seems always to have been a tendency for circus performers to follow a hereditary calling, the circus has often been a conservatory of techniques from the past. It is very possible that the high-stepping, dancing horses reported from Roman times went on dancing in fairs and market places right through the Middle Ages. Travelling animal trainers exhibited performing bears, monkeys, and dogs, and we know that in the 14th century they displayed performing horses. In two illuminated manuscripts of this period, the *Luttrell Psalter* and the *Romance of Alexander*, we find riderless, but in two cases saddled horses executing, at the direction of a trainer on foot, rough versions of the future "airs above the ground." All that may have been necessary to convert these to 16th century Dressage would have been to devise means to obtain high action and the various airs above the ground by the methods of the horseman rather than those of the animal trainer.

Whatever may be the facts, we should consider the first book to present a complete method of riding as signalling the beginning of educated equitation. And this is probably correct because, while nothing substantial was printed on the subject before Grisone, books began to appear in a continuous stream immediately thereafter.

The 16th century's cultivated approach to horsemanship originated in Italy as a part of that refinement of material living that accompanied the Renaissance.

In the preceding century Italy's art was already the greatest, her houses the most comfortable, her clothes the most elegant and her manners the most cultivated in the Western world. All classes that could afford it pursued an ideal of accomplished

Medieval animal trainers' horses from a 14th century manuscript. A tradition, doubtless kept alive from Roman times, was able to provide the Renaissance High School with ideas for "airs above the ground." The techniques of teaching these were probably at least partially borrowed from the same sources. The illustration shows rearing and kicking. *(From the* Romance of Alexander, *Courtesy of Bodleian Library, Oxford, England.)*

27

versatility. The courtier or the gentleman was expected not only to be an intelligent patron of the arts and to appreciate music, but to be able to turn out poems himself, to speak other languages than his own, to be a skillful swimmer and fencer, a graceful dancer and an educated horseman.

So much is certain, that in the sixteenth century the Italians had all Europe for their pupils both theoretically and practically in every noble bodily exercise and in the habits and manners of good society. Their instructions and their illustrated books on *riding*, fencing, and dancing served as the model to other countries. . . . *The important fact is that they were taught systematically.* (From *The Civilization of the Renaissance in Italy*, by J. Burckhardt, George Allen & Unwin Ltd., London. The italics are mine.)

Even if you have never held any old books of this period in your hands, you have probably seen reproductions of engravings from them. If so, you were perhaps curious to learn the state of mind that created and enjoyed the ambitious movements of the heavy, chunky horses of these illustrations—the high stepping, the formalized rearings and leaps into the air with legs drawn up underneath or kicking out behind, the pirouettes at a canter, etc. You may have also noticed that the riders in these engravings are superbly attired and that their horses are often very fancifully turned out.

But have you ever asked yourself what way of life produced this formality, and who were the people who could afford it in the days when even the bare idea of "a high standard of living for all" did not exist?

This is really a very important question, for without answering it one cannot understand the riding of the period. It was a Baroque way of life, which produced a stage setting for absolute monarchy and which required that even those not quite of the blood royal should impress the common man with their pomp and splendor. Riding, as most other activities of the ruling class, was made to serve this purpose. It was only the ruling class that had either the means, the leisure, or the effrontery to practice this elaborate game. For instance, Louis XIV's "prevailing occupation was splendor."

The airs above the ground as the 18th century depicted them.
The *Croupade* is a jump with the hind legs drawn under the body.
The *Ballotade* is a jump with the hind legs drawn under the tail with shoes facing to the rear.
The *Capriole* is a jump with the hind legs kicking out horizontally at the moment the forehand is at its highest above the ground. (*From* Ecole de Cavalerie *by de la Guérinière, 1st edition, Paris, 1733.*)

29

His great palace at Versailles, with its salons, its corridors, its mirrors, its terraces and fountains and parks and prospects, was the envy and admiration of the world. He provoked a universal imitation. Every king and princelet in Europe was building his own Versailles, as much beyond his means as his subjects and credits would permit. Everywhere the nobility rebuilt or extended their chateaux to the new pattern. A great industry of beautiful and elaborate fabrics and furnishings developed. The luxurious arts flourished everywhere; sculpture in alabaster, faience, giltwork, metal work, stamped

A fancy-dress hunt in northern Italy in the 17th century.
This picture is one of many similar illustrations in a book privately printed by the Duke of Savoy to commemorate a hunting house-party. As a matter of fact, from today's point of view the everyday lives of many of these people would seem little less than a costume party. Their riding necessarily partook of the same character. (*From* La Venaria Reale, *printed in Italy, in 1674.*)

leather, much music, magnificent painting, beautiful printing and buildings, fine cookery, fine vintages. Amidst the mirrors and fine furniture went a strange race of "gentlemen" in vast wigs, silks and laces, poised upon high red heels, supported by amazing canes; and still more wonderful "ladies," wearing vast expansions of silk and satin sustained on wire. Through it all postured the great Louis, the sun of his world. . . . (From *The Outline of History*, by H. G. Wells. The Macmillan Company, New York, 1921.)

The unfamiliar life of another time often comes more vividly before our eyes when described by a contemporary. In *The Complete Horseman*, first published in 1696, Sir William Hope, Knight, Deputy Lieutenant of the Castle of Edinburgh, writes:

This imposing construction is merely a 17th century hunting lodge of the Duke of Savoy.

Obviously, the hunting party that would emerge from these buildings would bear little resemblance to a field of modern foxhunters. The preceding illustration shows how they looked on occasion. *(From* La Venaria Reale, *Printed in Italy, in 1674.)*

The Art of Riding is so noble and genteel an Exercise, that it would require a whole Book, merely to deduce and express its Excellency; For as to Pleasure and State, what Prince or Monarch looks more great or more enthron'd, than upon a beautiful Horse with rich Furniture, and waving Plumes, making his Entry through great Cities, to amaze the People with Pleasure and Delight?

Or what more glorious and manly than, at great Marriages of Princes, to run at the Ring, Tilt, or Course in the Field? What can be more comely and pleasing, than to see horses go all their several Ayres? . . . But above all, what Sets-off a King more, than to be upon a beautiful and ready horse, at the Head of his Army.

While few if any continental gentlemen of those days would dispute this approach to horses and riding as a source of pomp which separated the chosen few from the rest of humanity, the English country squire, whose traditional pleasure was riding to hounds on the basis of experience rather than education, objected to manege riding. The Earl of Shaftesbury, in his 17th century description of an old-fashioned squire furnishes the background against which the majority of Englishmen then rode:

Mr. Hastings was an original in our age, or rather the copy of our nobility in ancient days, in hunting and not warlike times. He was low, very strong, and very active, of a reddish flaxen hair, his clothes always green cloth, and never all worth when new five pounds. . . . He kept all manner of sport-hounds that ran buck, fox, hare, otter and badger, and hawks long and short winged . . . a house not so neatly kept as to shame him and his dirty shoes, the great hall strewed with marrow bones, full of hawks' perches, hounds, spaniels and terriers, the upper sides of the hall hung with the foxskins. . . . The parlor was a large long room . . . in a great hearth paved with brick lay some terriers and the choicest hounds and spaniels; seldom but two of the great chairs had litters of young cats in them, which were not to be disturbed. . . . The windows which were very large, served for places to lay his arrows, crossbows, stonebows and other such like accoutrements. . . . He lived to a hundred, never lost his eyesight, but always writ and read without spectacles, and got to horse without help. Until past fourscore he rode to the death of a stag as well as any.

The typical English squire was particularly annoyed when manege schooling was presented to him as essential basic training even for a hunter: ". . . what is a horse good for that can do nothing but dance and play tricks?" Answering this evidently frequent derogatory remark, William Cavendish, Duke of Newcastle, wrote in the preface to his famous book, *A General System of Horsemanship*, first published in 1657:

> . . . I presume those great wits (*the sneering gentlemen*) will give Kings, Princes, and persons of quality leave to love pleasure-horses, as being an exercise that is very noble, and that which makes them appear most graceful when they show themselves to their subjects, or at the head of an army, to animate it; so that the pleasure in this case is as useful as any thing else, besides the glory and satisfaction that attends it.

These quotations indicate differing attitudes of the period toward riding of the kind that today we call Dressage. It can certainly be said that the first form of educated riding was devised for the nobility. If one appreciates this, one is not surprised to find in the subtitle of de Pluvinel's classic, *Maneige Royal* (1623), the assertion that this book contains "all exercises worthy of Princes."

Psychologically this was almost inevitable. Just put yourself (if you can) in the place of one of these gentlemen with a strong sense of his God-given position in the world. Once you are convinced of this, once you are dressed in silks and satins, with a plume in your hat, gilt spurs at your heels and fringed gauntlets in your hand, once you live in a marble palace surrounded by liveried flunkeys, you will find it as incongruous to go for a simple morning hack along the muddy lanes as it would be to tear around a course of five-foot jumps. Although undoubtedly quite sure of your innate superiority, you will feel obliged to manifest this in every action of your very public life. You will have to do everything in a more refined, elaborate and impressive way than your social inferiors.

Books which were written for Princes were naturally bought by Princes; the list of subscribers to the *Déscription du Manège Moderne*, written in French by the Baron d'Eisenberg, but published in London in 1738 and dedicated to the King of England,

An agreeable way of showing horses to friends.
The company is comfortably seated at a cloth-covered table, drinking wine, while musicians play and the horses are led up for inspection. The aristocratic period of equitation possessed many amenities—at least for the few. *(From* Hof-Kriegs-und Reit-Schul, *by E. von Löhneisen, 3rd edition, Nürnberg, 1729.)*

clearly illustrates this fact. Some seventy-five per cent of the names are titled. To take only those under the letter A.

S.A.S. Le Margrave de Brandebourg d'Anspach.
His Grace, the Duke of Ancaster.
His Grace, the Duke of Argile.
The Right Honourable, the Earl of Albemarle.
The Right Honourable, the Lord Ashburgham.
Le Marquiss d'Aix, Envoye de Sardagne.
Le Baron d'Alberg.
Le Baron d'Alberg Vicedom.
Le Baron d'Alvensleben.
Monsieur d'Asfelt.
M. Arundell, Esq.

One has only to look through enough old books on riding to find all this confirmed again and again. For instance, de la Guérinière in his book *Ecole de Cavalerie* (1733) has five full-page equestrian portraits of his distinguished pupils. Only one of them is just M. de Kraut, while the rest are:

The Marquis de Beauvilliers.
The Count de St. Aignan.
The Marquis de La Ferté.
Charles, Prince de Nassau.

Naturally, most of these books are dedicated to kings, princes, or great nobles. Although from the point of view of merely financing the book (something essential in those days), a rich merchant would have done as well, his name would not have carried prestige with those for whom these books were written—nor would he have had the time at his disposal nor the manner of life that would have enabled him to pursue this type of riding.

· · · · · · · · · · · · · · · ·

Even in England one of the persuasive arguments for learning riding was simply pointing out that kings and princes enjoyed it:

Many people say, That all Things in the Manege are but Tricks, Dancing, and Gambols, and of no Use. . . . The next Thing is, that they think it a Disgrace for a Gentleman to do any Thing well. What! be a Rider. Why not? Many Kings and Princes have thought themselves grac'd by being good Horsemen: Yea, our present and most gracious King is not only a very Graceful Horseman, but also taketh great Delight in riding, and I dare say, thinketh it no Disgrace that he is reputed a good Horseman. (*The Complete Horseman*, by Sir William Hope.)

This aristocratic period of Dressage, incomplete though the latter may still have been technically, represents the most glorious phase of this form of riding—a phase during which it was truly fulfilling its purpose.

CHAPTER 4

Early Dressage Teachers

. . . .

T HE last chapter gave a glimpse of the nature of the horsemen who enjoyed manege riding from the middle of the 16th century to the end of the 18th. Of the men who taught this type of equitation there were many, but I shall discuss only those whose contributions to riding are generally considered milestones in the development of the art. These are:

Federico Grisone, Italian, whose important book was published in 1550

Solomon de la Broue, French, whose important book was published in 1594

Antoine de Pluvinel, French, whose important book was published in 1623

William Cavendish, Duke of Newcastle, English, whose important book was published in 1657

François de la Guérinière, French, whose important book was published in 1733.

Federico Grisone's book, which inaugurated the new kind of riding, was not an isolated event even in its time. The next work on manege riding, by Cesare Fiaschi, appeared six years later, and in the course of the next twenty-five years perhaps as many as a dozen volumes were published in Italy alone. Thus Grisone's book was merely the first of those produced by the Italian Renaissance, with its new approach to riding as well as to most other things.

In reaction to the general ignorance of the Dark Ages people searched for at least a rational basis for what they were doing, and the pompous movements of the High School suited the grandiose taste of the time to perfection.

The early writers on riding were also riding teachers. Grisone helped to establish the fame of the riding school of Naples, and Fiaschi founded one in Ferrara. It was in the latter school that another great Italian of those days, Pignatelli, received the education which he later passed on to his pupils in the school of Naples. To this school came many ambitious young men from other countries, among them two eventually famous Frenchmen—de la Broue and de Pluvinel. De la Broue later taught riding in France and his book on equitation, *Le Cavalerice François*, was the first to be written by a Frenchman. De Pluvinel wrote a classic of the early 17th century, *Instruction du Roy*, and was the teacher of the French King, Louis XIII.

The traffic was both ways, Italians also going abroad to teach in different European countries; many came to France, some to England. However, the period of complete Italian supremacy in horsemanship lasted less than a century. With de la Broue and de Pluvinel, the fountainhead of equestrian thought moved from Italy to France, where it remained for a long time.

These early days of educated riding were thus described by Sir William Hope in his book, *The Complete Horseman*, from which I have already quoted:

> ... let us ingeneously acknowledge, that this noble Art was first began and invented in *Italy*: So that it is the *Italians* who have given the first Directions for putting in practice

those Rules, which they invented for Dressing of Horses, and making them capable to serve advantagiously in War; and also, to give all the Satisfaction and Pleasure imaginable in the Carreer and Manege.

And as they themselves did much practice this noble Art, so was it also upon that Account that all the French, and other Nations went thither to be taught; the Seat of Horsemanship being first at *Naples*, and Afterwards at *Rome*, whither a great number of all Nations repaired, to make themselves Horsemen: But those who design'd to come to a greater Perfection in this Art, went to Naples, where they were kept two or three Years, before the Masters so much as told them, whether they were capable either to learn, or become Teachers of it; so well did these Gentlemen know how to esteem their Talent, of which they were more frugal, I assure you, than People now adays are.

The first who ever writ of it was one Frederick Grison, a Neapolitan, and truly he writ like a Horseman, and a great Master in the Art for those Times, it being then but in its Infancy; for we may see to what Perfection it is brought, since that Time and seeing it is an easy Matter to follow a beaten Path, it is therefore no great wonder if the *French* have, since that Time, brought this Art to some Kind of Perfection, seeing other Persons gave them Matter whereupon to work; However, it was nobly done in Grison to have been the first whoever writ on this Subject, and for which he is much to be commended, seeing (considering the Time his Book was publish'd) what he writ was so good. Henry the Eight sent for two *Italians* that were his Scholars, to come to him into *England*. . . .

The old Earl of *Leicester* sent for an excellent Rider out of *Italy*, call'd *Signor Claudio Curtio*, who writ a Book of Horsemanship, which is quoted by several *Italian* Writers; but I think that very much of his Book is stol'n out of Grison. . . . There is likewise *Casar Fieske* who writ a Book much out of Grison too. . . . There is another Book of Horsemanship, call'd *Gloria del Cavallo*, with long Discourses, and much out of *Grison*, especially as to what concerns the Dressing of Horses. . . . There is also another *Italian* Book of Horsemanship called *Cavallo Frenato de Pietro Antonio, a Neapolitan*, much stol'n out of Grison. . . . But the most famous Horseman that ever was in *Italy*, was a Neapolitan who liv'd in Naples, Call'd *Signior Pignatel*, but he never writ, altho' he could certainly have done it very well, being one of the ablest Masters that ever was in *Italy; Monsieur La Broue* rid under him five years, *Monsieur de Pluvinel* nine years, and *Monsieur St. Anthoine* many Years; . . . These three last mentioned Frenchmen, who rid under *Signior Pignatel* filled *France* with *French* Horsemen, which before was filled with *Italians; Monsieur la Broue* was, I believe, the first that ever writ on Horsemanship in the *French* Language. . . .

De la Broue was a gentleman who started life as a page to the Count d'Aubijoux, and later became an equerry in the royal stables, where his friend, St. Antoine, was in charge. The end of his life was most unfortunate, as both he and St. Antoine were imprisoned without ever knowing either their crimes or their accusers. De la Broue was in prison at the time of the printing of his book, and when he was, in his own words, "old and almost useless . . . having nothing in this world but a used cavesson."

De la Broue indeed seems always to have been unlucky; the first manuscript of his book was lost. He rewrote it during a long illness, but tells us that the copy that was actually printed was not as full or as polished as the original one.

De Pluvinel fared much better. Also a gentleman, he successfully served three French kings, Henri III, Henri IV and Louis XIII. He was not merely a master of horsemanship but a courtier as well; on several occasions he was sent to foreign countries on the king's business and was to some extent employed in the education of the future king, Louis XIII. About 1594 de Pluvinel founded an academy in Paris for young noblemen. This was not only a riding academy; mathematics, literature, poetry, painting and music were also taught. It was a kind of "finishing school" for gentlemen.

As to Pluvinel's famous book—it is rather confusing that it came out under two different titles. This was caused by a curious incident. For some unknown reason he kept his as yet unpolished manuscript with his friend and pupil, René Menou. When Pluvinel died, evidently unexpectedly, the artist Crispin de Pas, who was in the process of making the engravings to illustrate the book, and who already had half of the plates ready, became

The invention of double pillars is usually attributed to de Pluvinel.

Boxed between pillars and whips, the horse had no place to go but up. With the help of two pillars, the Piaffe, Levade and airs above the ground were taught.

On the left—de Pluvinel and the future king, Louis XIII. (*From* Maneige Royal, *by de Pluvinel, 1st edition, Paris, 1623.*)

worried for fear all his work would be lost. So he succeeded in procuring from Pluvinel's servant a garbled, incomplete copy of the manuscript that Pluvinel kept at home. He quickly finished the job of illustrating it, and published it in 1623 at his own expense, under the title, *Maneige Royal*. Then Menou, much upset by this, edited the manuscript that had been entrusted to him by the author. He published it two years later as *Instruction du Roy*, illustrated with the same engravings by de Pas. Since the plates were by then somewhat worn they did not produce such perfect prints. So it is said today that if you wish to enjoy really fine engravings procure the first book, and if you wish to read de Pluvinel, buy the second one. However, neither is easy to obtain, for both editions are now extremely

A lesson given by de Pluvinel (who is touching the horse with a whip) to the future king, Louis XIII (mounted). The subject is a series of Courbettes on a circle.

Showy movements were essential to a horse who played his part in that continuous theatrical performance of the Baroque period, in which the royalty and nobility were the leading actors. (*From* Maneige Royal, *by de Pluvinel, 1st edition, Paris, 1623.*)

rare, and I was lucky to have acquired the first one after a search of at least ten years.

This book was written as a dialogue between the future king and his teacher—a literary form which gave de Pluvinel, the courtier, an opportunity to pay homage to his master. In the beginning de Pluvinel addresses the dauphin: "It will be very easy for your majesty to understand it [Dressage] and to execute it. For God gave to you as much as or more than to any prince in this world an accomplished body, and endowed you with such great and fine judgment that all that will be needed will be to choose horses worthy of so perfect a master. . . ."

Not only are the dauphin's answers always the correct ones and always distinguished by his "great judgment," but he even correctly anticipates some of the questions, to the continual admiration of his teacher.

A single pillar was used for lessons on a circle. Here the longe is no longer tied to the pillar, which indicates that the training is in an advanced stage.

The title of this book is *Court, War and Riding School* and in this picture the courtly background is quite apparent. *(From* Hof-Kriegs-und Reit-Schul, *by E. von Löhneisen, 3rd edition, 1729.)*

In this respect the book contrasts with one written shortly after the French Revolution of 1789 by another riding teacher, Charles Thiroux, an ardent convert to the new republican ways of thinking. Thiroux claimed constantly that he wished to instruct the servant more carefully than the master and that he was writing for everyone, for fear he would be classified with the "infamous Pluvinel, who had dared to vaunt that he had mounted a young tyrant."

French equestrian literature is simply enormous. A bibliography of it completed in 1921 by General Mennessier de la Lance, which describes every book on horses and riding published in French up to that date, contains about sixteen hundred pages of very small print; several thousand books must be listed in it. Here, as I have said, I am mentioning only those that were important events in the history of riding. In this respect another horseman-writer, de la Guérinière, who was active about one hundred years after de Pluvinel, deserves particular attention.

Again a nobleman, de la Guérinière, whose famous book, *Ecole de Cavalerie*, appeared in 1733, maintained an "Academy" in Paris from 1715 on; in it was taught not only equitation but "everything pertaining to the science of the horse." Representative of the sophistication of the 18th century French court, de la Guérinière's book, when compared to Grisone's, de la Broue's or even de Pluvinel's, illustrates the growth of the general cultural level of the French aristocracy. As to its technical content, it is interesting to note that one can read in a pamphlet on *The Foundations of the Classical Art of Riding*, written by the chief of the Spanish School, Colonel A. Podhajsky, that the doctrines of both de la Guérinière and de Pluvinel "are still in force at the Spanish School in Vienna." In a later chapter I shall quote at length from the *Ecole de Cavalerie*.

Zealous teachers have always complained of a lack of serious pupils and of an ideal method; de la Guérinière was no exception. Perhaps it was his keen sense of this shortage of theory in riding up to his days that caused him to work on it himself to the extent that this became one of his great contributions in the field.

Every science and every art possesses principles and rules by means of which discoveries are made which lead to its development. Riding is the only art for which, it seems, nothing more than practice is necessary. Practice, however, devoid of true principle is no more than routine, the results of which are a forced and uncertain execution and a false brilliancy which impresses the half-educated, who are often more surprised by the willingness of the horse than by the merit of the rider. This is the cause of the small number of well-schooled horses and of the meager capabilities one finds today among those who call themselves horsemen.

This dearth of principles prevents pupils from distinguishing faults from perfections. They have nothing to fall back on but imitation and, unfortunately, it is easier to turn to bad practices than to acquire good ones.

What about English writers on riding? The English equestrian literature is also very large—particularly in the 19th century—but its subject is sport rather than the techniques of schooling and riding at collected gaits. The English always preferred hunting and racing to manege riding, and the latter had only one important champion, William Cavendish, Duke of Newcastle. His book, *A General System of Horsemanship*, was first published while the Duke was living on the continent as a refugee from the Cromwellian regime. There he evidently developed a great taste for the French manege riding, which he had already studied in his youth.

When Newcastle moved from France to Flanders "... No stranger of note thought of passing through Antwerp without coming to see Newcastle's riding house ... which, though very large, was so often full that 'my esquire, Captain Mazin, had hardly room to ride.' . . . He relates in detail the compliments of some of his more important visitors, tells us how he himself mounted and performed before them, whilst Spaniards 'crossed themselves and cried Miracule.' " However, when he was in his sixties his riding was curtailed by his wife, Margaret, who wrote his biography, *The Life of the Thrice Noble, High and Puissant Prince William Cavendish.* In it she says: "His prime pastime and recreation hath always been the exercise of manege and weapons; which heroic arts he used to practice every day; but I observing that when he had overheated himself he would be apt to take cold, prevailed so far, that at last he left the frequent use of the manege." (The first part of this paragraph is taken from the editor's preface to the book.)

As any cultivated gentleman of the 17th century, Newcastle

The Duke of Newcastle, one of the wealthiest peers of 17th century England, used his various castles as appropriate backgrounds for the illustrations to his famous book. Here he is shown performing a Ballotade on the lawn before his castle of Bolsover. (*From* A General System of Horsemanship, *by William Cavendish, Duke of Newcastle, with 17th century plates. Edition of 1743.*)

had many interests besides horses. He wrote a few plays and poems and was a patron of several writers, scientists and philosophers (Dryden, Descartes, Hobbes, and others). In many instances his book reflects these hobbies. For example, defending High School against the remarks of some who found it useless, he thus philosophized:

"If these gentlemen will retrench everything that serves them either for curiosity or pleasure, and admit nothing but what is useful, they must make a hollow tree their house, and clothe themselves with fig leaves, feed upon acorns, and drink nothing but water, for nature needs no greater support."

A true child of the Renaissance, he looks down on many superstitious concepts and practices inherited from the Middle Ages; he already points to the errors in beliefs which were to remain for long after his time. In the chapter on breeding he says:

... I am no friend to astrological remarks in this case. The moon's aspect, or that of any other celestial body, are equally absurd in affairs of this kind; and it matters not whether the moon is increasing or decreasing, or whether any of the other planets are in conjunction or opposition; for horses are not begot by astronomy, or by the almanack. Such observations are as ridiculous as those relating to the point from whence the wind blows, to produce a male or female colt; ... or another of the same nature, which is, that of placing a cloth before the mare's face, of what color you please, that she may conceive a colt of the same. . . .

Sir William Hope enthusiastically describes the Duke of Newcastle:

After all these came the Prince of Horsemen, the great Duke of *Newcastle*, who may be justly said to have given the very last and master Strokes for the perfecting of this subject;

for it was he who first describ'd the natural and artificial Motions which should be made by the Legs of all Horses, when they are performing such and such an Ayre, which is the Foundation and very ground-work of Horsemanship. . . .

The Duke of Newcastle would have readily agreed with the compliments paid him by Sir William and, as a matter of fact, at the end of his own book he evaluates it thus:

". . . if this work pleases you, I shall be thoroughly well satisfied; if not, I shall be content in my own mind; because I know certainly that it is very good, and better than any thing that you have had before of the kind."

Modesty was no part of the 17th century nobleman's mental equipment. The Duke of Newcastle could conceive of himself as mounted on Pegasus executing a Capriole, with the gods of Olympus looking down, and the horses from his own stables paying homage in a proper High School manner. *(From* A General System of Horsemanship, *by William Cavendish, Duke of Newcastle, with 17th century plates. Edition of 1743.)*

.   .   .   .

This enviable self-assurance reminds one that a sense of superiority would have been a natural characteristic of almost every aristocrat of those days. We must remember that every equestrian writer mentioned in this chapter was a nobleman. Newcastle was more than that; he was a duke and one of the wealthiest peers of England; the others belonged to the minor nobility and were not rich. Despite this, they all represented a single class in which the man at the bottom and the man at the top had the same ideals. The "noble" art of riding in the 16th, 17th and 18th centuries was both developed and practiced by noblemen. These circumstances gave it certain forms which I shall describe in the next chapter.

The epithet "noble" for a horse is also a survival from a past when it was almost always the attribute of his rider. This attribute can be traced much further back than the Middle Ages. Into the ancient world, which means the Near East and the Mediterranean basin, the horse came as an import from the pastures of the North. As an imported article, not too well suited to his environment, he remained a luxury, and a luxury of primary value in warfare. As a luxury and a piece of equipment as precious as first class armor he was the prerogative of the ruling class. Some vague aura of all this still clings to him and increases the pleasure of many people who ride horseback today.

Early Dressage's Place in Life

. . . .

As I have shown in a previous chapter, educated riding—in the strict sense of the term—did not exist before the 16th century or, if it did, we have no knowledge of it. The simple, practical riding of the Middle Ages was based merely on individual ability to handle the horse and on experience while, outside of war itself, mounted warlike games and hunting were the only activities in which to demonstrate one's horsemanship. Therefore a horse's schooling would necessarily be limited to what would enable the warrior to use his weapons with skill, or the hunter to follow his quarry, or to what made a pleasant hack for the road.

There can be few riders of the Western world who have not at one time or another titillated their imaginations by fancying themselves knights in armor. I am no exception. But from the horseman's point of view it has always proved a frustrating experience. I find myself incased in steel from head to foot, looking out at the world through a narrow slit; I am literally wedged in a high wooden saddle; only one hand is free for the reins, since the other guides and supports a long, heavy lance; the stiff saddle and still more, the horse's armor if he is wearing it, prevent my communicating with his sides in any but a hit or miss fashion at the end of my eight-inch-long rowelled spurs.

It becomes quite evident that I not only cannot hope to obtain a good movement from the animal under these circumstances but that if I should do so no one would see it under all the trappings. I myself cannot tell whether the horse's neck and head are in the proper attitude, whether his mouth is open or his sides yielding. As a matter of fact, all this would be quite unnecessary for the sole purpose of unhorsing my opponent and, with luck, bringing down his horse as well.

Mid-16th century German armor for man and horse; the knight's armor weighs 56 pounds and that of the horse (saddle included) 92 pounds. This type of armor, which first began to appear in the 14th century, was preceded by chain mail for both mount and man—a form of protection equally cumbersome, and usually more so. The 13th century horse might also be covered to below his hocks by a trapping of heavy fabric or leather, but it is said that this reduced the efficiency of his rider to that of the slowest infantryman. *(The Metropolitan Museum of Art)*

This German armor (c. 1500) is for a joust run in the open field without a barrier between the combatants, the object being to unhorse one's opponent and splinter one's lance. This armor weighs 85 pounds.

The straw-filled cushion worn over the chest of the horse prevented injury to the horse's forehand and the rider's legs, should the two horses collide.

The 12' to 14' lance made of pine (since it was meant to break if properly aimed) was supported on a heavy rest bolted to the knight's breastplate. The jousting lance frequently had a head consisting of three prongs arranged in a crown. These prevented its slipping on the smooth helmet and enabled the full force of the impact to be used in pushing. The riders passed left arm to left arm.

It is clear that, with the weight and rigidity of this armor and the contestant's primary preoccupation with unhorsing his rival, it would have been impossible for the rider to obtain refined or elaborate movements from his horse; these were, in fact, unnecessary. *(The Metropolitan Museum of Art Rogers Fund, 1904)*

All I need for combat is a bold, strong horse that can be trained to go without hesitation straight toward the horse that is galloping at him and not to be dismayed when the lances hit the shields. After this, if my opponent is still in the saddle, my horse must be one which I can turn readily in order to resume the attack.

Moreover, it is obvious that to carry an armored knight, a heavy saddle and, often enough, armor of his own, a heavy horse was needed. It is also clear that once such a combined weight got rolling it would require strong measures to stop it in a hurry—hence the brutal bits. Again, to overcome the initial

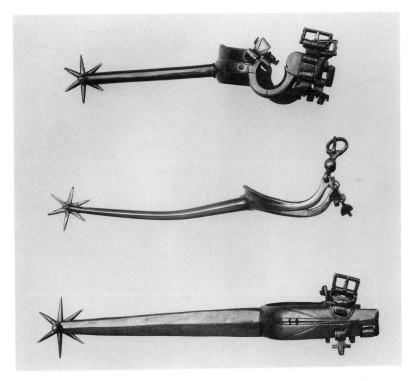

These 15th century spurs indicate the remoteness of the rider's heels from the horse's sides, hence the difficulty of refined control of a medieval war horse. *Top*—Italy, neck 5"; *center*–Germany, neck 6¾"; *bottom*—France, neck 7¼". *(Courtesy of the Metropolitan Museum of Art, New York City)*

53

inertia of all this weight, very sharp incentives were needed—
hence the vicious spurs. These were not means by which to
obtain elegant or precise movements, even if the horse in question would have been able to perform them, loaded as he was.

When riding changed, and in the 16th century High School
movements including formalized kicking, rearing and "ayres
above the ground" such as Capriole or Ballotade were introduced, some of their sponsors liked to claim that these were
practical for war or tournaments. I suspect that they made these
claims simply to sell their methods to the hard-headed, practical
man. It seems they were not always successful. For instance, an

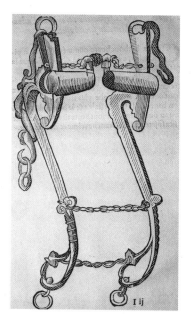 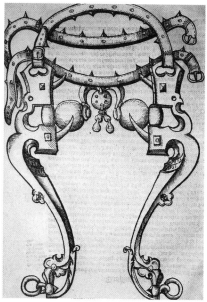

(Left) This mild bit was invented by Antonio Pignatelli, famous instructor at
the school of Naples. *(From* Traitté des Emboucheures, *by Samuel Fouquet,
Paris, 1663.)*

(Right) This bit, with part of its headstall, was recommended for teaching a
horse that was stiff in one side to make a turn, the spikes bearing on the opposite
side of the head when the rein was pulled. Spikes might be placed only on one
side. *(From* Gli Ordini di Cavalcare, *by Federico Grisone, German edition of
1608.)*

Englishman, Thomas Blundevill, at the time of Queen Elizabeth wrote:

> ... unless your horse be naturally light of his body and nimble of his legs, it is unpossible by Art to make him to do any of these things well; and to say the truth, they be things that may be very well spared, and specially in horses of service, which being once used to such delighting toies, do forget in time of nead their necessarie feats. For when they are spurred to go forward, or to passe a cariere, they fal a hopping and dansing up and down in one place. Likewise, when in their manege they should make a speedy round, and just turn, either single or double, they will not turn but leisirely with the Corvetti: and therefore I would wish none of the Queenes Majesties Horses to be used to the Corvetti but such as are onely left for pleasure, where of it is sufficient to have in her highnesse stable two or three at the most. (*The Art of Riding.*)

There is another reason why the High School jumps were impractical for war. Although the chief of the Spanish School of Vienna, Colonel A. Podhajsky, in his booklet on the Spanish School, says that the Courbette was taught for use in battle, since it would help a rider surrounded by infantrymen to rid himself of them, he goes on to add that the difficultness of this movement is attested by the fact that it may take years to find a stallion with an aptitude for it. This indicates how rare was the happy horseman who could hope to escape the enemy if relying mainly on airs above the ground.

Historically, such claims of High School riders have no real factual foundation, except perhaps in isolated cases. Long before High School originated, the type of warfare for which such a movement as the Courbette was supposed to be useful was becoming obsolete. By the time the first books on equitation were written, the lance and the sword were losing to fire-arms.

The period of early artistic riding coincided with the decline of individual or small-group fighting with "cold arms."

... At Crécy the horse proved the weak link in the French organization, for of the next great battle, namely Poitiers (1356) we find John le Bel writing of the French knights: "All fought on foot, through fear that, as at the battle of Crécy, the archers would kill their horses." ... From the battle of Poitiers onward cavalry fell into a rapid decline; the French knights learnt nothing, and as the bow and pike destroyed them a new weapon arose in the crude bombard of the 14th century, which was destined to revolutionize the whole art of war ... the knight exchanged his lance for the petronel, a type of hand cannon, in order to fire on infantry in place of charging them. This form of attack was first used by the French at the battle of Cerisoles, in 1544, and proved effective. ... Soon the petronel was replaced by the arquebus-a-rouet, and a little later on by the wheel-lock pistol, which was first used by the German cavalry at the battle of St. Quentin, in 1557. (*The Encyclopaedia Britannica*, 14th edition, in the article on "Cavalry.")

It was not until the first half of the 17th century that the cold arms of the cavalry regained their importance, but by then warfare was entirely altered and light cavalry charged in large organized bodies supported by infantry and artillery fire.

In answer to the common question whether High School horses of this period were used for hunting, equestrian history indicates that this was not a general practice. Fully schooled manege horses, trained at slow, extremely collected gaits, were not in the habit of galloping fast nor of coping with uneven terrain. It is also hard to see why a nobleman rich enough to have "parade" horses in his undoubtedly large stable should have used them for every kind of service; he certainly had others that were more suited to the chase.

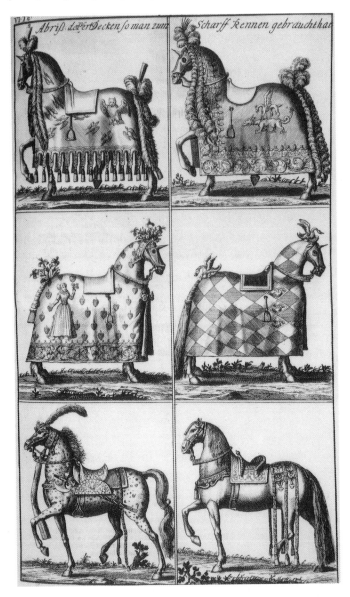

Horses turned out in a manner appropriate for 17th century jousting in Germany.

It is interesting to compare these definitely flat saddles with the earlier deep tournament saddles *(From* Hof-Kriegs-und Reit-Schul, *by E. Von Löhneisen, 3rd edition, Nürnberg, 1729.)*

The principle of specialization of work for horses, depending on their suitability, is very old. The Romans had different categories of horses: *itinerarii* for travel; *gradarii* for hacking; *venedi* for hunting; *cantherii*, pleasure horses.

This practical system would be bound to obtain wherever the horse was extensively used and put to various purposes. Therefore it is safe to assume that it continued throughout the Middle Ages, wherever and whenever there was enough prosperity and security to permit it. In fact, we know that it existed in the Middle Ages. In the England of Chaucer's time, for instance, there were palfreys, amblers, coursers, steeds, dexters, hackneys, capuls, etc. The palfrey was a good-quality general purpose riding horse; the ambler an animal which ambled, popular with the elderly or infirm or for long distances; the courser was a fast horse for informal racing and hunting, the steed or dexter a warhorse; the hackney a poor quality three-gaited riding horse, and the capul a draft horse.

The Duke of Newcastle explained at length that one cannot expect either a human being or a horse to be equally good at all services:

> ... one is capable of being a bishop; another is hardly fit to be a reader, or school-master in a country parish-church. In like manner, some are good astronomers, and others are not capable of making an almanack or sun-dial; some understand algebra perfectly, and others know nothing of addition and subtraction.... If the horse is fit to go a Travelling, let him do it. If he is naturally inclined to make Curvets, he must be put to it ... if he be not cut for that, use him as a drudge to do errands. If none of these suit him, he will perhaps be good for racing, hunting, or travelling, or for the portmanteau, ... so that it is the fault of the horseman, and not of the horse, if he passes for a jade; for really there is no horse but what is fit for some use or other....

The concept of an "all-around horse" on a high level of riding is a product, by the way, of the military domination of riding in the 19th century. The average cavalry officer had two horses; with these, which had necessarily to be trained to the parade and formation riding, he also wished to participate in the various equestrian sports open to him: hunting, steeplechasing, etc. Out of this arose the conception of the ideal officer's charger, and this is the origin of the Combined Training Tests of today.

It is not easy to reconstruct the riding of the Middle Ages, since books on horsemanship did not exist for the simple reason that most noble knights were illiterate, while learned clerks did not participate in equestrian games. But the elementary riding that I have described would be in perfect harmony with the simple and often brutal mounted contests of the period. As early as about the year 1300 regulations began to appear intended to make tournaments (combats between two groups of knights) and jousts (combats between two individual knights) less bar-

Jousting in Paris at the beginning of the 17th century.
A wooden barrier (tilt) separates the two contestants.
This "knightly exercise," which served a practical purpose in the Middle Ages, was now preserved only as a part of pageantry, and was soon to die out completely. (*From* Maneige Royal, *by de Pluvinel, 1st edition, Paris, 1623.*)

59

barous. Swords with points, pointed daggers, clubs and maces were gradually prohibited. Jousting lost many of its dangers after the invention of the "tilt"—at first a stretched cloth and later a wooden barrier along either side of which the two contestants galloped to meet each other. Many old-timers must have passed remarks about the effeteness of the new generation. But tournaments still were frequently bloody affairs. Perhaps the last important victim was Henry II, King of France, who died from a lance stroke in a tournament in 1559.

It is indeed hard to agree with the usual claims of early High School riders that refined manege horsemanship could be helpful to the knight in tournaments or jousting. The great French chronicler Froissart devotes many pages to detailed descriptions of some thirty individual jousts between English and French contestants during a meet of several days at Saint Ingylbertes in France, in 1390. The general pattern was the same in every encounter. The two contending knights would first occupy their respective positions and then would gallop at each other. Some horses, knowing what to expect, naturally did not want to gallop straight at the other horse, hence in many cases they "crossed" or "refused." It was obviously not easy to keep a horse galloping straight against an expected unpleasant experience, guiding him with one hand and supporting a heavy lance with the other, while bracing the legs forward in the stirrups in preparation for a heavy blow. But when the knights did meet they struck each other with their lances once, then returned to their places to repair damages and prepare for the next run.

Froissart says:

Than came forthe an exquyer of Englande, called Blaquet, and sent to touche an the shelde of the lorde of Saynt Pye, who was ready to answer. . . . The first course they taynted eche other on their helmes, and loste their staves; they toke their staves agayne, and in the aprochyng their horses crossed, and so passed by, and returned agayne to their places: they taryed not long, but ran eche at other: with that course Blaquet strake the lorde of Saynt Pye a hye on the helme, and gave hym a sore stroke, and Saynt Pye strake him in the sight of the helme a sorer stroke, so that therwith he was unhelmed that the bocle behinde brake, and the helme fell to the grounde: than Blaquet returned to his company, and justed no more that day; and the lorde of Saynt Pye sate styll on his horse abyding other comers. (Lord Berners' translation, printed in 1523.)

The pageantry of the dying tournament was gradually transferred to its direct descendant, the relatively gentle carousel. In this the competitive spirit was satisfied by harmless feats in which the skill of contestants with pistol, sword, and lance was tried individually on inanimate objects. The knights no longer broke lances fighting each other; at most the combat of former days was merely simulated. Now the contestant would ordinarily essay to hit the head of a mechanical wooden figure with his lance; if he struck it other than in the right place it would quickly swing around and give the horseman a blow on the back with a wooden sword, undoubtedly to the delight of the audience. This dummy was called the Quintain.

This arena contest was the ancestor of our horse show. The tournament of the Middle Ages, the carousel of the 18th century, the military 19th century competition in the use of the sword and the lance, and the horse show of today, have all satisfied the human desire to exhibit skill and win a game. The difference in form is merely the result of different ways of life.

But let us return to the 16th century, the century that gave birth to scholastic riding with artistic aims. The Renaissance in Italy was already more than a century old, and the upper class of society no longer resembled its rude ancestors. The refinement of those, at the top at least, was evident not only in Italy but, in varying degrees, all over Europe. The sharp distinction that had existed throughout the Middle Ages between the literate clerk and the warring baron was almost eliminated, and the well-rounded gentleman was supposed to combine the learning of the one with the masculine virtues of the other.

In the second half of the 16th century in Italy, and later in other parts of Europe, the more restrained forms of the Renaissance began to be superseded by the lavish ones of the Baroque, that is of a style based on a tendency toward exaggeration and ostentation. Art, with new knowledge at its command, exploited every trick to achieve the dramatic and the effective; painting was full of writhing bodies, striking highlights, and dark shadows; architecture bulged and billowed in unrestrained virtuosity, palaces covered more and more acres, their gardens swarming with statuary and erupting with foun-

Louis XIII riding at the "Quintain," one of the games that replaced real jousting. The Quintain was a mechanical figure which, if not struck in the correct spot, automatically swung around and delivered a blow to the rider. (*From* Maneige Royal, *by de Pluvinel, 1st edition, Paris, 1623.*)

tains. With new talents and new brains coming up in the world, the old ideal of "noblesse oblige" was replaced by unabashed self-advertising. In this the horse played his role. Conveyances have always been a status symbol, whether they were cart, chariot, carriage, or Cadillac, hackney or lively charger. The rich man's pampered steed was apt to be fat and bouncy, prancing and cavorting all over the lot, while the poor man's jade-of-all-trades moved along at a sober, dogged pace. In the popular imagination the spirited animal represented power and wealth. What High School did was to take the prancings and rearings and cavortings, to label and regularize and control them, and put them into a system to serve the purpose of the age—the glorification of the great.

Not only did the various airs above the ground, the Ballotade, the Capriole, etc., suit the needs and the taste of the times to perfection, but even the clumsy horses with bulging curves seen in contemporary pictures appear to have been expressly bred for the Baroque era.

But if riding took Baroque forms it was not because the horsemen of the time consciously aimed at being up-to-date but because they schooled their horses for events of a decidedly Baroque nature—for pageants at royal or princely courts. The new type of riding at highly collected dramatic gaits was used mainly then for parades and carousels, and the latter included individual exhibitions. None of this was practiced in blue jeans.

Edward Phillips in his *New World of Words*, printed in 1658, gives a contemporary definition of *Carousel*.

"*Carrousel*, a magnifecent Festival made by Princes and Great Men, upon some occasion of public rejoycing, and consists in a Cavalcade of Nobility sumptuously apparel'd, and clad after the manner of the ancient Knights, who repairing to some public Piazza, shew their activity in running at the Ring, Jousting, Turnaments, and such other noble Exercises."

In the great equestrian fête given by Louis XIV in 1662 to

It would hardly have done for the horses who pulled these Baroque sleighs to move at a free, relaxed pace. One artificiality calls forth another, and a measured prancing would have been the only appropriate gait here. *(From* Hof-Kriegs-und Reit-Schul, *by E. von Löhneisen, 3rd edition, Nürnberg, 1729.)*

celebrate the birth of the heir to the throne, the King himself and a great number of the princes and nobles of the court participated. They were divided into groups, each group representing a nation, classical or exotic; Romans, Persians, Turks and even Americans—these being among the exotic. The King was dressed as a Roman, in silver brocade enriched with gold and decorated with diamonds; his casque, boots, saddle and reins were all gilt and studded with precious stones. The other important personages participating in this quadrille were attired in a correspondingly sumptuous manner; even the pages and grooms were elaborately costumed for the occasion.

De la Guérinière thus described the carousel of the first half of the 18th century:

> The carrousel is a military fête or a sham combat presented by a troup of horsemen, divided into several quadrilles [teams] in order to participate in contests for which prizes are given. The spectacle should be ornamented with chariots, floats, decorations, concerts, recitals, devices and mounted ballets, whose diversity forms a magnificent sight. . . .
>
> As the subject matter of the carrousels is historical, fabulous or emblematic, the defendents and the challengers ordinarily assume names conformable to the subject they represent. For example, those who represent illustrious Romans take the names of Julius Caesar, Augustus, etc. . . .
>
> For a warlike harmony trumpets, drums, cimbals, oboes and fifes are used . . . as for the music which accompanies the chariots and floats, it is composed of violins, flutes, bagpipes and oboes. Dances and horse ballets are also made to the sound of these instruments. . . .
>
> Of all the courses that were anciently run . . . in the carrousels have been preserved only the "Course de Têtes et de Bagues." When running at heads the lance, the dart, the sword and the pistol are used. (*Ecole de Cavalerie.*)

The "Course de Têtes" consisted of attacking a painted plac-ard or the head of a wooden figure, past which one galloped, with any one of the above arms. The "Bague" was a suspended ring to be pierced with a lance.

That part of the carousel from which exhibitions such as that of the Spanish School of today are descended was the horse ballet. In 1667 Kaiser Leopold of the Holy Roman Empire was himself the main actor in an elaborate horse ballet held in Vienna:

> . . . there were forty-nine riders with the Kaiser, of whom nine rode courbetting horses, four rode horses which two-tracked at a canter, and four horses which executed High School jumps [such as the Capriole, etc.] . . . The Kaiser

A carousel was an elaborate affair and included not only jousting and the horse ballet but a parade. Hundreds of men and horses sometimes participated.

Horses were decked out for the latter in the "Roman fashion" *(above)* and in the "Turkish" *(below)*.

To people whose daily dress and customs were elaborate in the extreme only exotic trappings from antiquity or remote lands could give that added sense of festivity for special occasions. Hence the popularity of "costumes" in this period. *(From* Hof-Kriegs-und Reit-Schul, *by E. von Löhneisen, 3rd edition, Nürnberg, 1729.)*

made his entrance in the first figure with several elegantly executed Courbettes. . . . As soon as the trumpets blew again four of the riders who had entered with the Kaiser also making Courbettes flew back and forth with high Passades until, by the end of the air, they had surrounded the Kaiser, who had stationed himself a little forward of them. This was the first turn. [There were twenty more "turns."] (From Löhneisen's *Hof-Kriegs-und Reit-Schul*, revised edition of 1729.)

The same German book suggests prizes for such affairs:

1st   A diamond ring.
2nd   A gold repeating watch.
3rd   A dagger set with precious stones.

The horse ballet always formed part of a carousel.

The horses in the center are making Levades, while two horses at the side execute Caprioles.

The four groups of horsemen outside the ballet area are the musicians. Below is a plan for all the movements of this particular ballet.

The performances of today's Spanish School of Vienna are directly descended from such spectacles. *(From* Hof-Kreigs-und Reit-Schul, *by E. von Löhneisen, 3rd edition, Nürnberg, 1729.)*

4th   A gold snuff box set with diamonds.

5th   A pair of pistols mounted with silver and gold.

No other type of riding would have suited the pomp and circumstance of the period so perfectly as Dressage. Even today, in a very different setting, well-executed Dressage on the level of the Grand Prix is a beautiful sight. Perhaps still more impressive than any individual performance are such horse ballets as those of the Spanish School of Vienna and of the Saumur Cavalry School in France. Everyone who visits the Vienna School today falls under the spell of the white horses dancing in a columned hall. I am only sorry that the riders of Vienna now wear sober Empire costumes and that the Lipizanners do not carry plumes on their polls.

The type of riding I have just described obtained throughout most of Western Europe from the Renaissance to the end of the 18th century. Riding in England, however, would have presented a rather different picture. This is because England herself presented a different one.

At the end of the 15th century the great nobles who had eaten each other up during the Wars of the Roses began to give place, under the Tudors, to an ever more numerous country gentry. The English gentleman of that day possessed a love of rural life quite remarkable to continental visitors; he was also a member of a far less rigid class system than those visitors; and after the time of Charles II the royal court was not important enough to form a focus for society. Hence the English gentleman hunted the deer and when, as a result of the reduction of forest land, that quarry grew scarce, the hare, and later still the fox as well. His riding was primarily riding to hounds. Thus, rather than concentrating on the scholastic side of riding, the Englishman developed a sporting attitude toward it.

"Sir Edward Harwood presented to Charles I a memorial setting forth the great scarcity of good and stout horses for the defence of the kingdom . . . and he ascribed this state of things to the popularity of racing and hunting, which called for lighter and swifter horses." (William Ridgeway, *The Origin and Influence of the Thoroughbred Horse*, 1905.)

The principles of the English school are rather vague. Furthermore, there were few English horsemen [educated] and they wrote little. The genius of the nation leaning much more toward practical and utilitarian than toward theoretical.

The English school made a complete revolution in the equestrian world. It founded speed racing and regenerated the breeds of horses. But if at first they had a method and masters, it soon fell into a latent state. A very developed taste for horses exists in this country; as to equestrian principles, they have completely disappeared. Horsemen have an incontestable boldness but no method. (*Origines de l'Ecole de Cavalerie*, by Captain L. Picard, 1890.)

The scholastic approach to riding on the continent, on the one hand, and the sporting attitude in England on the other, resulted in the fact that even today many equestrian technical terms in the English language are of Italian or French origin, while a considerable part of the French equestrian sporting vocabulary is English. For instance, we use such terms as passage, piaffe, courbette, capriole, appuyer, volte, pesade, manege, ruade, cavesson, amble, cadence, cavaletti, equitation, dressage, etc. On the other hand, the French today employ such English terms as steeplechase, jockey, gentleman-rider, meet, hunter, "cross" (for cross country), oxer, etc. The French also use the English word "jumping," and it is rather startling to read a report of a Paris show under the heading of "Jumping de Paris." The old French word "sauteur," that is literally a jumper, is limited by 400 years of use to designate a High School horse that performs such jumps as the Ballotade or the Capriole.

But more important than this exchange of terms was the fact that English practical cross-country riding eventually influenced the theoretical continental manege. A blend of both made its appearance in France at the end of the 18th century. Today the reverse has taken place; at least some of the English who have fallen under the influence of German Dressage riding have imported its practices into England and promoted a mixture of the two schools, with the further addition of a few modern ideas.

The Substance of Early Dressage

. . . .

SINCE the beginning of educated manege riding many generations of horsemen have worked to improve it. In the course of this long process better techniques were conceived and the crude methods of the early horsemen were gradually replaced by more refined means. The 16th century masters of equitation are often accused of being cruel. The vast number of illustrations of vicious bits of the time, as well as many passages in contemporary books, testify to the justness of this indictment. But, of course, we must not forget that this was three hundred years before a humane society was thought of.

This cruelty stemmed not only from the general cruelty of the times but also, ironically, from an attitude towards the horse that credited him with a more human type of mentality than we ascribe to him today. Grisone and his followers believed that the horse's disobedience arose from wilful stubbornness rather than from fright or inability to understand what was asked of him. Hence the severity of the punishments was morally justified. Grisone compensated for them to some extent by rewarding an obedient horse with caresses, but among some of his followers the punishments were more severe and the rewards less frequent. For instance Grisone writes:

> If the horse, either from fear of work or on account of obstinacy, etc. does not wish to approach the mounting block in order to be ridden, you will hit him with a stick between the ears on the head (but be careful of the eyes) and on all parts of the body where it seems best to you, and also threatening him with a rude and terrible voice, so that, realizing that you are as obstinate as he, he will become as easy to mount as a lamb and will approach without making any more resistance; but you must also pat and caress him every time he comes willingly and does what you wish.

To cure a horse who has a tendency to lie down in water when passing through it Thomas Blundevill says you should

> Cause a servant to ride him into some river or water, not over deepe, and appoint three other footemen with cudgels in their hands, to follow him hard at the heeles into the water, to the intent that when the horse beginneth to lie down, they may be readie to leape upon him, and with the helpe of the rider to force him to ducke his head downe under the water, so as the water may enter into his eares: not suffering him to lift up his head againe of a good while together, but make him by maine force to keepe it still under, continually beating him all the while with their cudgels, and rating him with lowde and terrible voices: that done, let him onely lift up his head to take breath and aire. During which time, cease not also to beate him still upon the head, betwixt the eares: which done, ducke his head with like violence once againe into the water, and then let him rise up upon his feet: and whilst he is passing through the water, let the men follow after him, beating him and rating him all the way, untill he be cleane

72

out of the water, and then leave, for otherwise it were dis-
order. (*The Art of Riding*, about 1560.)

The number, variety, and extravagance of the means devised
at the time to make a horse simply *move forward* make one
wonder if the animal was indeed as stubborn and cold-blooded
as the authors make him out to be, or if he was not so uncom-
fortably bitted that he moved in any direction with reluctance.
For instance Blundevill also suggests how a rider who "lacketh
arte, and knoweth not by order of riding how to get the maistrie
of his horse" may correct his stubbornness and make him move
forward:

Let a footman stand behind you with a shrewd cat tied at
the one end of a long pole, with hir bellie upward, so as she
may have hir mouth and clawes at libertie; and when your
horse doth staie or goe backward, let him thrust the cat
betwixt his thighs, so as she may scratch and bite him, sometimes by the thighs, sometimes by the rumpe . . . and let the
footman and all the standers-by threaten the horse with a
terrible noise, and you shall see it will make him to go as
you will have him, and on so doing be ready to make much
of him. Also, the shrill crie of a hedgehog being strait tied
by the foot under the horse's taile is a reminder of like force,
which was proved by Master Vincentio Respino a Neapolitan,
who corrected by this means an old restive horse of the King's
in such sort, as he had much ado afterward to keepe him
from the contrarie vice of running awaie. The like correction
also may be given with a whelpe, or some other loud-crieing
and biting beast, being tied to the crupper, so he may hang
downe under the horse's taile, having a long ende fastened
unto him, which ende, passing between the horse's thighs,
the rider shall hold in his right hand to molest the horse
therewith by pulling it and letting it go as he shall see it

73

needful. Or, instead of such a beast, there may be tied a piece of iron of a foote in length, or more, and three fingers broade, made full of prickles like thornes.

Despite this to us extraordinary callousness towards beasts both great and small, Blundevill still believes that they have better natures which can be appealed to, and when the horse yields to these complicated coercions he often suggests that he should "be made much of."

Blundevill's cruelty may have been obvious and stupid but, unfortunately, one cannot say that cruelty was confined to the early period of educated riding alone. The same human stupidity and the same resultant cruelty may be encountered, although in different forms, today. Only people now practice it behind the barn and do not write about it. However, another kind of cruelty—the accepted, hence to many invisible, cruelty inherent in asking of the horse much more than he can do with ease— is as widespread today as it was in the 16th century; the forms alone have changed. The very severe bits, the vicious spurs, the pillars, the attendants with whips, etc., of the early High School were necessary because people were requiring too much of the horse, and knew no other means of achieving the desired results. And although later, with improved techniques, many cruel practices were eliminated, the attempts to force nature remained. Horses were never monkeys in their past, and acrobatics can hardly appeal to them as much as they do to us. Today the cruel aims have switched from manege riding to sport, and people who wouldn't kill a fly cripple horses on the track or in the jumping arena in pursuit of the barely attainable. Since this kind of cruelty is more widespread and at the same time less apparent to most people, it is really a greater menace than the obvious beating of a horse.

But to return to Grisone—his text is not well constructed. On the one hand it fails to give general principles; on the other, it

16th century schooling.

Since the horseman of that period pursued highly artificial aims, but possessed as yet imperfect techniques, he needed help from the ground (at least at the beginning of schooling).

The role of the dismounted men here, holding the horse back with raised whips while he is being urged forward, was later played by the pillars. These are an illustration of early efforts to teach the horse collection—a study he can hardly ever have enjoyed. (*From a German 16th century edition of* Gli Ordini di Cavalcare, *by Federico Grisone.*)

contains too many confusing details. All this, of course, is to be expected from a pioneer. But it does describe such basic things as teaching the horse to move on the bit, collection, backing, side-stepping, suppling the horse, obtaining softness, etc.

Early High School trainers, among them Grisone, evidently experimented with many methods of trying to persuade the horse to do what they wanted. One approach that would seem strange to us today in the teaching of Dressage was the means by which they claimed to appeal to the horse's visual sense. A straight path, bounded on either side by heaped earth or brush-wood, would terminate at either end by circles of the desired diameter, similarly inclosed and with stakes in the center. The horse going back and forth along this clearly marked channel would acquire the habit of moving straight and, being forced to make his voltes (or whatever other type of turn was required) within a firmly defined area, would also become accustomed to execute very small circles with considerable precision. To us these walled corridors seem more like a painless form of coercion than an appeal to the visual senses. At all events, they were obviously not a permanently successful way of schooling a horse (perhaps because both he and the rider came to depend upon them too much) and they were abandoned by the 17th century trainers.

De la Broue, one of Grisone's French followers, working with the advantage of time and a larger body of experience to draw upon, and probably assisted by the lucidity of his French mind, was able to go so far as to define good hands as those "which knew how to resist and how to yield at the proper moment, and to control with precision the action produced by the legs." Among other things, he improved the bits suggested by Grisone, introduced three types of flexions of the neck, investigated causes of resistance in the horse and the reasons for a hard mouth, and worked him in a less confined manner.

De la Broue was one of the first to recognize that such prim-

76

itive means as those described in the quotations above could lead neither to precision in obedience nor refinement in movement. He also considers that the majority of horses disobey through misunderstanding or as a *result* of such abuse and, speaking of animals with naturally difficult dispositions, he specifically says:

> I could add a large number of remedies which I once practiced to make stubborn horses go forward, either by fire or water applied in different ways to their most sensitive parts. . . . and even by means of animals and other things attached to the tail or under it. . . . but because I am an enemy to those little secrets which have been invented for lack of skill, I shall leave the description and the practice of them to others who lay more importance on them than I do.

De Pluvinel, who came after de la Broue and who invented the double pillars for training horses to High School airs, is credited with having done more to instruct the French nobility in advanced horsemanship than any of his predecessors, both through his own teaching and through the numerous schools founded throughout France by his pupils. Thus the ground was gradually prepared for the appearance of de la Guérinière who, working in the first half of the 18th century, substantially improved Dressage and brought the hundred and seventy-five-year-old method to the height reached in his day. He represents the acme of early High School.

His most important book, *Ecole de Cavalerie* (the word "Cavalerie" here means horsemanship) was published in 1733. Its three parts deal with conformation, riding and schooling, and diseases of the horse. The table of contents of the riding and schooling section lists the subjects that were taught and thus helps us to reconstruct the picture of manege riding in his day. I quote it in full from Chapter VI on (the previous chapters

77

merely explain the equestrian vocabulary, give a description of gaits, and furnish other introductory matter):

CHAPTER VI   Of an Elegant Seat in the horseman.
CHAPTER VII   Of the Hands, Reins and their effects.
CHAPTER VIII   Of the Aids and Punishments necessary in Schooling horses.
CHAPTER IX   Of the necessity of the Trot for suppling young horses, and the usefulness of the Walk.
CHAPTER X   Of Halts, Demi-halts and Backing.
CHAPTER XI   Of the Shoulder-in.
CHAPTER XII   Of the Croup at the wall.
CHAPTER XIII   Of the usefulness of Pillars.
CHAPTER XIV   Of the Passage.
CHAPTER XV   Of the changes of hands and the manner of doubling.
CHAPTER XVI   Of the Gallop.
CHAPTER XVII   Of Voltes, Demi-Voltes, Passades, Pirouettes and Terre-a-Terres.
CHAPTER XVIII   Of the Airs above the ground:
                  Of the Mézair.
                  Of the Courbette.
                  Of the Croupade and the Balotade.
                  Of the Caprioles.
                  Of the Step-and-Jump and of the Gallop-Gaillard.
CHAPTER XIX   Of War horses.
CHAPTER XX   Of Hunters.
CHAPTER XXI   Of Coach horses.
CHAPTER XXII   Of Tournaments, Jousting, Carrousels, etc.

This unadorned list, of course, does not paint a full picture. To have a better understanding of 18th century riding the definitions of some of the movements mentioned in the table of contents should be added. I shall let de la Guérinière describe them in his own words, and I have chosen those movements which may be less familiar to some of my readers.

THE PASSAGE . . . is a measured and cadenced walk or trot. In this movement the horse is obliged to hold his legs for a longer time in the air, one behind, the other in front, diagonally as at the trot, but it should be much shorter, more sustained and more pronounced than the ordinary trot.

THE PIAFFER. When a horse passages in place without moving forward, back, or sidewise, and when he raises and flexes his legs high and with grace in this action, it is called Piaffer. This movement which is very noble and very prized in carrousels . . .

VOLTE . . . In France the word volte signifies going sideways on two tracks, the horse [i.e. his hooves] executing two parallel circles or a square with round corners.

TERRE-A-TERRE. His Grace the Duke of Newcastle has well defined the Terre-a-Terre: a gallop in two beats which is executed along two tracks. In this action the horse raises the two forelegs together and puts them down in the same manner; the hindlegs follow and accompany the forelegs, which produces a lively low cadence, which is like a series of little low jumps, close to the ground, moving always forward and to the side.

PASSADE. To execute Passades is to ride a horse back and forth along a specified length of ground changing at the ends from right to left and left to right, passing and repassing always on the same line. There are Passades at the little gallop and there are furious Passades.

PESADE. The Pesade is an air in which the horse, remaining in place, raises the front very high, keeping the hind legs firmly on the ground without advancing or moving them.

MEZAIR. The Mézair is nothing more than a half-cour-

· · · · · · · · · · · · · · · · ·

bette, the movement of which is less detached from the
ground, lower, brisker and advancing forward more than
that of a real courbette, but also more raised and pronounced
than the Terre-a-Terre.

Some Dressage movements as practiced in the 18th century.
The *Passage* is a slow, highly collected and cadenced trot with accentuated high
   action.
The *Gallopade* was the term for a slow, highly collected canter.
The *Volte* at that time consisted of two tracks on a circle.
The *Pirouette* is still a turn on the haunches at a collected canter. *(From* Ecole
   de Cavalerie, *by de la Guérinière, 1st edition, Paris, 1733.)*

COURBETTE. The Courbette is a jump in which the horse rises higher in front in a more pronounced and more sustained manner than in the Mézair, and in which the hindquarters strike the ground and accompany the front in an even cadence, low and lively, at the moment that the legs of the forehand return to the ground.

CROUPADE and BALOTADE. The Croupade and the Balotade are two airs that differ from each other only in the position of the hind legs. In the Croupade while the horse is in the air with all four legs, he tucks up and draws in his hind legs and feet under the belly without showing his shoes; and in the Balotade, when he is at the height of his jump he shows the hind feet as if he would like to kick back, as he does in the Capriole.

CAPRIOLE. The Capriole is the most elevated and the most perfect of all jumps. When the horse's front and hindquarters are both raised in the air he kicks back vigorously, the hind legs at this moment are close to each other, and he extends them as far as it is possible to stretch them; the hind feet during this action are raised to the height of the croup; and often the hocks creak from the sudden and violent extension of this part.

THE STEP-AND-JUMP. This air is comprised of three tempos of which the first is a shortened gallop or Terre-a-Terre; the second a Courbette; the third a Capriole, and so forth in sequence.

I wonder what my readers may think of these airs above the ground during which sometimes "the hocks creak." To me they are as unattractive as any other extreme physical effort, on the part of either horse or man. These airs, by the way, look better in still pictures than in actuality; the former fail to reveal the strain and violence of the motion. Human beings have an unfortunate propensity to carry anything they undertake beyond the sensible limit and up to the barely possible point of achievement. This is where horses frequently suffer. The human impulse behind these airs was probably very much the same as that which today promotes Puissance jumping and such gruelling cross-country tests that horses sometimes even die attempting them.

Many people might be inclined to think of these High School movements as being those of the circus. From the ordinary layman's point of view they would be correct; for the difference between a movement in classical High School and that same movement executed in the circus may be purely one of technique, and apparent only to the initiate. The main distinction lies in the fact that classical High School movements are the end-product of a long and consistent course of training; they are not taught in a vacuum. The Piaffe in High School, for instance, should come as the natural result of the physical dexterity that the horse has acquired, while in the circus a horse may be taught the Piaffe without any preparatory work, as a trick is taught. In my time, however, I have witnessed many poor examples of the Piaffe in the classical manege and sometimes seen quite good ones in the circus. The barriers between these two approaches to High School have been further lowered by the fact that at different times outstanding Dressage riders have found the circus a more rewarding field than the pure manege and have entered it.

There are two more chapters in de la Guérinière's book which I would like to discuss. They concern the war horse and the hunter. These are short chapters, of only three and five pages respectively. They seem particularly short when compared with the chapters on such details as the "Shoulder-in" and the "Volte" to which four pages apiece are devoted. Evidently the chapters on the war horse and the hunter were mere additions to a book whose subject was High School.

Almost all manege riders, from the very beginning of scholastic equitation up to our day, have tried to prove that their art is not only a beautiful and extremely difficult one but that it also has practical application. Early writers claimed, as I have mentioned before, that many High School movements were useful in war, tournaments or jousting; later ones extolled the practicality of the simpler parts of their method for the cavalry. Some of our contemporary manege riders insist that at least the early stages of Dressage are a good preparation for jumping and cross-country riding. I have never been able to understand why Dressage riders seem to feel obliged to justify their art by making practical claims for it. Why can't they simply practice art for art's sake? De la Guérinière shared this compulsion when he wrote recommending his method of riding for the army:

> The art of war and the art of horsemanship are reciprocally indebted to each other. . . .
> The Passage, for example, makes the action of a horse that is at the head of a troup high and noble. . . .
> By means of Voltes one attacks the croup of the enemy and surrounds him diligently. . . .
> Passades help one to go against the enemy and return promptly at him. . . .
> Pirouettes and Half-Pirouettes make it easier to turn more swiftly in battles.

A score of years later, the success of Frederick the Great's cavalry, trained both individually and in formation to cover rough country at a gallop, must have cast doubts on all this wishful thinking. And it was completely confuted soon after the end of the century by the Napoleonic cavalry, which had had no elaborate manege preparation, in the first place because there was no time for it and, in the second, because ideas on the subject had begun to change even before the French Revolution. And so, with very elementary means of handling horses, Napoleon's cavalry "made the tour of Europe."

I, myself, as an ex-cavalryman who participated in cavalry

charges during the First World War and heard many on-the-spot accounts of others, can assure you that the success of an attack does not depend on refinements of equitation but rather on the moment being rightly chosen and on the adequate weight of the charge. The latter is a combination of the number of its

One of de la Guérinière's pupils, typically attired for an 18th century informal ride. *(From* Ecole de Cavalerie, *by de la Guérinière, 1st edition, Paris, 1733.)*

swords (in relation to the enemy's strength), its speed, and its determination to win. As to the actual hand-to-hand fighting, which is physical chaos and emotional and mental confusion, riding during it can only be of the most primitive kind.

De la Guérinière's short and completely atypical chapter on hunting was probably written under the influence of his familiarity with the English scene. It is perhaps to the relatively democratic basis of English society, hence to the popularity of racing, that we paradoxically owe the high standards of modern horse-breeding. For High School was the product of a rigidly stratified society which had the leisure to savour refinements and was more interested in the quality of an elaborate performance than in what horse might have won by a nose. Moreover, even connoisseurs' tastes differed, and there was no such simple and clear-cut test of the animal's capacities as on the turf. Breeding in this field could hardly hope to keep up with that in racing circles. In 1607 English race horses had already been imported into France and "in 1673 Sir William Temple met a French buyer who had purchased twenty horses in Ireland for the French army at from twenty to sixty pounds apiece." (W. Ridgeway, *The Origin and Influence of the Thoroughbred Horse*, 1905).

It is no wonder that de la Guérinière knew the English horse and admired it. After pointing out that it is really nature that produces great gallopers by giving them good shoulders he says:

"English horses more than any other European ones have this quality; . . . English hunters are often out for a whole day without being unbridled and always on the tail of the hounds in their fox hunting, jumping hedges and ditches which can be found in a country as populous and cut-up as England."

As for riding to hounds, de la Guérinière suggests that both the trot and the gallop of a hunter should be more "extended than raised." He also says that during the "hunting gallop" the rider "should not insist on the position of the head, on the principle of keeping it perpendicular from the forehead to the tip of the nose, as in manege horses; the hunter should be given more liberty, so that he can breath and open his nostrils."

In this chapter de la Guérinière also makes a suggestion which would be approved by any modern trainer of cross-country horses:

When one begins to gallop a horse destined for hunting, one should not first ask a fast gallop; because he is not yet in the habit of galloping freely, he will lean on the hands;

English foxhunters of the 18th century.
The horses are ridden in plain snaffles, and they undoubtedly will be permitted to keep their necks extended at all gaits and on the jump. When the hands and the legs of these riders interfere with their horses it is not because of a desire on the part of the horsemen to execute finer control, but simply through failure to maintain a good position in the saddle.
The great freedom and initiative given to the horse in this type of riding when compared with contemporary Continental equitation are closer in spirit to today's attitude than the rigid control that the latter demanded. *(From George Stubbs and Ben Marshall, by Walter Shaw Sparrow. Pub. by Cassel and Co. Ltd., London, and by Charles Scribner's Sons, New York, in 1929.) (Courtesy of the Earl of Yarborough)*

but neither should one ask a collected gallop, which will prevent him from using himself as he should; but he should be maintained in a united gallop, without restraining him nor pushing him forward, *as he would gallop by himself without being mounted.* (The italics are mine.)

These ideas which had unconsciously been put into practice by English squires are particularly interesting in view of the fact that somewhat later similar ones, but much expanded, were advocated by many educated continental horsemen. In this respect parts of de la Guérinière's text foreshadow the future. Unfortunately the harmonious effect of the chapter is spoiled by some unnecessary manege riding advice and by the insignificance of what de la Guérinière says about jumping. The latter evidently did not interest him at all, and he disposes of the subject by repeating, in eighteen lines, what de la Broue had said one hundred and forty years earlier. Here is his text on the subject in full:

The quality that a hunter should possess is to jump hedges and ditches so as not to stop in his tracks when such obstacles are encountered. Monsieur de la Broue gives a lesson on the subject which I believe to be practical and good. Take a wattle fence about 3' to 4' wide and 10' to 12' long; lay it first on the ground, and make the horse jump it at a walk, at a trot and then at a gallop: and if he puts his feet on the wattle, instead of jumping it, punish him with a whip and spurs. Then raise the wattle about one foot and as the horse jumps it freely, raise it more and more up to its full height; then trim it with branches and leaves. This method, which he [de la Broue] says he often practiced, certainly teaches a horse to extend and lengthen himself for jumping over hedges and ditches, but this lesson, which is necessary for a military horse and for a hunter should not be used until he obediently turns in both directions and not until his head is set and his mouth accepts the bit.

To me, and probably to you, this almost complete disregard of jumping is disappointing, but de la Guérinière is not really at fault; he merely represents the attitude of his century. Nobody at the time was seriously interested in negotiating obstacles.

Jumping, as anything else, must attract interest and furnish competition before its standards can be raised to those of an art. With jumping this has happened only during my lifetime. To be sure, some interest, although quite unscientific, was manifested in it as early as the year 1800 by the English. The great master in this field, however, was to come from another nation.

CHAPTER 7

The Last of the Old Regime

. . . .

I N the previous chapter I indicated that during the 18th century manege riding reached a point of great sophistication, and that on the whole this type of riding, already traditional, was characteristic of the time. But history does not move in a logical fashion and at an even pace in a single direction. More often than not various new tendencies and innovations, appearing side by side with the popular trend, break the uniformity of the period. Some of these departures from the main current, impractical or premature, perish soon after they are born; others survive and grow to start a new era. These eras in the history of riding, or in any history, seldom correspond exactly to the reign of the king whose name they carry, nor do they begin or end precisely with the century. Equestrian thinking in the 18th century did not concentrate exclusively on the old manege of display; occasionally it deviated. In several respects developments typical of the 19th century had their roots in the 18th. Thus before the year 1800 dawned a new pragmatic approach to riding had made its appearance. Although it became particularly prominent in France in Napoleonic times, its origin can be traced to Germany and England.

When Frederick the Great ascended the Prussian throne in 1740 he remarked that his "cavalry is not even worth the devil coming to fetch it away." This was a cavalry trained on the principles of manege riding. With the help of two of his cavalry generals, Seydlitz and Zieten, both of them original thinkers, Frederick retrained his mounted troops so as to be able to fight rather than to parade. Work in the manege was largely reduced (although collection was still preserved) and replaced by galloping in the field, both individually and in close formation. One of Frederick's favorite sayings was that "one who cannot gallop for a long time is useless as a rider." As a result of this training, at least fifteen out of twenty-two battles were won by Frederick's army, thanks to the cavalry's acting in close cooperation with artillery and infantry. The achievements of the Prussian cavalry in the Seven Years' War (1756–1763) made a great impression on the continent, and aroused doubts among many officers concerning the old manege equitation.

You will remember that parts of de la Guérinière's chapter on hunting were written under the influence of the achievements of this sport across the channel. Only a generation later, in 1762, a little book, written by Henry, Earl of Pembroke, was published in London. It was entitled *A Method of Breaking Horses and Teaching Soldiers to Ride, Designed for the Use of the Army*. Forty years later an English riding teacher, John Adams, wrote about this book:

> Another small tract I have seen, wrote by the Earl of Pembroke. This his lordship intended solely for the use of the army. It contains only a few general rules, absolutely necessary for the discipline of the cavalry. His lordship, knowing the aversion a soldier has to study, and the shallowness of the common soldier's capacity, most certainly thought that much would never be attended to, though the little he wrote might.

True enough; Pembroke's is a very small and unimportant book, but it represents the appearance of ideas which have little in common with de la Guérinière's chapter on "War Horses." I would like to quote some of them:

It would scarce be possible (neither is it at all necessary) to teach the many more difficult and refined parts of horsemanship, to the different kinds and dispositions, both of men and horses, which one meets with in a regiment; or to give the time and attention, required for it, to such numbers. . . .

This lesson of the *Epaule en dedans* [shoulder-in] I would only have taught to such people, as are likely to become useful in helping to teach men and to break horses . . . none others should ever be suffered upon any occasion to let their horses look any way, besides the way they are going, which is a very rare thing now to be seen in most regiments. . . .

However highly I approve of pillars, I would on no account admit of any, unless constantly under the eye and attention of a very intelligent teacher; which is a thing so difficult to be found in regiments, that I think pillars are better banished from amongst them. . . .

The above excerpts should be sufficient to make it clear that the Earl of Pembroke, although a follower of the French school (he even uses the French word for shoulder-in) was practical enough to suggest its considerable simplification for the army.

The next similar move in the same direction was made in France itself, by another practical man of Scottish origin who served in the French army. This was Count Drummond de Melfort, Inspector-general of the Light Cavalry. He published his book, *Traité sur la Cavalerie*, in Paris in 1776. The short list of subscribers to the book contains only sixty-three names, all but six of which are titled—the revolution was still thirteen years away. This thick and very beautiful folio is primarily concerned with cavalry maneuvers; only about sixty pages are devoted to horsemanship. In these one finds such sensible statements as the following:

I am of the opinion that, providing a rider knows how to make his horse go forward, to make it stop when he wishes, to make it back, turn to the right and the left, walk, trot and gallop, this is precisely all he should know; . . . I repeat that I believe, that one should not push instruction in the art of riding too far and that one should preferably stick to working in formation.

De Melfort did not seek to change the precepts of classical riding, he merely abridged its practice in view of the special circumstances in the army. In this respect he and the Earl of Pembroke were alike, and far ahead, of course, of de la Guérinière and his conservative followers. But collected gaits, halts that put the horse down on his hocks, shoulder-in, croup-to-the-wall, etc., still had a place in Count de Melfort's book as cornerstones of equitation. As to jumping, like de la Guérinière he repeats what de la Broue had said long before, adding only a few insignificant remarks of his own. The fact that the first men to abridge the full program of manege riding did so especially for the army is of particular significance, since in the next century educated riding was to be primarily military, and civilians were to imitate it.

Count de Melfort was not the only French cavalry officer of the period who wrote about the necessity of simplifying and adapting manege equitation for the army; there were others. Thus, for instance, in a book which was printed the same year as de Melfort's, Mercier Dupaty de Clam wrote:

"The military horse is ordinarily used only for fast work; hence it is necessary to school him to go forward and not to give him a slow, shortened pace which does not move ahead. Parade horses are the only ones that should possess this showiness." (*La Science et l'Art de l'Equitation*, 1776.)

A few years earlier he was telling soldiers in his company that:

"Manege horses are good only for hacking and for the occasions when brilliance is necessary; few people are in a position to have horses especially for parades, and, furthermore, only a few know how to complete their schooling."

In one more thing Dupaty de Clam anticipated the following century: in trying to put riding on a solidly scientific foundation. He went so far as to explain equitation by geometry and physics, and produced works, "learned and conscientious, but often obscure and, more often still, boring." (*Essaie de Bibliographie Hippique*, by General Mennessier de la Lance, pub. by Lucien Dorbon, Paris, 1915–1921.)

There was also, at the end of the 18th century, the Chevalier de Boisdeffre who already made a distinction as well for the *hunter*: "There is a difference between schooling a manège horse or making one for hunting or for war. The latter needs only to be prepared for movement forward; his gaits should be only free ones and the development of his strength is half the job; in all he requires far less exactness."

Thus the 19th century trends in equitation really started before the year 1800. The century proper began in Europe with Napoleonic campaigns which turned old-fashioned ideas on riding upside down; but this temporary upheaval also started a few years earlier in 1789, with the French Revolution. The Count d'Aure, writing close to the middle of the 19th century, described this significant period:

When the revolution came, equitation suffered cruelly; of all the arts it was the one to suffer the most. Its sanctuary at Versailles, supported by royal munificence, disappeared with royalty. The other schools fell away also and our horsemen became exiles or found refuge in military camps.

When France, after a long period of anarchy, became military, she felt the necessity of organizing the cavalry, and reestablished a school. Versailles was destined to educate our cavalry. It was no longer the academic manege of the past, which was suffered to preserve the old traditions while making progress; it was now only a question of hurriedly educating instructors for our regiments.

Jardin and Coupé [instructors], as all horsemen, knew very well that the more freedom is given to the horse and the less is demanded of him the less one provokes resistances. The use of the hands and legs, necessary when one needs it to collect a horse and to master him, is that much more dangerous when employed by people who may not be familiar with its effects.

Riding at this period consisted, with few exceptions, in permitting horses to go freely. Once secure in his saddle the rider learned, often as much by instinct as by precept, how to control his horse; closing in his legs to make it go forward, pulling on the bridle to stop it or diminish the speed; when the horse was going more or less as he wished he let the reins float. The substance of almost all the lessons given at this period was to say: stop and yield; it was simply a question of stopping on time and yielding at the right moment. Since the riders had neither the time nor the ability to supple their horses nor to put them on their haunches, and horses were left to themselves to a considerable extent, they remained in balance as well as they could but assumed each time and in every situation the position that was the most suitable to their physique. It was with such an unscholarly education, in which instinct often took care of everything, that our armies made the tour of Europe. (Count d'Aure, *Traité d'Equitation.*)

However, as I have said before, the over-all equestrian picture of the second half of the 18th century was far from being uniform. The High School of de la Guérinière still found both partisans and occasions for application. But, significantly enough, its specialized character was beginning to be recognized even by its masters. Thus a German, the Baron de Sind, wrote in 1762:

Those horses destined only for public functions should be exercised only at the Passage and the Courbette so that they will not mix them with other airs.

I gave my master the Elector of Cologne a dapple-grey horse to ride on the day of the coronation of his brother Charles VII in Frankfort. The magnificence of the imperial procession attracted an immense number of spectators. The whole cortege moved at the passage, but the attitude of the horse ridden by the elector was the most effective of all. He continued to execute the passage from the Römer to the church and, on the return trip, from the church to the Römer without losing a beat. Moved by a brave and noble pride, he adorned his action with two or three courbettes after a few steps of passage, and by alternating the two movements at appropriate intervals he was the admiration of all Frankfort. (*L'Art du Manège.*)

Although in France the requirements of military preparedness made it imperative to simplify riding for the army, in England manege riding from its introduction met civilian opposition from the hunting squires and from the gentlemen whose pleasure was racing. Occasionally there appeared in England a master of classical equitation who taught the complete manege, including High School. But even some of these were obliged to make concessions and to admit that manege riding might not be the answer to better riding in all branches of horsemanship. One of these teachers, John Adams, who worked at the end of the 18th and the beginning of the 19th centuries, wrote a book, *An Analysis of Horsemanship*, published in London in 1805, from which I quote:

How strange . . . that the art of riding and managing horses should be so much neglected, that very few, indeed, know or think that any such art exists. . . . I believe it will be found to originate, for the most part, in the masters themselves. For certain it is, masters of old taught only one style of riding, which was the *manege*. . . . The obvious consequence is, that gentlemen are as emulous of riding fast, as of riding well; and finding persons who learned to ride in a style so ill calculated to travel far, or fast, or endure its fatigue, they ridiculed the idea of learning to ride at a school, but preferred, or sought to copy, a hunting groom, or racing-jockey.

Nevertheless, the study and knowledge of the *manege* has many advantages; for you are not confined to ride in the *manege* style when you find it most convenient to ride in any other; and certainly, if you ride fast long distances, or a hunting, the *manege* style is not calculated for your own ease, or that of the horse. But whenever you adopt the proper style for these extended paces and suffer the horse to take a support and ascendency of the hands, you can, when you find it necessary, more readily recover the superiority of the hand than those who are totally ignorant of the science.

Adams' conviction of the superiority of classical Dressage was very strong; he ends his book with a description of how to school a horse to execute such movements as the Capriole, Ballotade, etc. But at the same time he admits, as previously mentioned, that there are other forms of equitation. Consequently he devotes many pages to a seat especially designed for hunting. He was also, I believe, the first one to present the technique of jumping at any length (12 pages). Thus he was more advanced in his thinking than either the Earl of Pembroke or Count Drummond de Melfort, who changed nothing but merely abridged the program of the old school.

Adams' description of the hunting seat contains amazingly

.   .   .   .

modern ideas; as a matter of fact, he can be considered a precursor of Caprilli, who developed the Forward Seat one hundred years later. Out of some twenty pages on the hunting seat I shall select certain phrases and assemble them so that you will immediately recognize the modern Forward Seat. Adams does not actually connect these points in an orderly fashion, nor has he any logical explanations for them. Furthermore, he includes opposite and contradictory points among his sound ones. But however vague his description may be, it is the first appearance in print of some of the basic ideas of the Forward Seat.

> ... The hunting seat is that of riding in the stirrups. ... the intention of this style of riding is ... to relieve yourself from that friction and heat which the bottom would receive from such strong and continued gallop, if seated close down on the saddle. ... the first thing to be considered is the length of the stirrups, which must not be too short, though somewhat shorter than what was recommended for military or road-riding. ... When the horseman is raised in the stirrups he must have a forward inclination from about twenty to forty-five degrees short of a perpendicular, as the rider shall find most pleasant and convenient for himself; but whether the body has a great or small inclination the position otherwise must be the same as when upright; that is the breast open, the shoulders down, the back hollow, the head firm. ... when you ride in the stirrups (I do not mean under the toe, as you may do in manege-riding without inconvenience) under the ball of the foot, you have the play of the instep, which acts as a spring, as does also the knee, and the joints, next below the hip, which save the body from a great part of the roughness which the action of the horse occasions. ... If you find it necessary you may turn your toes out a little to strengthen your hold ... and when the thighs are not suf-

ficient then the legs are applied, which is a deeper and stronger hold . . . the hands must be kept low.

This seat Adams intended for the gallop only. He did not go so far as to work it out for the jump. This privilege was reserved for Federico Caprilli who, around the year 1900, conceived a completely new method of riding and schooling horses (field horses and jumpers) of which the Forward Seat was an integral

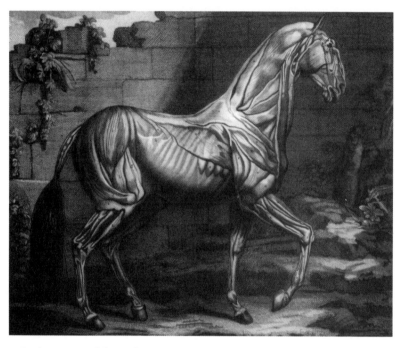

In the course of the 18th century, the horse's anatomy was studied in greater detail than ever before. This knowledge was one of the factors which later permitted horsemen to attempt to give riding a scientific basis.

Of the books on this subject, the *Cours d'Hippiatrique,* published in 1772 by a French veterinarian, Philippe E. Lafosse, is by far the most sumptuous. It was said to have cost the author 70,000 French livres to print it.

This book is profusely illustrated by plates of the high quality of the one here reproduced. It is characteristic of the 18th century that science had not yet begun to depict the objects of its study in a severely clinical fashion, but considered that they should be as pleasingly and decoratively presented as possible. *(From the* Cours d'Hippiatrique, *by Philippe E. Lafosse, Paris, 1772.)*

part. It is interesting to note that Adams approached his seat from the point of view of the rider's comfort, while Caprilli did it from that of the horse's.

Caprilli's method today is sometimes called the "Natural Method," because it is based on the natural, ordinary movements of a calm horse. This idea also can be traced to the 18th century. Baron de Bohan, then a Captain in the French cavalry, wrote in 1781:

> ... Nothing is so dangerous as an ignorant artist. He makes mistakes methodically and goes stubbornly astray: of such are the great majority of those who make a business of schooling horses; they are, for the most part, incapable of giving correct definitions of the simplest operations in the art they profess. One has only to open our treatises on equitation to find *nature everywhere coerced and contradicted*, how many horses have been crippled or worn out before one has been found capable of executing the *antics* that Newcastle and de la Guérinière have described for us under the baroque names of passades, terre-a-terre, pesades, mézair, balotade, etc. It is this meticulous jargon that I particularly intend to avoid in my school; *the horses will learn no artificial gaits and I will apply all the resources of art to perfect those which nature has given them.* (From *L'Examen Critique du Militaire Français.* The italics are mine.)

In two other respects characteristic elements of the 19th century were foreshadowed in the 18th. For one thing, attempts at a scientific analysis of the mechanics of the horse's movements were then first made. Baron de Bohan, whom I have just quoted, suggested in his book that the horse does not move solely by the muscular efforts of the legs, but that the loss of equilibrium to the front plays an important part in locomotion. On this basis a theory of how the horse should be schooled to acquire a good balance under the weight of the rider was later evolved. This theory forms the foundation of today's Forward Schooling, which I shall describe later in this book. Speculative thinking about the horse's locomotion was to continue throughout the 19th century, particularly in France, and a most important step forward was to be made in the United States during the seventies and eighties by Eadweard Muybridge's photographic study of the horse's and other animals' movements.

In the second place, the High School in England, lacking the support of the royal court and of wealthy sponsors, began to play a paramount role in the program of the circus. This position, first assumed in the 18th century, was maintained through the 19th throughout Europe.

The English circus became important and popular for the first time under Philip Astley (d. 1814), who kept a circus in London at the end of the 18th century. Ducrow succeeded Astley in this field and established the circus tradition. It was only much later that the mammoth three-ring American circus with its emphasis on large-scale performances, relegated individual equestrian feats to the background. In none of today's circuses are the traditions of the father of the modern circus, Astley, maintained. His amphitheatre was primarily a combination of riding-school and music hall, and it preserved much of the old dignity of horsemanship.

Like his illustrious predecessors, the court High School riders, Astley practiced Pesade, Capriole, Croupade, etc. And like them, he tried to sell his method (at least the simpler parts of it) to amateur riders and, of course, to army officers. In this respect his ambition was that of the great circus riders of the succeeding century. This is what he wrote in his *Astley's System of Equestrian Education*, published in London, in about 1800:

"It is a known fact that many gentlemen have purchased commissions in the cavalry, merely because they could ride a fox-chase, or horse-race; but a little actual DASHING SERVICE in the field of honor soon convinced them of the necessity of being taught to ride on pure scientific principles, and under able professors."

In ending the period of early Dressage riding it may not be amiss to summarize in a few words the course it followed for almost two hundred and fifty years, up to the time of the French Revolution.

Starting during the transition from the Middle Ages to the Renaissance it followed the elaborate forms of the succeeding

The frequent attendance made possible by a permanent circus, and the excellent visibility of the small, intimate arena, in which the audience's interest was concentrated on one act at a time, combined to produce a group of circus-going connoisseurs who knew what they were looking at. These circuses could afford to pay great High School riders, and the riders were aware that they were performing before a discriminating public. This is how the best circus High School of the 19th century could come to be of very high calibre. *(Astley's Amphitheatre [circus] from Pugin and Rowlandson's Aquatint in Ackerman's Microcosm of London, 1810.) (The Metropolitan Museum of Art)*

periods and served kings and their nobles for entertainment and parade. Cruel in its practices at first, it was ameliorated considerably as the accumulation of knowledge made more refined techniques possible. However, requiring the horse to perform in a more artificial manner than any animal was capable of doing with ease, remained characteristic of High School to the end of the period. This form of equitation remained supreme as long as kings and nobles ruled Europe, and had the means to employ this elaborate riding to ornament their lives.

Towards the end of the period, in the second half of the 18th century, increased emphasis on efficiency in warfare compelled armies to simplify riding and to take it out-doors. After this, pure manege riding, while still practiced by many, ceased to be the universal ideal. A reasoned approach to riding began to be applied not only to the manege horse but to the trooper's horse and the hunter, and there was appreciation of their special problems.

At about the same time a popular increase in interest in science resulted in the first attempts to base equitation on physical laws. This attitude was to develop considerably during the next two centuries. Curiously enough, this very learned approach was seconded by the absolutely unscholastic riding of the English who, in their empirical fashion, followed many laws of nature. The English success in cross-country riding was noted by continental horsemen, and the means by which it was achieved were at least taken into consideration.

All these elements of the equestrian scene will continue to struggle against each other throughout the next century, and it is only in our time that new principles, much developed and improved, will actually begin to win out over the old-fashioned ones. The riding world has always been a conservative one, and it has always taken a long time for a brand-new idea to be generally accepted. One of the reasons for this is the fact that practically nothing in riding is black or white, and that a really

. . . .

talented horseman can often successfully school a good horse by highly unorthodox or old-fashioned means.

Another interesting thing that occurred at the end of the 18th century was the appearance, at a high level of riding, of men from nowhere, like Astley. Significantly enough it first happened in relatively democratic England; after the French Revolution riders of simple origin, who were destined to become great, also appeared on the continent. These new men, who had to look for new fields in which to display their talents, discovered the circus. *Supreme* High School in a circus was something new in the history of the "noble art." But in the 19th century some of the horsemen in this field were to advance High School to new and unparalleled heights. These men, fighting for a better place in life, had to progress or go into oblivion, and so they produced a modern 19th century High School as opposed to the old Classical High School which had remained practically static since the days of de la Guérinière. Thus High School, which had moved from the circus to the royal court, after two hundred and fifty years found itself once more in its old home.

In many ways the second half of the 18th century was the beginning of a new era.

THE MILITARY
PERIOD

·　·　·　·　·　·　·

CHAPTER 8

Baucher versus d'Aure

. . . .

I have described how, in France during the Napoleonic regime, the necessities of war simplified military riding to bare essentials. It took time for France to return to normal (whatever this may mean) and up to the end of the period called the Restoration (the restoration of the Bourbons, 1814–1830) riding remained much as it had been under Napoleon. But as soon as the new order had settled down, and military schools again had time to begin to give a thorough training to future cavalry officers, equitation once more took on an educated form. This is where the struggle started between two schools of thought—one that emphasized manege Dressage and another that promoted cross-country riding. The great leader of the first movement was François Baucher; that of the latter, an equally great man, the Count d'Aure.

Educated riding was now represented by the peacetime army, which supported the restored but much-diminished royal throne. It was natural that cavalry officers under these conditions should feel nostalgic for the days of splendid courts and should wish to revive the manege riding and equestrian traditions of the previous century. This sentiment made it possible for Baucher, a circus High School rider of great talent, and an energetic promoter of his own method, eventually to become the chief spokesman for the century. "Baucherism" is still remembered. On the other hand, the Count d'Aure's ideas, while less followed in the mid-19th century, were closer to those which would obtain fifty years later. Riding in France during the Restoration period, which was the background for the work of both Baucher and the Count d'Aure, was thus described by the latter:

When the Restoration came and peace promised to be durable, the youth of the country, trying to give themselves martial airs, copied everything that was military. Since our officers had got into the habit of riding with dangling reins [i.e. during the Napoleonic Wars], all the young people thought it was the thing to do to ride with their legs forward to an absurd degree, and to let their horses go loose.

Then there appeared a vigorous and energetic form of riding, quite unscholarly, perhaps, but in harmony with the tastes of the period. Tournaments and carrousels, where horses had paraded with forceful, shortened movements, having been replaced by racing, hunting and steeplechasing, those principles [i.e. scholarly ones] which seemed only to make the horses hesitant could not be appreciated by our young people.

The majority of the teachers rigidly opposed the change that was taking place. They only modified the useless movements of manege equitation, and remained faithful to collected movements; they did not demonstrate ways of developing speed, and left their pupils under the illusion that the surest way to attain speed was to close in the legs and yield with the hands. On the one hand, they lost all the prestige that a brilliant execution of the old forceful High School airs brought with it, on the other they inspired little confidence in pupils who were learning from experience that to make a horse bold and to develop speed one should, on the contrary, give support to the horse's mouth, etc. From now on all the young people ceased to have faith in the manege and tried to fly with their own wings. Consequently, they produced a riding of their own, which consisted in negotiating obstacles, in making a bold horse, without bothering otherwise whether he was correct or incorrect, properly placed or not, straight or crooked.

This very natural, very bold equitation, once it came into fashion, only asked to be regularized by principles. (*Traité d'Equitation*, third edition, 1847.)

Under these circumstances, Baucher and d'Aure began to develop their two very different methods.

François Baucher was born in 1796. His equestrian education started at fifteen, with lessons from one of his uncles, a professional horseman. Later he studied horsemanship in the principal schools of France, then worked in one of them, and finally opened a riding school of his own in Rouen. At the age of thirty-eight he became a partner in a Paris riding school. While teaching there he exhibited his High School horses for ten consecutive years in the circus of the Champs Elysées, and his outstanding performances earned him the reputation of a great master.

Possessing unusual talent, both as a trainer and as a rider, Baucher taught his horses High School for circus performances in incredibly little time. Only in rare cases did it take him more than a year to prepare a horse for public exhibition, while most of his horses performed in public after only a few months of schooling. His outstanding achievements in this respect were *Gericault*, schooled in twenty-seven days, and *Kleber*, schooled in one month; the latter feat was done on a bet.

The army became interested in Baucher's method and in 1842 twenty-six cavalry officers were studying in Paris under him. At the same time his son was instructing another group of officers in the provinces. The next year Baucher, with his son,

(Top) Baucher, on Capitaine, making an abrupt halt.
(Bottom) Baucher, on Capitaine, making what he termed a Pesade. *(From* Souvenirs Equestres, *by F. Baucher; reproduced from* Journal de Dressage, *by James Fillis, Paris, 1903.)*

was invited to the Cavalry School of Saumur to give a demonstration course. It was then that he succeeded in arousing great enthusiasm among the officers and in converting many to his method. Soon afterwards, however, a special commission of officers, formed to consider his system, pronounced an unfavorable verdict and rejected it for the army. About this episode Baucher wrote in the preface to his book, *Méthode d'Equitation*: "... my works were translated into several languages, and everywhere amateurs and intelligent army officers adopted my principles. I have already related what prevented my method from being introduced into the French cavalry, in spite of the unanimous decision of the officers consulted. Let my pen be silent on the sad past."

Baucher continued his private teaching and his regular work in the circus. He exhibited his horses in Berlin, Vienna, Venice, Milan, etc., and, of course, always in Paris. In 1855, as he was about to mount a green mare he was schooling, the circus chandelier fell on him. He escaped death, but his right leg was smashed, and he never rode for an audience again. Yet until 1870—that is, three years before his death—he continued to ride mornings during the training of the circus horses which were still in his charge.

Baucher devoted his life to the creation of a new and better method of riding. Even on his death-bed he took hold of the hand of his pupil, General l'Hotte and, setting it in the proper position and squeezing it strongly said, "Always do this, never bring your hand back to your body when attempting to restrain a horse."

While Baucher was the first great French master of equitation to come from the common people, his chief opponent, the Count Antoine-Henri d'Aure (1799–1863), was born of an aristocratic family and started his life accordingly. Graduating from the military school of St. Cyr as a lieutenant at the age of sixteen, d'Aure joined the Royal Body Guards, and became attached to the Royal Manege of Versailles. When the school of Versailles was closed in 1830, he retired from the army and opened his own riding school in Paris.

The Count d'Aure believed that in horses "the qualities which blood produces come to our aid for the simplification of equitation, because nature gives a well-bred horse flexibility, suppleness and, above all, energy, which horsemen of former days did not always find in their horses." (A consideration on which today's Forward Schooling is largely based.) Consequently, at his school he organized an association for the improvement of French breeds. One of his pupils at this time was the Duke of Nemours, later an influential member of that commission of cavalry officers that rejected Baucher's method. In 1847 d'Aure was appointed chief instructor to the Cavalry School of Saumur; but this victory over Baucher lasted only a few years, and he retired in 1854 when "Baucherism" had definitely gained ground. D'Aure's last job was that of chief inspector of the national breeding establishments.

While at Saumur the Count d'Aure encouraged hunting, racing and cross-country training. He himself could always serve as an example of a strong, courageous, bold rider in the field. His old teacher, the Chevalier d'Abzac, frequently said of him that he would always be a "break-neck." By the way, the moment he retired from Saumur, hunting—which he introduced without official authorization—was prohibited.

As a matter of comparison, it may be interesting to quote what James Fillis wrote about Baucher: "The fact is that Baucher never rode outside. Without being his pupil, I followed and studied him during his journeys to Austria, Italy, Switzerland, etc. from 1847 to 1850. But during these three years I never saw him go outside on horseback." (*Breaking and Riding*, second edition, 1911, Hurst and Blackett, Ltd.)

General Mennessier de la Lance in his *Essai de Bibliographie Hippique* (Lucien Dorbon, 1915), from which the above biographical notes were partly taken, says: "there exist several portraits of Count d'Aure. Ledieu painted two. One of them represents him jumping a ditch. I used to have it . . ." A portrait of Baucher jumping anything, and in the fields, would be highly unlikely.

The clash between the personalities and the methods of Baucher and d'Aure resulted in many arguments in print, not only between themselves but between their respective followers; it even occasioned several duels.

At first d'Aure often went to the circus to watch Baucher ride, and afterwards always held short but polite conversations with him. On the other hand, Baucher saw the Count d'Aure mounted only once, when he went to see d'Aure ride, on the pretext of buying a horse. The experiment resulted in an argument which soon became violent, and the two horsemen parted, never to see each other again.

Today people who oppose the modern method of schooling jumpers and hunters often say that there is nothing new in equitation, and that there is nothing to add to the old art. This feeling, however, was never shared by the great Dressage riders of the past. The men who took part in developing the art of riding were all innovators, and said they were. Baucher's attitude toward his work, as well as the attitude of his contemporaries toward his accomplishments, serve as perfect illustrations of this fact.

The 14th (1874) edition of Baucher's, *Méthode d'Equitation*, starts with a chapter entitled, "The Latest Innovations." In it he says:

> During the forty years that I have occupied myself with the art of schooling horses I have always understood that the unique problem to be resolved by the trainer was to perfect the natural balance of the horse, and my whole life's efforts have had no other aim but to make the problem simpler.

Each of the thirteen editions of the method is distinguished by progress which makes the trainer's work easier. . . . (The italics are mine.)

It is interesting to note that even after three hundred years of educated riding the matter of the balance of the horse in motion remained an open question. As a matter of fact, Baucher himself, in spite of his claims, never solved this problem theoretically, although in practice he knew how to obtain the artificial balance that goes together with full collection.

In the same book Baucher lists the "innovations" which he introduced into the art of riding. Among these are sixteen new manege movements, such as instantaneous transitions from the slow to the fast Piaffe, trotting backwards, cantering backwards, etc. He also enumerates thirty improvements in the technique of manege riding. Some in the latter category were considered by Baucher to be basic to his system. Here are a few of them:

The distinction between *instinctive* and *imparted* forces of the horse [imparted by the rider].

The abolition of the *instinctive* forces of the horse and their substitution by the forces *transmitted* by the rider.

The definition of true collection and the means of obtaining it.

The means of suppling the lower jaw, the neck, the loins and the croup [mostly in hand].

Baucher claimed that working on the basis of these principles led to *all horses* being supple in the mouth, neck, loins and back; to their being *all* light in hand at the three gaits; to giving them a regular walk, and a united, extended or cadenced trot; to reining back as easily as moving forward; to an easy gallop, and to every degree of collection.

Some of the horsemen of the century were doubtful about Baucher's claim that his method would work wonders with *all horses*, while others were very much impressed by the results obtained by Baucher himself.

"... I wish to say that both officers and non-commissioned officers unanimously approve Baucher's procedure for schooling young horses. In fifteen days Monsieur Baucher obtains better results than those obtained in six months by the old methods." (Correlet, Colonel of Paris' Municipal Guard.)

"Monsieur Baucher's antagonists wish to present him as an imitator of Pignatel, Pluvinel, Newcastle, etc. But did these famous horsemen, while preaching suppleness and equilibrium, ever teach a theory as clear, as precise, and as well-reasoned as Baucher's? No." (de Novital, Commander of the Saumur Cavalry School.)

Baucher's method, based on his novel principles, can be summed up as follows: two forces combine to produce the horse's movement—weight and muscular effort. The first is passive, the second active. If the latter is used by a horse of his own will, Baucher calls it *instinctive* force, while if the muscular action is produced at the will of the rider, he calls this force *imparted*. In the first case the rider is dominated by the horse; in the second the horse becomes an *instrument* in the rider's hands. Once the horse has been mounted he should move only as a result of *imparted* force. Consequently, the first aim of the rider is to "destroy the *instinctive* forces" and the second is "to replace the *instinctive* forces by *imparted* ones." Thus Baucher began his schooling by completely abolishing the horse's *instinctive* forces and will, and only after accomplishing this did he begin to build a completely new structure upon this void. To achieve this, Baucher, by his new combined effects of hands and legs, would shift the horse's weight rearward and engage the quarters under the new artificial center of gravity, always holding the neck high and the head perpendicular to the ground. His goal was to gather the horse to the point where he felt as if the animal was ready to raise himself in the air with all four feet simultaneously. This accomplished, *he would carry the horse forward* (with imparted forces), maintaining the same position. Needless to say, all this is not easy to do, and if the rider succeeded in destroying the natural forces of the horse but was unable to produce the artificial ones, what would remain? Baucher himself performed miracles with his method and many of his outstandingly talented pupils were also successful with it, but obviously, for the majority of riders, it was much too difficult. A serious French equestrian historian, Captain L. Picard, wrote at the end of the 19th century:

> Monsieur Baucher was an admirable High School horseman; no one surpassed him, nor even equalled him in obtaining from the horse the maximum it could give. . . . He set down the means by which he searched for and obtained these results, and from this point of view he formulated a logical theory. But as a result of ambition, he wished to make his method universal, and to create an equitation of the future, and there he was completely wrong. There is an abyss between the method of schooling used for a horse destined exclusively for the High School, who repeats the same performance every day, and the method which is suitable for war horses and hunters. (*Origines de l'Ecole de Cavalerie.*)

Dismounted work in hand, which required great tact, and which formed the basis of Baucher's method, was one of many other items hardly practical for the army. About ninety years earlier the Earl of Pembroke had written in his little instruction book for the cavalry: "As for working a horse in hand without a rider, I cannot but condemn and reject it: Two people indeed in my life-time, and amongst the many I have observed, but only two did I ever see who have succeeded in it . . ."

The three pages of Baucher's book that concern jumping and the four on field riding do not say much. James Fillis, who knew him personally, wrote about this neglect:

Baucher being a reformer and consequently a seeker, had no pleasure in leaving a horse to himself, as is done when hacking. He devoted all his life to his work in order to show us the way, which was the only thing that interested him. Riding without working was only weariness to him. Therefore he never studied the character or manner of riding a hack or hunter; or the enormous difference between a "closed-in" school horse and an ordinary saddle horse, which is left a good deal to himself. (*Breaking and Riding.*)

Were I to write a history of the development of equestrian techniques, rather than to describe the various forms educated equitation took as a result of the varying circumstances in which it found itself, I would here dwell upon how in the latter part of his life Baucher changed some of the principles of his original

Work in hand, flexing the horse's neck and head directly and laterally, was a part of every serious horseman's education in the 19th century. These illustrations show the sort of work in place developed by Baucher. *(From* Origines de L'Ecole de Cavalerie, *by Capt. L. Picard. Milon fils, Saumur, 1890.)*

method, how he developed a new way of obtaining full collection, etc. Since such things, however, do not belong to the main
theme of this book I pass them by.

As to his simplified method for the army, since it was still
based on the principle of collection, although of a lower degree
in this case, it could lead to nothing but smart gaits on parade
grounds. Because this sort of thing was much admired at the
period, "Baucherism" remained in force for a long time, and
even today some Dressage riders are influenced by it. On the
other hand, "few men were ever as violently attacked as was
Baucher. One has only to glance through the heated polemical
writings stirred up by his teaching before and after 1840 to
appreciate the number of his adversaries and their vigour."
(*Bibliographie Hippique*, by Mennessier de la Lance.) To this
should be added that few men had as many devoted followers:
both friends and enemies are naturally made by every successful
innovator.

The most formidable of Baucher's adversaries was the Count
d'Aure. The thinking of both men had its roots in the 18th
century. On the one hand, Baucher was introducing new methods into the old classical manege, and on the other, was working
on abridging it for the army (an old idea by then). The Count
d'Aure, although an excellent High School rider himself, was
primarily interested in outdoor riding, hence his aim was greater
naturalness. As you already know, the germ of this idea also
existed even on the continent at the end of the 18th century. In
his own words, his basic principles were:

The art [of riding] in becoming more general should be
simplified: it should no longer consist of producing elevated
gaits and forced movements, which serve only to display the
skill and patience of the rider. Today, on the contrary, it
should be applied to regularizing gaits and to controlling the
horse, while permitting him to retain all his natural energy,

and to helping him to develop almost by himself those qualities which are proper to him.

Fifty years later the essence of this paragraph was expounded by Federico Caprilli, and today it is one of the basic principles on which modern horsemen school hunters and jumpers. It was also fundamental to the Count d'Aure's teaching, and he repeats this statement in different words several times in his book. Wanting equitation to be as simple and natural as possible, so that it could serve many horsemen instead of a few, he was particularly critical of Baucher's theory of the destruction of the natural forces of the horse. In his manege teaching d'Aure was very simple. The main theme of his work, as stated, was to make riding more natural; hence in his book one finds ideas such as:

> ... England and Germany differ in their principles: the former (the English) are occupied with racing and hunting, and consider speed as the most important quality. In training young horses they employ means that serve to push them forward; also, generally English horses are more on the shoulders than on the haunches. ... The Germans, on the other hand, work particularly in the manege and are occupied with military riding. They want to have horses that are sloweddown and handy. To obtain this result they make their horses carry more weight on the hindquarters than on the forehand. ... We, in our riding should look for a middle way, and do something to come closer to the English principles, without taking over what is bad in them; as we also should modify the German system, which is the one to which we are the closest. These results should be that much easier to obtain in *that they are closer to nature*. (The italics are mine.)

And, describing the canter departure, the Count d'Aure again refers to nature:

119

. . . .

Work on straight lines, devised to some extent for the trot, becomes difficult as soon as it is a question of practicing it at a gallop. . . . the order in which the legs move at the gallop *naturally entails a gallop departure from an oblique position*. . . . in order to depart on the right lead the horse needs to have the right shoulder further forward than the left. . . . We cannot hope to go *against nature* to the point of changing the order of her equilibrium; perfected work alone may diminish this tendency and render it almost imperceptible. (The italics are mine.)

Concerning this same point General Harry Chamberlin of the U.S. Army wrote one hundred years later:

". . . no attempt to compel a canter with the quarters directly in rear of the shoulders should be made. This is neither natural nor beneficial, although it is considered important in high-school work." (*Training Hunters, Jumpers and Hacks*, pub. by The Derrydale Press, New York, 1937.)

Here it may be appropriate to say a few words about the two terms, "artificial" and "natural," as they are variously interpreted in riding. Because a free horse when excited may exhibit collected gaits and, if sufficiently stimulated, even some airs above the ground, there is a superficial reason to call all movements of High School natural. And in a way this is correct. A living being cannot learn to do what is completely unnatural to him; humans cannot learn to fly, nor can a horse be taught to climb trees or to stand on his head.

Certain movements, such as the ordinary (travelling) walk, trot or canter, will be performed all day long by calm horses at liberty, as a part of the routine of living. Collected movements, and leaps in the air, however, being strenuous, will only be the result of excitement in a free horse. Manege riding is particularly interested in the latter category of movements and its aim is to obtain them from a horse sufficiently calm to be obedient. To

120

execute with precision and calmness and at the direction of the rider those movements which in nature are produced only by excitement is completely artificial for the horse.

Furthermore, in nature a free horse will not keep up any collected movement for any length of time, nor follow any of the artificial rules for its execution laid down by human beings for the sake of beauty and precision. When a free excited horse makes a few steps of Passage he does not care to what degree his legs are bent, whether he preserves the evenness of his steps, or whether his head and neck remain in the *correct* position— he just wants to raise hell. The transformation of short moments of simple *joie de vivre* into hours of regular, systematic procedure is, to a horse, fully and disturbingly artificial. This is why, of course, it is so easy to upset a horse when attempting collection without the necessary gradual preparation for it.

In some other instances we use these two terms again without any consideration of the horse. For instance, we say that the legs and hands are natural aids, while the spurs and the whip are artificial ones. Obviously, to the horse, the legs of the rider are as artificial as that addition to them—the spurs. And the hands, acting through the reins and the bit, with which the horse was not born, are an artificiality of the highest order.

Of course one may say that since riding a horse is artificial to begin with, the whole of riding must be. This is correct, but there remains the matter of degree.

The least artificial and least abusive manner in which we can ride the horse, once we are determined to ride, is to ask him only to move at his normal easy gaits, maintaining the calmness that is natural to those gaits. This is, as a matter of fact, the most efficient way of riding from the point of view of covering ground. On this basis we may ride slow or fast, we may ride across country, change speeds, gaits, halt, make different types of turns, rein back, even require precision in the execution of all this, and jump up to the height suitable to the particular horse. The horse, even in his present form, has a history over a million years long; it was passed on the prairies. But the manege is a recent and entirely human invention.

This is not necessarily to say that the artificial is not often to be admired, but simply to point out that it should be recognized as artificial.

The Count d'Aure's *Traité d'Equitation* is an absorbing book, and one is tempted to go on quoting it indefinitely. I shall, however, limit myself here to one more excerpt, which I include because I believe many of my readers may be interested to know the origin of "posting" to the trot:

> It is only recently that a long-striding trot has been included among the gaits of saddle horses . . . but in altering the gait the riders have not been permitted to rectify the discomfort produced by its effects [that is they continue to sit in the saddle at the fast trot as they did at the slow]. It is from England that this long-striding trot has come to us. The English, in order to profit by the advantages of speed while seeking to avoid its tiring effects, have invented for practical use the period of suspension which, while giving the means to avoid discomfort, permits the rider to preserve the delicacy of his aids, the firmness and accuracy of his hand. This is an advantage one cannot obtain when subject to violent shaking-up.

The posting trot to which d'Aure refers had, however, been introduced into France as early as the last quarter of the 18th century but was opposed by the old masters for a long time.

It is generally believed that the long-striding trot and the posting that went with it originated in England when post-chaises appeared on improved roads around 1730. The word "post" does seem to reflect the postillions or "post-boys" who rode one of the forward horses. However, nowadays in England the word "post" is seldom used; the English say "rise to the trot." But the word "post" may have come to this country with English settlers, and it may reflect the word as used then in England.

It is quite obvious that Baucher, with his inclination toward the artificial, and the Count d'Aure, with his pursuit of simplicity and naturalness, could never agree. Possessing quite different temperaments they even argued differently. Characteristic of Baucher was his self-assurance. For instance:

"I say it out loud that full collection was never either understood or defined before me, because it is impossible to execute it perfectly without having applied successfully those principles which I have been the first to develop."

The Count d'Aure, on the other hand, presented his arguments in a mild manner, and occasionally with humor. This is how, for example, he treated some of Baucher's "inventions" —in this case the trot and the gallop backward:

Today all we are concerned about are the aids to use when we wish to make a horse sit on the haunches and rein back; but no mention is made of those required to make him go forward. It is perhaps a strange and rare thing to see a horse trot and gallop backward but, as use still requires a horse to move forward, and today perhaps more than ever, these are principles which it may be well to know.

The struggle between these two horsemen ultimately resulted in the following situation described (in 1890) by Captain Picard: "The mixture of the two methods is the theme of the present instruction at Saumur, and it is in this spirit, more or less modified by the one or the other method, that the teaching of the different instructors who have succeeded each other may be summarized."

It may be appropriate to mention here that the fundamental theme of today's major argument is the same—elaboration and artificiality as opposed to simplicity and naturalness. And some people still try to find a solution by mixing the two.

Although d'Aure and Baucher were making headlines in equestrian news, the High School of de la Guérinière was still practiced by a few, some of whom rode in the circus. Franconi, who was a renowned circus rider and an example of all the refinement of classical equitation, agreed with Baucher's critics that the latter's method was "a disarticulation of the horse, by mechanics, rather than by horsemen." Naturally, the old school could not look kindly at Baucher.

While these various arguments about methods of riding were going on, the life and customs of the 19th century were acquiring certain new characteristics which were to make this period in equitation a military one. All the essential causes of this started, however, earlier.

The influence of the French Revolution did not perish with Napoleon's empire. In the countries conquered by France the authority of the church had been abolished and the privileges of the nobles liquidated, to be replaced by religious tolerance and the equality of all citizens before the law. The *ancien régime* was over.

Although aristocratic attempts to restore the old order began, of course, with the fall of Napoleon, the new democratic ideas kept growing. This clash of ideals and of material interests eventually culminated in the revolutions of the forties. These revolutions were suppressed by the army, but the restoration of the old regime also failed. The newly evolving order led in many ways to an eventual compromise.

The nobility, whose supremacy had rarely been challenged in the past, had now to share their political power, and to some degree even their social prestige, with a new class of prosperous and educated bourgeoisie, created by the industrial revolution and colonial trade. The term "society" became vaguer in its meaning, often covering the whole of the upper and professional classes, or at least their well-educated, well-dressed and well-mannered members. Armies underwent a comparable democratization; they became less exclusively aristocratic and more professional and national.

By the middle of the century imperialism was growing rapidly in all major European countries, and the competition which arose from imperialistic trends led to the creation of large standing armies, with an effective peace-time strength equal to their former war-time one. All this resulted in an "Armed Peace"

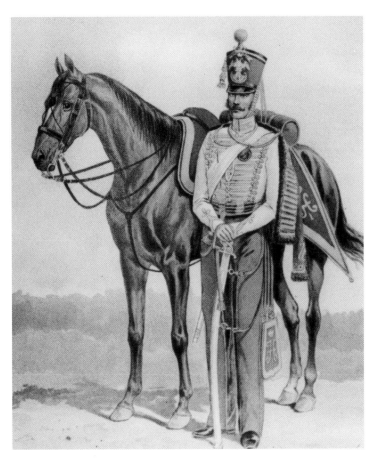

This uniform of my regiment in the middle of the 19th century is rather typical of the European cavalry uniforms of the period. In those days the army fought as well as paraded in such elaborate clothing. *(From the* History of the Sumsky Hussar Regiment, *Moscow, 1901.)*

preserved, up to a point, by a "Balance of Power." The armies were the backbone of it.

Although the first half of the century after Napoleon was free of large-scale wars, there were enough lesser wars (some with grave consequences) in the second half of it on the continent, and enough fighting in the colonies to preserve the importance of armies in the popular imagination. And official militaristic propaganda raised the prestige of the officer in all strata of society but the liberal ones. It taught that "the uniform of the officer is the dress of the sovereign; only those who belong to the chosen of the nation have the right to wear it. There is no position higher than that of an officer; it is greater than any civilian rank." This indoctrination survived until the First World War and I was brought up under it myself. For example, on my first day in the regiment, a senior officer, briefing me

At the beginning of our century colorful uniforms were still worn (though no longer in war). It may be noted that the formality was extended to moustaches and expressions. These are the executives and instructors of the Officers' Cavalry School, St. Petersburg, Russia, in 1906, but they would be typical of most similar bodies throughout continental Europe in the last half of the 19th century. Under such leadership, riding was bound to be formalized, standardized and relatively static. (*From the* Russian Cavalry Messenger, *for 1906.*)

.   .   .   .

on my future behavior, told me "by virtue of being a Sumski hussar you can do no wrong, but if you do anything wrong we shall kick you out." This illogical statement meant that only the officers' corps could henceforth judge me.

The romanticism of the period also found the dashing young cavalry officers in their brilliant uniforms, who still spent a great deal of time (and money) on the pleasures of life, quite irresistible. They were painted in spirited and heroic action by Gericault, Gros and others, their conquests both military and romantic enlivened the fiction of the time. They were bound to be envied and admired, and their manner of riding became the ideal. The old incentive to "ride the way princes ride" was replaced by the new one, "To ride the way the cavalry rides."

All this, of course, is why Baucher, in the first half of the century, and Fillis, in the second, made such strong efforts to be recognized by the cavalry. For if one's method was accepted by the army, it was accepted by the nation.

CHAPTER 9

Lesser Lights

· · · · · · · · · · · · ·

Later in this chapter you will read about the scientific research on the mechanics of the horse's movements that was conducted in the 19th century by many horsemen and scientists. Some of this research, such as the analysis of the dynamic balance of the horse, raised hippological knowledge to a new high. When we realize this, and also take into consideration the fact that all the armies of the period searched for better ways of riding and schooling so as to enable their cavalries to make longer and faster marches, then it becomes seemingly incomprehensible that they did not abolish collection. In other words, why didn't a Caprilli appear on the scene earlier?

All of us who have schooled horses on the principle of free going know that a green colt who has trouble in carrying the weight of the rider is heavy on the front, and hence moves badly and stumbles often. To a rider his movements feel uncomfortable and even unsafe. It is only later, after the colt has developed sufficient agility and strength to carry weight properly that his natural free gaits, based on natural balance, may become very pleasant to the rider. But, if from the very beginning of schooling, attempts are made to collect the colt, the trainer will never even have the chance to experience the pleasure of good free gaits. In this case he will remember only the awkwardness of the horse before he could be collected and his smoothness after he learned to move at collected gaits. This narrow experience with horses that had been taught only one kind of balance led horsemen to erroneous conclusions.

It is difficult to comprehend why continental horsemen did not experiment. They had, after all, very early in the century at least two examples of other ways of doing things: England and Russia. I suppose it was easy for an army officer to discard English sporting riding with the superficial remark that what may be good for foxhunting is not necessarily good for war. But what about the Russian cavalry which, in the course of the Napoleonic Wars, covered itself with glory on so many battlefields all across Europe? There are many contemporary prints showing Cossacks watering their horses in the Seine (in Paris in 1814), or bivouacking in the Bois de Boulogne. These Cossack horses were not schooled to collection, nor were the horses of my regiment of the regular cavalry—which, by the way, entered Paris at the head of the vanguard that had charged and destroyed the last resistance of the Napoleonic troops outside the city. But despite the experiences of the recent wars, the French army returned to collection; other countries had never abandoned it; and the victorious Russians, in their desire to become as cultured as Europeans, imported among other things the Western form of riding which ruined their cavalry for several generations.

All this seems incomprehensible until one takes into consideration the fact that the taste of the period was strong, and the horsemen's logic often weak.

In all European countries throughout the 19th century, the aristocracy, wherever it could, still clung tenaciously to the past. While the noble families had lost much of their power and some of their wealth, they still retained a great deal of their social prestige, and most remained able to continue to live in a formal manner in their old castles or palaces. Even the diminished scale was still a grand one.

At the same time the new industrial and commercial bourgeoisie was trying hard to imitate its betters. A rich industrialist or banker or shipping magnate lived now in a large city house, staffed by an army of servants and decorated in an eclectic style. The constant search for novelty, the low ebb of the creative arts, a sentimental infatuation with the past, and the new attraction of the remote and exotic were producing Gothic halls, Louis XVI dining rooms, Louis XV boudoirs, and Turkish smoking rooms at a rapid rate. The revivals were endless.

To the unpracticed eye of the new rich of the period the elaborate was often synonymous with the beautiful. The new machinery was also now capable of turning out complicated

This contemporary plate shows the entry of the Allied Armies into Paris in 1814.

The troops on the left are Cossacks, riding on snaffles with the necks of their horses completely extended.

These rough and ready troops were civilized Europe's only glimpses of men virtually born in the saddle. But, although the West was fascinated and admiring, its horsemen took no hints from their practical but primitive methods. (*From* An Illustrated Record of Important Events in the Annals of Europe, during the years 1812, 1813, 1814, and 1815. *Pub. by R. Bowyer, London, 1815.*)

decorations which could be and were applied indiscriminately to anything and everything. Exposed to this in quantity, even the old selective eye of the upper classes eventually became uncritical. As the bewildering number and diversity of material objects continued to increase, taste declined, and the 19th century, although it always continued to strive to be genteel, was frequently to be vulgar.

But formality continued and was manifest in the black frock coats and high hats of the gentlemen, in the tightly laced corsets and high shoes of the ladies, in the dozens and dozens of buttons and hooks and eyes and snaps on their elaborate, long-skirted dresses. It was visible in the colorful uniforms and gold braid of the military, in their white gloves and in the rigid cummerbunds some of them wore to set off those uniforms. It was a period when children were still seen and not heard, when the little girl's governess was immediately succeeded by the young

British uniforms issued in 1856. These were considered an improvement in the direction of simplicity and practicality over the ones previously worn by "that most brilliant arm of the service, the cavalry," as the *Illustrated London News* calls it. These officers certainly would not have considered themselves properly mounted except on collected horses. *(From* The Illustrated London News, *April 12, 1856.)*

lady's chaperon, when maid-servants wore starched aprons and stiff caps, men-servants were in livery, and carriages had footmen.

The pomp and ceremony may not have been as great as in the preceding centuries, but restraint and formality still sufficiently governed the horse-owning classes in all they did; they would certainly have continued to prefer the elaborate movements of a collected horse to the free-going simplicity of a well-developed field horse, had they ever had occasion to choose between the two—which on the continent they did not. If we ask ourselves again why the cavalry never developed a more

The entrance to the stables of Prince Galitzine, built in Russia in 1820. Musicians sat in the tribune behind the statuary. 19th century riding still could be a formal affair.

Children of that period briefly visited such stables accompanied by their governesses, but mounted their horses from the block at the porte cochère, whither the latter were brought by grooms. (*From* Starie Gody, *St. Petersburg, January, 1910.*)

These pictures of a German cavalryman during successive phases of the jump, taken before the invention of the motion picture camera, are instantaneous photographs. They were included among the illustrations in a Russian cavalry cadet-school text book published in 1889, as examples of how one should jump. They are indicative of what jumping was at a time when Dressage still flourished. *(Photographs by Ottomar Anschutz. From* Hippological Atlas, *by Major General Bilderling, St. Petersburg, 1889.)*

efficient and less fatiguing method of covering ground, we can only answer that in a period when some infantries were goose-stepping and others marching with less exaggerated but still stylized movements, one could hardly expect the most resplendent branch of the army to move in a natural and simple way.

I began the story of the 19th century with a description of what was happening then in France because, once Baucher and Count d'Aure became active, France resumed her interest in equestrian science and maintained it for the rest of the period. For almost forty years after Waterloo Europe enjoyed peace. Military thinking, as usual when there is neither any pressure of emergency on it nor any practical field in which to put its ideas to the test, stood still. Russia presents a striking illustration of this tendency.

Until 1815 [in Russia] there was no method of schooling a cavalry horse; the line cavalry was almost entirely mounted on "steppe" horses, and field service was all that was required. There were no maneges and therefore there was no manege riding. . . . The regiments of our cavalry were known for their uniformity only in action; they were capable of long marches, swam wide rivers easily, traversed mountains and ravines and in battle displayed a boldness and an enthusiasm by which they accomplished miracles. . . . In 1815 [the end of the Napoleonic Wars] we began to imitate the West . . . and from this time on we began to train our mounted troops by the standards of the German cavalry. . . . The cavalry received this announcement and the order had to be obeyed . . . our officers found themselves in a great predicament, for they had merely heard of the manege and the special art of horse-trainers, but did not have any idea how to start the work. . . . Someone translated de la Guérinière's book on High School into Russian, which being a very poor book for the line cavalry-man, did not even mention the snaffle, but primarily described superior circus riding and was illustrated by the piaffe, ballotade, capriole, etc. .... the young commanders jumped at this book, assuming that with the help of its information they would be able to organize the schooling properly. .... Fast gaits at that time were eliminated. In 1820 it was announced in the order of the day of one of the cavalry regiments that "during regimental and troop exercises the full gallop should not be employed but rather the smooth movements of the formation should be achieved at a walk, collected trot and not-too-fast gallop." ... The incorrect conditioning and schooling of horses became evident in the war of 1828–1829 [Russo-Turkish—a minor war] when horses, crippled by intensive manege breaking, lost flesh during the very first marches, began to collapse, and the great majority was found to be completely incapable of field service. (From contemporary recollections in an article in the *Russian Cavalry Messenger* for the year 1906.)

Few books on riding were written in Russia, particularly in the first half of the 19th century; I happen to have one of these, written by Colonel Ivan Bobinsky and published in 1836. In spite of its approximately five hundred pages of rather small print it is entitled *A Short Hippology and Course in Horseback Riding*. Its contents are not original and merely repeat the principles of the old Western European manege riding, presenting them as the basis for cross-country riding. According to it the horse should not be allowed to relax even when simply travelling along the road.

The field or travelling cavalry walk is very different from the natural one which an unschooled horse employs. So long as the horse in his natural movements does not know how to bend the joints of his hindquarters, he carries the croup high and the forehand low; hence the shoulders and other

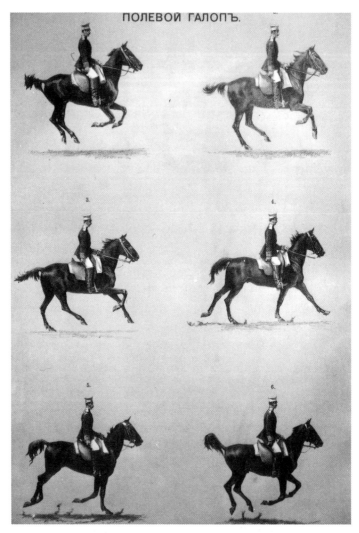

ПОЛЕВОЙ ГАЛОПЪ.

Another series of the German pictures which illustrated a Russian army text book of 1889.

The Russian caption at the top of the plate reads "field gallop." This gallop was used by the Russian cavalry at the time in conditions which today would call for a "hunting pace." This horse however, who is to some extent collected, is moving rather at the "extended gallop" of Dressage than at an easy, natural and fast field gallop of today. (*Photographs by Ottomar Anschutz. From* Hippological Atlas, *by Major General Bilderling, St. Petersburg, 1889.*)

136

members cannot move freely and the walk of the horse is slow and heavy ... the rider, forcing the horse to use the [schooled] walk for travelling, should lift the front, without checking the horse: and urge the quarters. ...

It is little wonder that these unfortunate animals, with mouths pulled and ribs kicked by the hour on long road marches, fell apart in war. Since this book was based on the German military interpretation of classical equitation, it gives some idea of what was happening in parts of Central Europe in the first half of the 19th century.

It is worth noting that among the seven hundred and fifty odd subscribers to this book all but eight belong to the army. The list is a roll of generals, colonels, captains, etc., and in the case of the comparatively few titled names, the rank precedes the title. How different from the 18th century; times have changed, and the army has taken over.

On the other hand, England continued to present quite a different picture; there foxhunting and racing flourished rather than military reviews.

After Waterloo, a small standing army was maintained, but its popularity came to an end with the war. Though no longer regarded as a menace to the Constitution, it was regarded as an unnecessary expense by the economic anti-militarism of the new age. Moreover, the reformers now rising to influence disliked it as an aristocratic preserve. Such indeed it was; but the reformers, instead of proposing to reform it and democratize it, preferred to starve it and cut it down. Meanwhile the respectable working classes continued to regard enlistment in the army as a sign of failure in life, if not of positive disgrace. Nineteenth Century England, having the good fortune to be safe from attack for several generations, conceived that so long as her navy was efficient her army could safely be neglected. . . . (From *Illustrated English Social History*, by G. M. Trevelyan, 4th vol. Longmans, Green and Co., 1952.)

The great majority of English 19th century riders then were civilian rather than military, and riding continued to be for sport rather than for parade or the manege, and the flashy hacks of Rotten Row were not schooled horses in the Continental sense.

This was the time in England when the ranks of the hunting field, previously made up largely of local gentry and farmers, were swelled by well-to-do business people from the fast-growing industrial centers. Their town-dwellers' manners and often erratic performances out hunting gave Robert S. Surtees an excellent opportunity to make fun of these newcomers in such books as *Jorrocks's Jaunts and Jollities* and *Handley Cross*, which immediately gained wide popularity. Indeed, sporting literature as a whole, glorifying racing and foxhunting, and with a strong accent on manly courage, was growing fast. C. J. Apperley's (Nimrod) famous *Memoirs of the Life of the Late John Mytton*, still cherished by foxhunting men, was only one of the many books on the subject then appearing. Spirited illustrations, such as those of the Alkens and John Leech contributed much to these books. They also produced colored plates to hang on study and inn-parlor walls, depicting the chase as one great rollicking adventure, which involved a series of bone-shattering but presumably enjoyable falls.

More serious artists, like George Stubbs (in the 18th century) and Ben Marshall, J. F. Herring, and others later, painted the first real portraits of horses and their owners. The results were often charming, and for the first time the horse entered the drawing room on his own merit.

Paintings, prints and books, all widely collected today, are to be found in many American homes and libraries. From them it is easy to see that the atmosphere of 19th century sporting

England was hardly conducive to a scientific approach to riding. This sporting rather than scholastic attitude of English horsemen was thus expressed by John Lawrence in his book *History of the Horse*, American edition of 1830:

"Nothing can be more obvious than that the *menage* is chiefly ornamental; and that the thoroughly dressed horse is rather an object of luxurious parade than of real utility. . . . the grand *menage* is an antique and cumbrous superfluity, which ought to be laid aside, or exhibited only in a depository of heavy carriages and heavy starched apparel. . . ."

But in the second half of the 19th century in France much work was being done toward putting equitation on a sound scientific basis. This, of course, could be achieved only after the

A lesson at Jules Pellier's riding school in Paris. Jules Pellier came of three generations of professional horsemen of that name. For a time François Baucher associated himself with Jules Pellier's father and worked in the latter's riding school. They collaborated on a book, *Les Dialogues sur l'Equitation.*

This picture illustrates the formality of Victorian manege riding, which fostered stylish collected gaits. The formal group ride, executing elaborate figures, often to music, was a logical civilian counterpart of the brilliant cavalry review of the period; it was another one of the descendants of the old carousel. *(From* Le Langage Equestre, *by Jules Pellier, Paris, 1889.)*

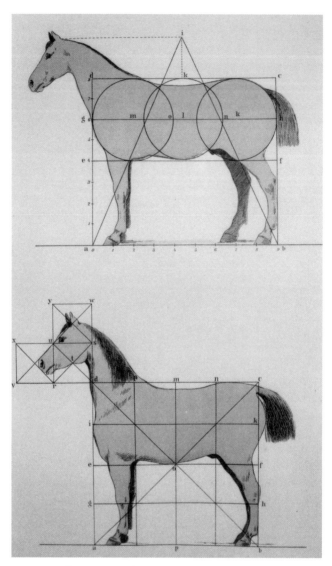

These are not illustrations of "how to draw a horse" but a mathematical approach to conformation, typical of many 19th century efforts to reduce everything concerning riding to a science. *(From* Hippological Atlas, *by Major General Bilderling, St. Petersburg, 1889.)*

The top drawing by V. Ritter; the lower by Dominik.

horse's locomotion had been thoroughly analyzed. Many horse-men worked towards this end, often assisted by scientists. One of the latter, for instance Professor M. Marey, invented a "graphic" method for the study of the horse's gaits. A book of the period claims that with this method "he has determined in an almost definite manner most of the principles [of locomotion] previously doubtful." There were others who participated in this research, some French, some German, many of them pro-fessors of veterinary science. To mention a few: Vincent, Goiffon and Lenoble du Tail of France; M. L. Hoffman, Ernst and Wilhelm Weber of Germany.

The outstanding contribution to the study of the mechanics of the horse's movements was made, however, in the United States in the seventies and the eighties of the 19th century, by a photographer, Eadweard Muybridge. A dispute over whether there is a phase of the trot during which all four feet of the horse are off the ground provoked Muybridge to make his first experiments with instantaneous photography of horses; these took place in California during the summer of 1872.

> It then occurred to him that a series of photographic images in rapid succession at properly regulated intervals of time, and distance, would definitely set at rest the many existing theories and conflicting opinions upon animal movements generally. . . . he devised a system for obtaining a succession of automatic exposures at intervals of time which could be regulated at discretion . . . experiments were carried on from time to time . . . it was not until 1878 that the results of any of them were published.

In that year some of Muybridge's photographs were repro-duced in several European magazines, and in 1886 a French artist, Aimé Morot, painted a battle scene representing galloping horses in attitudes based on this new knowledge. The painting stirred much controversy. People were not used to seeing horses in such positions, being accustomed rather to the conventional misrepresentations of the gallop and the jump typical of English hunting prints or of the numerous battle scenes that hung on the walls of a France still dreaming of her days of military glory.

In 1884 Muybridge, sponsored this time by the University of Pennsylvania, began his photographic study of the locomotion of animals in general (with a series of twenty-four cameras) and in 1887 published *Animal Locomotion*, containing some 20,000 figures of men, birds, lions, elephants, other animals and many horses in motion. (This information is taken partly from the

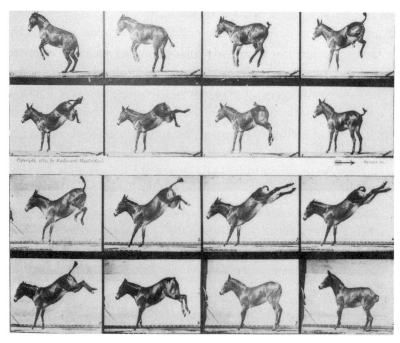

In the last quarter of the 19th century photography supplanted learned conjecture in the analysis of the horse's movements, and many facts were discovered upon which modern theory could build. An American, Eadweard Muybridge, using a battery of cameras, took pictures of successive phases of the movements of various animals. *(From* Animals in Motion, *by Eadweard Muybridge, first published 1887.) (Reproduced from a reprint published by Chapman & Hall, Ltd., London, 1925.)*

142

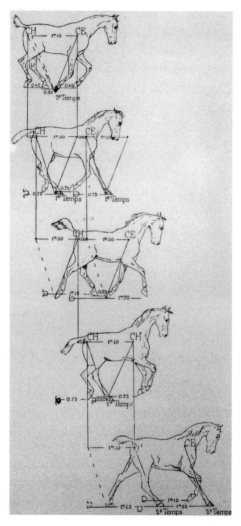

An example of the many 19th century efforts to analyze the horse's locomotion. This series of pictures shows transition from canter to trot and back to canter. The horsemen of the last century were very serious about such things and made no attempt to popularize them. The text illustrated by these drawings is an excellent example of how complicated this scientific approach could be. *(From* L'Art Equestre, *by E. Barroil, Paris, 1889.)*

preface to the abridged edition, reprinted in London in 1925, under the title *Animals in Motion*, by Chapman & Hall, Ltd.)

About this time Ottomar Anshutz of Lissa, Germany, also produced a series of instantaneous photographs of the horse's gaits and of jumping. In 1889 these photographs illustrated one of the text books of the Nicholas Cavalry School in St. Petersburg, Russia, where I later was a cadet. The word had spread fast. These 19th century photographs are of little practical value today, not only because we now have motion pictures, but also because the horses in them move awkwardly, as a result of exceptionally bad riding.

Animal locomotion in general, and hence the horse's in particular, is a total of two forces: muscular effort and constant redistribution of weight. While the muscles of the quarters push the horse forward, the weight, momentarily switched to the forehand, pulls him forward. Then, just before the instability in front can cause a fall, a leg comes forward to support the body. This phenomenon is repeated at every stride. The ability of the horse to keep himself upright while playing with his weight in order to produce movement, and particularly speed, constitutes "dynamic" balance. The "static" balance of a horse standing still is a very different thing; in this case stability is merely the result of a certain constant distribution of weight on four feet.

In the course of the latter part of the 19th century many horsemen attempted to analyze the balance of the horse, and they gradually arrived at the conception of "dynamic" balance. Two professors of veterinary science, Armand Goubaux and Gustave Barrier, thus formulated the idea in their book, *The Exterior of the Horse*, published in 1892 by J. B. Lippincott Co.

The movement of the body over the ground implies displacements of the center of gravity and, consequently, a destruction of the initial equilibrium, which incessantly compels the members to form new bases of support. Hence the members, each in their turn, come forward and prop it in front ... the rapidity with which they succeed each other is so much more frequent as the imminence of a fall is greater. Here is the reason of the correctness of the expression, that the *instability of the equilibrium*, in these gaits, *gives the measure of the velocity*.

The progress in thinking accomplished in the course of the century becomes evident if one compares this definition with what Baucher had to say on the same subject:

In our 19th century, when all things should be treated scientifically, it was natural that science was asked the secret of equilibrium. Science replied with a problem: to put your horse in equilibrium, look for his center of gravity. This answer did not fail to arouse a noble enthusiasm. Everyone went to work. The center of gravity is sought after everywhere, all the time ... but it is not to be found. ... It unquestionably exists, but in a passive state. What you set up as a cause is merely a result ... abandon the center of gravity to the influences which govern it ... mount a real horse, and you will probably approve the principles which I am about to use for obtaining and maintaining the equilibrium of the horse.

In this paragraph, Baucher, completely disregarding the horse's natural ways of balancing himself in motion, refers exclusively to the artificial equilibrium forcefully given to a collected horse by the rider; this equilibrium was the only one recognized by Baucher.

Later in the century many horsemen came to realize that forward movement in a free-going horse results from a combination of muscular effort and a loss of equilibrium to the front, but they either did not know, or chose to disregard the role played by the neck and head as "balancer" during the walk

145

and the gallop and in jumping. It was easy to overlook this, since at collected gaits, prevalent then, the balancing "gestures of the neck and head practically do not exist." Thus, at one time the chief of the Saumur Cavalry School, Captain A. Gerhardt could write:

"Experience proved that 'ramener' should be the object of the constant preoccupation of the rider. Ramener consists in raising the neck and in placing the head in an approximately vertical position. This attitude is sought not merely because it is graceful . . . but above all because it favors regularity of action and the force of the bit." (*Dressage et la Conduite du Cheval de Guerre*, 1862.)

"Ramener" is the first step toward collection; the latter term refers not only to the attitude of the neck and head but to a certain redistribution of weight, and the resultant high action. The term "ramener" has never been translated into English, and uneducated riders who dabble in Dressage often confuse it with collection, which in French is called "rassembler." The rassembler itself may be of different degrees.

A rigid neck and head at collected gaits are quite correct, for in this case the horse's motive power is predominantly muscular and, in the absence of constantly repeated moments of instability, the auxiliary balancing efforts of the horse's neck and head are unnecessary. It is different, however, at fast gaits.

There is one more point concerning "ramener" and "rassembler" that may be worth mentioning here. Probably due to the fact that riding in our century began by following and, to a certain extent, continues to follow the principles of manege riding, hence of collection, one often meets horsemen who are confused enough to think that the horse is in a state of equilibrium only when collected. There is no question but that a collected horse is in a state of equilibrium. But the fast-moving horse, with neck and head extended, may be in equally good equilibrium. The first kind of balance is more often than not artificial, while the second is always natural. Many horsemen

146

of today are still working to improve the method of schooling hunters and jumpers on the basis of natural balance. There will be more about this in later chapters.

The scientific approach to the study of the horse's locomotion, so typical of the century, manifested itself also in attempts to present riding as an almost exact science. To illustrate this let me quote again from Captain A. Gerhardt's *Dressage et la Conduite du Cheval de Guerre*:

> The animal mechanism may be considered as a reservoir of forces from which the horse draws indifferently those which he requires to begin or to maintain this or that gait; let a stand for the force necessary to produce the walk. Now let us suppose that the rider wishes to make his horse gallop; the latter, in order to respond to the urging of the aids, must draw from his reservoir of forces the amount b which, added to the first amount gives $a + b$, the total which is needed to enable him to go into a gallop. But in order to *persuade* the horse to take this gait, the rider must put him in a preliminary *position*, and he is unable to do this without using up n of the force a; the latter would therefore be reduced to the amount $a - n$ which added to b, would be insufficient to enable the horse to make a canter departure.
>
> In order to overcome this obstacle the rider, while he is using one of his legs to give the position to his horse, will use the other to induce him to draw from his reservoir of forces a new part $n' = n$ and then the amount represents $a + b - n + n'$ will be exactly equal to the one we arrived at by $a + b$; which is to say that the horse will employ a total of forces sufficient to enable him to respond instantaneously to the urging of the aids, if no other physical cause impedes him.

The mathematical approach to be found in some books resulted from a serious attitude toward the mechanics of the horse's movements—on the continent at least. It was traditionally different in England. There, fine sporting results were achieved merely on the basis of a rider's experience and boldness, and on the superiority of the horse-flesh. The English books of the time stress courage rather than mathematics:

> "He that would venture nothing must not get on horseback" says a Spanish proverb, and the same caution seems applicable to most manly amusements or pursuits. . . . "Where there is no fear there is no danger," though a somewhat reckless aphorism, is more applicable, I think, to the exercise of riding than to any other venture of neck and limb. . . . If the man's heart is in the right place his horse will seldom fail him; and were we asked to name the one essential without which it is impossible to attain thorough proficiency in the saddle, we should not hesitate to say nerve. *Nerve*, I repeat, in contradistinction to *pluck*. The latter takes us into a difficulty, the former brings us out of it. Both are comprised in the noble quality we call emphatically valour . . . (*Riding Recollections*, by G. J. Whyte-Melville, published in 1878.)

Now about the rest of Europe: the two countries, Germany and Italy, which were to exert the strongest opposing influences on 20th century riding throughout the world, did not play such universal roles in the 19th. In the beginning of this chapter I mentioned that early in the latter century the Russian cavalry was under the influence of German military riding; it remained so into the 'nineties. This statement, however, should be qualified by saying that Germany herself did not have a uniform school of riding. While, for instance, the horses of one Prussian regiment were trained by Baucher's method, that method was criticized by such important German masters as Louis Seeger and E. Seidler. The story of minor influences and counter influences is very complex, and in this book I shall avoid discussing them. Undoubtedly every nation that borrows ideas from another modifies them to some extent to suit its national characteristics and the needs of the moment. Nor should local influences be confused with those of national or international scale. In a period when so many rode, there naturally were outstanding horsemen in every country, who earned the admiration of their contemporaries and died without influencing equestrian techniques or leaving an enduring memory beyond the borders of their fatherland.

For instance, have you ever heard of Saint-Phalle? The other day, when leafing through the *Russian Cavalry Messenger* for 1908, I came upon his obituary. He was a French cavalry officer who died that year at the age of forty. In 1900 in Paris he won the "Championship of the Universal Horse." The

test consisted of the following: an endurance test of 50 kilometers, arena jumping, a steeple-chase 4½ kil., the speed to exceed 550 metres per minute, and a schooling test, during which the rider might exhibit anything the horse was able to do. Captain Saint-Phalle, riding his thoroughbred mare, Marcelle, was first in every test, and during the schooling phase of the competition demonstrated, besides the full program of ordinary riding, High School movements, including changes of lead while galloping backwards.

But Captain Saint-Phalle did more than ride; he wrote books, in one of which, by the way, he criticized James Fillis' method; and his comments were important enough for Fillis to answer them in his *Journal de Dressage*. Probably it was only an early death that prevented Saint-Phalle from playing a more lasting role than he did.

Or take the case of the French General A. l'Hotte who, according to his compatriots, was "one of the glories of French equitation," and who "knew how to obtain the most difficult *airs* of High School without making the action of his aids obvious to the eye of the spectator." As Baucher's pupil he advanced this kind of equitation even further than his famous teacher. But due to his unsociable character he had few pupils and thus did not exert wide personal influence during his life. His important book was published only in 1906, after his death and at a time when Caprilli was already teaching a completely new method of cross-country riding and jumping, and France had ceded her place as a source of original thinking to Italy. General l'Hotte was too late to influence the world. However, both his and Saint-Phalle's books remained as very important items in the teaching of the Saumur Cavalry School.

Language, too, often forms a barrier. The international equestrian language of the century was French, and thus the possible influence of some important German books, which were never translated into French, was curtailed then and there.

Considering all this, in describing the 19th century I stress the role of two countries, France and England. The first exerted her influence not only by the seriousness and the originality of her thinking, but also through the great number of first-class horsemen who were active in the search for better riding; while England was influential through her achievements in the field of sporting riding, and through her production of better horse-flesh. What England accomplished empirically, the continent achieved eventually on a scholastic basis; it was England, however, who had pointed the way.

Until very recently it was not sufficient merely to ride brilliantly in order to exert wide influence. All the so-called masters of equitation created their own methods or at least improved existing ones; they also taught, and wrote books. Their books survived, and their able pupils spread the new theories, often also writing about them. It is only with the great increase in the number and importance of competitive horse shows that

In 19th century England it was not riding itself which changed as much as the people who rode to hounds, and their manners and tastes. John Leech, the famous caricaturist, here emphasizes the social changes in foxhunting circles, from the "good old times" to the "present degenerate" ones. *(From* The Illustrated London News, *February 23, 1856.)*

outstanding winners, helped by the media, can influence young riders on a large scale. A recent German international team is a particularly conspicuous example of this. Even so, I wonder how long their names will survive. Who, for example, remembers today the names of those pupils of Caprilli who originally did so much by their successful riding to promote the doctrines of their famous teacher? Who even remembers the names of all the members of the Mexican international team who won the Olympic Jumping of 1948 and were victorious in Madison Square Garden for so many years? It is only in institutions like cavalry schools or the Spanish School of Vienna that the names of their great riders of the past are preserved.

Leaving aside the story of innovations and improvements, and simply tracing the conditions of riding in Europe at the end of the 19th century, it may be worth while to listen to a knowledgeable (although perhaps not entirely unprejudiced) contemporary. James Fillis thus described them in his *Journal de Dressage* (1903):

There is but one school in Europe where the real school [High School] horse is to be found: that is Saumur. Its horses are schooled in a manner to be ready for any kind of work because they are well-balanced, light, and obedient to the hands and legs ... the riders are quiet in their movements. They are united with their horses by a suppleness and ease which they owe to their seat and their attitude ... and it is only there that one finds the school horse as I understand it; that is, schooled so that it will be able at a moment's notice, without further preparation, to hunt, race, or go to war. ...

Vienna has two schools, one of which is called Spanish, in which there are only horses that have been schooled between pillars. These horses can only be used in the manege. Under these conditions I consider High School harmful. Once school horses not only cannot be used for all purposes but are not even the best among the good it means that the art is warped. The other school is military, with no school [High School] horses.

Germany has three large schools: Hanover, Dresden and Munich. At Hanover there are five or six school horses which are not distinguished for their brilliance. They lack delicacy and particularly suppleness. What is particularly noticeable is the complete lack of those coordinated movements by which the rider collects his horse and makes him very light. The reason for the inferiority of German riding, as far as High School goes, is the result of the lack of an outstanding rider. There was one, named Steinbrech, whose example has not been followed, and his only pupil seems not to have understood him. French equitation requires the horse to be schooled by the mouth, German by the neck. This is why German equitation appears so stiff and hard next to the French. The mouth is a piano, the neck is an organ. A horse schooled by the mouth can be kept in hand by a mere thread at the end of the fingers, but one schooled by the head and neck requires taut reins and even taut arms. This is why the first type of equitation is all delicacy, the second all force. Dresden and Munich are quite inferior to Hanover; in these places the iron glove has replaced the velvet glove. On the other hand, ordinary riding (in Germany) which they call country riding, is quite superior to that in other European countries in that it is far more widespread. In Germany everyone knows enough about equitation to school his horse without the help of a teacher. In every city in Germany there is a quantity of excellent schools. Berlin has several, with between 200 and 300 horses apiece. . . . In a word, civilian riding is as widespread in Germany as it is neglected in other parts of Europe. When it comes to military riding it is absolutely first class [in Germany]; the horses are as obedient as the men. I consider it one of the most perfected of Europe.

There is no artistic riding in England: there is only sporting riding.

I cannot speak for Italy, never having had the honor of visiting its schools.

I have lived in Belgium and Holland. As these two countries raise no saddle horses, the cavalry procures them from Ireland. Good horses and well schooled, but not school horses.

Should I speak of the Russian school? [At this time Fillis was chief instructor in this school.] We are twelve instructors and we have only twelve horses for our school [High School] lessons. These are not enough, because there should be reserve horses available in case of disability. And our horses are used for everything. After having used them in the school from October to May we put them in training for six weeks. They ran in July [in military races]; in August they made a forced march of 150 miles in two days carrying 175 pounds; then in September they were hunted. This proves the usefulness of rational schooling, because these horses did well in all these tests. . . .

This is probably neither an entirely impartial nor a completely comprehensive account of the state of riding in Europe at the time, but in view of the fact that, to my knowledge, no other horseman with the same opportunities for observation gave such a summary, makes it particularly interesting. By presenting Fillis' point of view it introduces the reader to the man we shall discuss at length in the following chapter.

CHAPTER 10

—

James Fillis

. . . .

FROM the point of view of wide-spread influence at the turn of the century, James Fillis was second only to Baucher. Fillis' first book, *Principes de Dressage et d'Equitation*, was published in Paris in 1890, and afterwards translated into several languages. Significantly enough, the title was rendered into English as *Breaking and Riding* (Hurst & Blackett, Ltd., London, 1902); the term "Dressage," often so glibly used today, was not in vogue in England some sixty years ago when the translation first appeared. (Many passages quoted in this chapter will be from this translation.)

Born in London in 1834, Fillis came to France as a youngster, lived there longer than in any other country, and died in Paris in 1913. It was to this city, his home for many years, that he dedicated his second book, *Journal de Dressage*, published by Ernest Flammarion, Paris, 1903. Fillis himself described the beginning of his riding career:

> I was eight years old when I was put for the first time on the back of a horse. My humble person was not very highly valued and as soon as a horse resisted or made trouble they shouted "put the boy on him." They put him on and made him push the horse forward with heels, crop and whip. He

stayed on as best he could, or rolled on the ground to be put astride again immediately.

Such were my first steps in the art of equitation. This is how from childhood I began to cultivate the great principle of *impulsion* which has since become so dear to me.

Later came empirical work, with all the experiment it entails, the searching, the gropings, the gradually corrected errors, the mistakes rectified with difficulty, the sterile or fruitful efforts, and the good and bad advice, amidst the confusion of which one must orient oneself. (*Principes de Dressage et d'Equitation*, third edition, 1892.)

After riding for dealers and working on the track, Fillis studied High School under Baucher's former pupil, François Caron, to whom he dedicated his first book. While still a young man he rode under Franconi in the circus of the Champs Elysées in Paris. In the course of his life he demonstrated his High School horses in many European circuses, and gave private exhibitions before the Emperor of Germany, the Tsar of Russia, the President of France, the Queen of Belgium, the King of Denmark and the Emperor of Austria. Fillis ended his showman's career in 1898, after an engagement in Ciniselli's circus in St. Petersburg, Russia. The founder of this circus was Gaetano Ciniselli "a high priest of la Haute Ecole" and, of course, a pupil of Baucher. Fillis was then earning the equivalent of $900.00 a month in roubles at Ciniselli's; only consider what this would represent today. The Ciniselli circus was at that time a very fashionable institution and could pay the price, particularly to the outstanding master of this then very popular form of entertainment.

The European circus of those days differed considerably from the American travelling three-ring one under a "big top." It was housed in a permanent building, and offered a performance every day of the season. Although the circus did not move, the actors changed. It had only one ring and the accent was rather on a high level of individual performance than on large-scale pageantry. Ciniselli's circus was an attractive stone building, with red velvet seats inside, and on many nights people in evening dress were to be seen in the boxes.

About riding in the circus Fillis wrote: ". . . it is as natural for a horseman to ride in a circus, as for a lyric artist to show himself at the opera. . . ." As a matter of fact, in those days, when public competitions in Dressage did not yet exist, the circus was the only place where a civilian horseman could exhibit his art. The high standards of equestrian performances at Ciniselli's were still maintained in my youth, and the cavalry school where I was a cadet went there yearly, in a body, to watch manege riding at its perfection.

Cantering on three legs while holding the fourth one up and extended in the air was one of the movements invented by Fillis. He writes "I have never seen it done by anyone else, and I have never met with its description in any treatise on equitation." (*From* Principes de Dressage et d'Equitation, *by James Fillis, Paris, 1892.*)

· · · · · · · · · · · · · · · · · ·

It seems to me that in the days when outstanding High School riders performed in circuses and some of the instructors of the Saumur Cavalry School practiced the canter to the rear, it was not easy to pinpoint the distinction between High School and circus. The argument that the canter to the rear is a circus trick but that movements above the ground, artificially taught between pillars, are not, hardly holds water for those who are not indoctrinated. There is a point of view, however, that maintains that classic High School is limited to the movements taught by de la Guérinière. The Spanish School of Vienna illustrates this attitude when it practices the Capriole, the Croupade, etc., but excludes from its program such a thing as the canter to the rear, which was invented later. Such a policy of conservation may be considered valid—we have to have museums, but art has to go ahead also. Baucher, Fillis and other High School riders of the 19th century developed new forms of the art, and in this they are to be congratulated rather than condemned.

An Englishman, Captain M. Horace Hayes, who knew Fillis personally, and who did not admire High School but much preferred foxhunting, wrote of Fillis:

> He is very much of the same kind of build as was poor George Fordham, and no doubt would have been a brilliant jockey, had he entered that line. He is very energetic and is always true to his favorite motto, *en avant*... Although he is a naturalized Frenchman, his heart is English, and I am sure that nothing would give him greater pleasure than to have his skill recognized in England.... The difficulty of course is that in England, riding means riding to hounds, which has not much in common with school performances. (*Among Horses in Russia*, 1900.)

In 1898 the Russian army invited Fillis to teach in the Officers' Cavalry School in St. Petersburg. Fillis held the position of chief instructor in this school until his retirement in 1910, at the age of seventy-six. Thus he succeeded in becoming officially important in the training of cavalry which, you may remember, had been Baucher's dream. Fillis based the teaching in the army on his own simplified method, and it is described in the Russian army regulations for schooling horses of 1908, which were translated in 1914 into French as *Réglement pour le Dressage du Cheval d'Armes* (pub. by Ernest Flammarion, Paris). Fillis' method re-

Two examples of the "gallop rearward," one of the new movements of 19th century High School, invented by Baucher.

An example of a movement that originated in the contemporary circus being adopted by cavalry officers who were great devotees of High School. *(From* Journal de Dressage, *by James Fillis, Paris, 1903.)*

. . . .

mained in force until the First World War, which really marked the end of the 19th century. The experiences on this practical proving ground, however, disappointed those who still believed in collection and in arduous manege schooling.

Fillis was a hard worker. He tells in one of his books how when young he rode some ten horses on a week day, and three or four on Sundays and holidays. At the time Baron Gustave de Rothschild employed him he would begin work at four o'clock in the morning in the summer, and at five in the winter. One exceptional summer, during all of July and August and part of September, he rode sixteen horses daily, riding from four in the morning until eight at night, without time out for a real lunch. What price glory! In 1903 Fillis estimated that up to that time he had made about forty High School horses.

In his High School work for the circus, besides demonstrating such usual movements as the Passage, the Piaffe or the Pirouette at the gallop, Fillis exhibited such exotic feats as the half-rear with one of the forelegs extended, the gallop to the rear, the Passage on two tracks, the Courbette and the Pesade. Fillis' actual repertory was very large and included many movements in both categories.

Fillis' books are illustrated by photographs of him riding, from which we gather that at least in his later days he had a far from elegant seat; his legs were often stuck forward, his body assumed many positions, the strong use of spurs caused his toes to point downward on occasions. But his horses are fully collected—that is, sitting down on the hocks with a sloping croup; and they perform with great vigor. As one of my older friends, a former pupil of Fillis, used to say, "His horses moved as if the devil was inside them." But despite this, Captain Hayes wrote,

> the horse he rode walked into and round the ring [of a circus] in ordinary style, and without a trace of excitement or ex-

aggerated collection, until he began his particular act. As soon as the animal had finished his *numero*, he resumed his placid way of going, which showed that his brilliance was not the result of his having been tortured. Fillis is certainly the greatest master of this kind of riding.

At that time thousands of people must have agreed with Captain Hayes, for in the days when good High School riding could be seen in every first-class circus, and every important city of Europe had at least one permanent one, Fillis was the shining star. And there must have been some good reason for inviting him to teach cavalry officers.

Dressage riders of today, while they may admit his artistry, are apt to look down on Fillis as on a mere showman. This may be so. But one should not forget that Fillis made many creditable High School riders—I knew several. At the moment I am curious to know how much of Fillis' teaching was behind

The caption to this picture in one of Fillis' books reads: "an ordinary trot." Fillis' conception of an ordinary gait was obviously very different from today's. (*From* Journal de Dressage, *by James Fillis, Paris, 1903.*)

the winning of the Grand Prix de Dressage by a Russian in the Olympic Games of 1960; a second Russian placed fifth. As a matter of fact, I was told by a Dressage judge in those Games that Russian performances in Rome were still a product of Fillis' school, rather than of the modern French school—and certainly not of the German school.

Today, with only books by which to judge Fillis, I am always particularly impressed by the simplicity of his presentation of High School, and by the originality of his thinking about this form of riding. This is especially apparent in his *Journal de Dressage*, a diary of the training of three horses. These three stories are vividly written, and Fillis' understanding of the animals and the ingenuity with which he solves different problems are very striking. On the other hand, I find that his most important book, *Principes de Dressage et d'Equitation*, which treats

The Russian army regulation seat at the end of the 19th century, of which the present German Dressage seat is very reminiscent; it was then rather typical of all continental European armies. This was an all-purpose seat at the time, and that is one of the reasons why the jumping of the period was so deplorable. *(From* Hippological Atlas, *by Major General Bilderling, St. Petersburg, 1889.)*

of both High School and ordinary riding such as hacking, hunting, and riding in army ranks, can be quoted to support very different points of view. This, of course, would be unavoidable wherever there is an artificial mixture of two kinds of riding. Such lack of consistency is typical also among those people today who try to combine Dressage and Forward Riding.

Actually both parts of Fillis' work have the same foundation, which is collection. It is merely by the degree of collection that he distinguishes his different uses of the horse—with the exception of racing. He himself (in the *Army Regulation*) says:

"If the Rassembler is the acme of the High School it is no less, although in a smaller degree, the basis of practical equitation."

In the preface to his *Principes de Dressage et d'Equitation* which, as I have pointed out, deals with High School as well as with "practical" riding, Fillis also states that collection is the basis of his method:

"My method of equitation consists in distribution of weight by the height of the neck bent at the poll and not at the withers; propulsion by means of the hocks being brought under the body; and lightness by the loosening of the lower jaw."

I can still recite this paragraph in Russian; in the cavalry schools of my days, the cadets were made to memorize it— which really was too bad for the cavalry. Let us analyze what these few lines mean. First of all, by building his method on a fixed distribution of weight Fillis completely disregarded the natural locomotion of the horse in which the weight (center of gravity) is constantly fluid. In the second place, by implying that the hind legs alone propel the horse forward, Fillis again disregarded the role which the horse's weight plays in moving the body forward. Thus this part of the paragraph really refers to the artificial balance of a High School horse, similar to that of Baucher's horses. As a matter of fact, Fillis considered himself Baucher's follower. But since he was also an innovator he did not accept Baucher's teaching in its entirety; in his books he frequently argues against Baucher's method. A characteristic point of Baucher's collection, during most of his career, was the low bend of the neck, and it is probably against Baucher that the phrase "neck bent at the poll and not at the withers" is directed. As to the last phrase, about the loosening of the lower jaw, you may remember that in the previous chapter I quoted Fillis' saying that the French school their horses by the mouth and Germans by the neck. This third item pointed out on which side Fillis was.

In the matter of the balance of the horse in motion Fillis, who most of his life practiced the artificial balance of High School, was confused when trying to simplify his system for ordinary riding. Thus, for instance, describing the army horse he says:

"The horse ought to be neither on his shoulders nor on his haunches; but should have his own weight and that of his rider equally distributed on both ends" (which is medium collection).

On the other hand, he also says:

"The army horse should be balanced in such a way, as to be skilful at displacing his center of gravity as necessity demands, that is: to be able to shift the necessary amount of weight forward at rapid gaits, and to shift it to the rear for slow ones. . . ."

This paragraph, although it clearly contradicts the previous one, expresses, of course, a correct idea. But again Fillis negates his own statement by completely disregarding the important part neck movements play in the shifting of weight. Instead of leaving the neck free to act he insists upon giving it a certain fixed position.

"For enabling the horse to carry his weight better and to facilitate the utmost liberty in his movements it is necessary:

a) To place the head and the neck correctly rather high . . .

b) To give the neck muscular strength to make it rigid at its base. . . ."

164

Obviously, if one were to work long enough on raising the neck and on developing those muscles that tend to keep it elevated with a rigid base, not every horse would be able to extend it again readily, while still remaining on the bit, on the rare occasions when he might be asked to do so—that is, of course, except for the calm walk on loose reins.

And, certainly unintentionally, Fillis himself illustrates this. In his *Journal de Dressage* there are pictures of him on Maestoso and Povero, demonstrating what he calls "an ordinary trot." In all these pictures the neck is high and stiff, the chin drawn in, in the manner of a collected horse. Two pictures of a "fast gallop" show the neck and head in the same high and fixed position. To us today, his horses in these pictures are collected. Obviously the term "ordinary" may mean two different things to a High School performer and to a cross-country rider.

On the whole Fillis' books give the impression that even in his simple work he remained primarily a High School rider who, in attempting to make his method practical for everybody, was ready to give up many of his regular practices but not all. It would have been the more difficult also for him to relinquish them since he had nothing with which to replace them. All of his predecessors who attempted similarly to simplify manege riding had run into the same difficulty. Dressage, developed for a certain purpose, is a logically constructed method. One cannot adapt it to other purposes by merely watering it down. The problems of cross-country riding could not be solved on the basis of the theories of manege riding. Riding on uneven terrain at fast gaits, over obstacles, and without unduly tiring the horse required an entirely new approach. Fillis' contemporary, an Italian cavalry officer, Captain Federico Caprilli, was the one who finally solved this problem.

One of the principles of his High School that Fillis could not give up, even for the army, was the belief that artificial balance (although Fillis did not call it artificial), with part of the weight permanently switched to the rear, should be given the horse before working him mounted at gaits. Consequently, Fillis' schooling began dismounted, "in hand." This work aimed to raise the neck, to give a perpendicular position to the head, and to shift part of the weight from the front to the rear. It was also in hand that flexions of the mouth, turns in place, backing, and two tracks were first taught.

A High School air popular in the 19th century circus (what the Austrians call *Pesade* and the French *Courbette*).

The lightness of the rider's hands and the relatively relaxed attitude of the horse are to be noted. *(From* Anglo-French Horsemanship, *by John Swire, published by Vinton & Co., London, 1920.)*

This dismounted work "in hand" along the wall (and it was only the beginning of schooling) was quite impractical for the army, for it required an amount of equestrian tact not likely to be found in many troopers. As a matter of fact, Fillis himself wrote: ". . . the flexion is such a delicate thing that an incapable horseman who practices it will often spoil a horse instead of improving him. . . ." Our soldiers, almost all of whom were used to heavy work in the fields, did not always have delicate hands. All this manege schooling resulted in my day in horses whose chins rested on their chests, whose mouths were of iron, and who moved very badly indeed. Although strong-armed soldiers handled them quite well at reviews, they could not ride them efficiently across country and their jumping was plainly abominable. Besides this, we had far too many cases of spavin. After our first month or so of fighting in World War I, we (in

Even in his "simple" method for army use Fillis preserved the usual practice of 19th century Dressage riders of beginning schooling by "work in hand."

Here, a Russian trooper in a Hussar uniform is working on raising the neck and bringing the head into an almost vertical position. *(From a Russian Cavalry Manual of 1908, which embodied the teaching of James Fillis.)*

167

my regiment, anyway) discarded our curb bits, retaining only the snaffles, and began to ride on long reins. But even before this minor revolution and as early as 1906 and 1907, a few articles criticizing the army's emphasis on manege riding appeared in the *Russian Cavalry Messenger*. One cavalry officer, for instance, wrote that:

"The work in hand is entirely impractical because of the scarcity of covered rings (good ground being necessary), and because of its difficulty. To teach this symphonic music to our peasant soldiers would require a great deal of time at the expense of other exercises."

In my regiment, the First Sumski Hussars, which was stationed in Moscow, we had two covered rings; but these were rarely used in my time as the general policy was to conduct all exercises outdoors and make good Spartans of us. There were no riding or schooling lessons during the summers, which were spent in the country practicing formation exercises, shooting, and taking part in regional maneuvres. In Moscow, riding was taught in out-door rings, and since the Russian winter set in early and lasted late, mostly between high snow walls, with a layer of straw-manure for the track—hardly ideal conditions for work "in hand." True enough, our horses had had one year of schooling, prior to joining the regiment, in so-called reserve regiments which were large training depots, after which the animals supposedly needed no further fundamental work. But even if some of us escaped teaching the preliminary work in hand, we all taught, both dismounted and mounted, two tracks along the snow wall—another of Fillis' favorite exercises. You can imagine what it was when our healthy country boys took a crack at it.

Concerning work in hand, the commander of a cavalry brigade, Lt. General Tsourikoff, wrote in 1908:

... Does it really give balance to the horse? I doubt it. In any case, this balance will be destroyed once the horse is mounted . . . and thus all the preliminary work will be found unnecessary. . . . One often hears "schooled, balanced, engaged the quarters," what profound naiveté to ascribe to oneself that which a horse achieves by himself in work. There in the field, . . . crossing little unevennesses in the ground, the young horse will naturally adjust his way of going so as to make it easier for himself to carry a rider, in other words he will acquire a correct balance. . . . Who has not seen a girl, almost a child, easily and freely carrying a yoke with two buckets of water? Take her yoke and try to walk with it, step over a log, cross a ditch—you probably will lose your balance and spill the water. The girl is used to it and you are not. It is the same with a young horse. No matter how much you work him in hand in a ring without a rider, as soon as you ride him out into the field he will have to adjust himself again. A horse, if worked correctly, will find his balance by himself. (*Russian Cavalry Messenger.*)

Before the 19th century much dismounted work was conducted with the help of one or two pillars to which the horse was attached. Dismounted work in hand, which was also used early, was adapted by Baucher to his particular purposes. By it he attempted to supple the horse's neck, his lower jaw, loins and hindquarters. He practiced it primarily in place, with occasional backing. Fillis' work in hand differed from Baucher's in that most of it was done while moving forward. Fillis thus referred to this difference between himself and Baucher:

Baucher writes: "During the first lesson the entire half hour should be occupied in stationary work, except the last five minutes, during which the rein-back will be practiced." Twenty-five minutes of stationary work and five minutes of reining back is a deplorable waste of time. For a lesson of half an hour's duration I would devote thirty minutes to forward work, without any stationary work or reining back.

169

Since he based his schooling on forward *impulsion* Fillis was naturally even more opposed to the use of the pillars than to Baucher's stationary work in hand. This was one of the reasons why he did not appreciate the Spanish School of Vienna of his days:

> The horse is tied to the pillars in such a way that he cannot make a step forward. Then his hindquarters are driven by the whip; since the poor animal cannot extend he draws himself together. It is easy to understand that after a horse has spent months, or even years, contorting himself in order to draw himself together, any extended movement is completely unfamiliar to him.

In the remainder of this chapter from the *Journal de Dressage*, Fillis further accuses the Spanish School of artificiality and of failure to develop good gaits: "the horses of Lippiza are not able to do anything outside the manege"; "these horses have neither [good] walk, nor trot, nor gallop"; "the trainers make a point of preventing these horses from utilizing what nature gave them," etc. Then Fillis describes how he obtained better results by schooling a Lippizaner according to his own method.

That a circus rider should compare his system favorably with that used in one of the generally recognized temples of classical High School may seem preposterous to many today. To appreciate this particular criticism one should remember that Fillis was not only the foremost High School rider of his time, but one who hunted and raced his High School horses. How successful he was at this I do not know, but he did it—I suspect badly by modern standards.

Great as Fillis' method in High School may have been, his system for army use met continuous criticism from officers in the field, and not only because of its work in hand. Many resented the emphasis on collected manege schooling and would have preferred more cross-country training. Then a cavalryman who hid his identity under the initials of J. J., wrote a series of articles which appeared in the *Russian Cavalry Messenger* of 1907, in which he expressed surprisingly modern ideas:

One must remember that the horse's neck and head play the same part in his movements as the arms do in the movements of a human being. We swing our arms one after another when we wish to walk fast, we thrust our necks forward and swing with both arms simultaneously when we jump and, in general, wishing freedom in our movements, do not tie up any one of our limbs in an unnatural position. . . . Manege riding at collected gaits does not assure control over the horse at a fast pace; many horses that are obedient while they are held to a slow pace begin to pull the moment they begin to move fast. . . . Here we are not speaking of such outstanding riders as Fillis, whose High School horses hunt and race; his is an exceptional talent; his method of schooling, called a short one, is too refined, and I doubt that it is practical for the multitude. . . . Freedom of the head and neck of the horse, a natural position of his center of gravity closer to the front, and the work of unobstructed hindquarters give the horse the least tiring and the fastest movement forward. . . . the term "to balance the horse" should sound absurd to the modern rider. . . . The horse himself will shift his center of gravity so as to carry the weight of the rider advantageously. . . . A great number of the horses that work under Cossacks, farmers, and hunters illustrate the three fundamentals of riding: (1) complete freedom of the neck and of the head, (2) a natural position of the center of gravity near the front; (3) work of the unobstructed hindquarters.

I would love to know whether this was written under Caprilli's influence, or whether the writer arrived at these conclu-

Examples of two very different types of riding in Russia, at the end of the 19th century.

(Top) A Cossack sits in his traditional manner and uses a plain snaffle. He keeps his rather short stirrups well under his body, so that he can stand in them (with body inclined forward) at all gaits except the walk. *(From* L'Armée Russe, *by MM. de Jongh Frères, Paris, 1895.)*

(Bottom) A mounted policeman, taught to ride on the basis of collection, exaggerates the point, as often happens. *(From* Among Horses in Russia, *by Capt. M. H. Hayes, London, 1900.)*

. . . .

sions by himself simply from observing Russian natural horsemen—Cossacks and various semi-nomadic peoples.

Natural horsemen, from Poland on east across the Russian and Asiatic plains, have been cross-country riders for better than two thousand years. Their bits were usually simple and their traditional position in the saddle is often reminiscent of the modern Forward Seat. Russian Cossacks, for instance, always rode with short stirrups, in which they stood, keeping the seat low above the saddle and the torso inclined forward; they sat fully in the saddle only at a walk. This type of riding is not based on any theory of equitation; it has developed through centuries of living in the saddle. The Cossacks' aims were simple and if, on occasions, they used their horses hard, they never tortured them the way the artificially ambitious West did by persistent and complicated schooling. As a matter of fact, there

Tartars racing in Kazan, Russia, around the year 1800.
An example of the Forward Seat which, with no name attached to it nor theory behind it, was practiced for centuries by the horse-breeding peoples of the Eurasian steppes. *(From* Les Peuples de la Russie, *by le Comte Charles de Rechberg, Paris, 1812.)*

was no schooling at all in our sense of the word, but just the primitive breaking of a herd horse to the saddle.

This simple form of riding may even produce quite substantial sporting results. Harrison Salisbury, in one of his articles on Outer Mongolia, in a 1959 *New York Times*, describes a junior cross-country race. Four hundred and forty children, six to fourteen years old, participated in this race, some twenty-eight miles long, over cattle trails in the open fields, and only a handful failed to finish.

With such riding still very much a part even of the European Russian scene in my days, it was natural for Russian horsemen to become enthusiastic about the Italian method. At the time the articles quoted above were written there were already a few followers of Caprilli among sportsmen in our cavalry. By the time of Fillis' retirement the prestige his army method had formerly enjoyed was considerably diminished. Had there been no revolution, the old army would probably have altered its riding method in the twenties.

CHAPTER 11

Federico Caprilli

· · · · · · · · · · · · · · · ·

A T the beginning of this book
I wrote, "Something new and important has happened in the
riding world in the course of our century, that is, the sudden
rise of interest in competitive jumping." The chapters that followed described how and why educated riding in the Western
world changed its forms, its uses and its exponents over the
period from the 16th century to the beginning of the 20th. Now
the story has reached the point at which riding has taken a
really different road.

Before starting to describe contemporary riding, I would like
to survey briefly what was accomplished in jumping in previous
centuries. If one wishes to be laconic one may simply say: "Nothing."

You will remember that even de la Guérinière in the 18th
century was still repeating what de la Broue taught at the end
of the 16th. The first mention of jumping in French cavalry
regulations appears in 1788, and it does not say much. Baucher
in the 19th century wrote only four pages on the subject, sug-
gesting, among other things, that "Hop" uttered at the moment
when the horse should take off would give him the necessary
encouragement. Then he explained how the rider, with a "soft
opposition of hands, should help the horse to lift the front,"

and how the hands should act again to hold the horse up in landing. The idea of lifting the horse over the jump has persisted for a long time; even now one occasionally hears people seriously discussing it. It was prevalent long before Baucher's time. As early as 1762 the previously quoted Earl of Pembroke advised that in jumping "the riders must keep their bodies back, raise their hands a little in order to help the foreparts of the horse up. . . ."

Strangely enough, the Count d'Aure, who, as you may remember, actually promoted cross-country riding, does not include even a short chapter on jumping in his *Traité d'Equitation*. Fifty years later Fillis wrote:

> If the horse, when jumping, raises his forehand a great deal, as in a half-rear, the rider ought to lean proportionately forward at the moment the horse raises himself; . . . but as the horse comes down, he should bring his body back, for three reasons: first, not to be thrown forward by the propulsion given by the horse; second, to lighten the forehand, which on coming to the ground will have to bear all the weight of both horse and rider; and third, to keep his seat and support his horse in case the animal's forelegs give way. (*Breaking and Riding*, Hurst & Blackett, Ltd., London, 1902.)

I do not have to tell you that none of the reasons alleged for sitting backward on the landing comply with those laws of nature that govern the movements of living beings on this planet. In the first place there is no propulsion during the downward flight of the jump; in the second, no matter what position the rider may assume, the full, combined weight of horse and rider will still be borne by the first leg to land; thirdly, the rider cannot do anything to help a horse whose "forelegs give way" in landing. A monkey riding on your shoulders could not help you, either, if you stumbled, by jerking and pulling on your mouth, or by leaning back.

176

Fillis' suggestion to lean forward at the take-off, which was then generally practiced by the European military (although not in the way we do it today), created doubts in the minds of many amateurs:

According to military instruction the body is to be inclined forward as the horse rises and backwards as the horse alights, but that is a feat that only a long-practiced horseman can perform. The chances are that the pupil who attempts it, if he does not get a black eye or a bruised nose from the horse's neck, will find himself jumped out of the saddle from not having timed his change to the backward motion accurately.

The same pamphlet gives the recipe for safe jumping:

When a horse leaps he throws the unprepared rider forward. The object then is to resist or neutralize, by his position in the saddle, the impetus forward created by the horse's bound. As the horse approaches the leap the rider should bend his body back, from the hips upward over the cantle of the saddle, while keeping his seat firmly in its place by the grip of his legs and thighs. At a great down jump the best horsemen almost touch the horse's croup. (From a pamphlet published, in 1891, by Mark W. Cross & Co., Saddlers.)

People in those days did not know what good jumping was (pictures of the time illustrate this), and consequently did not have any idea what kind of work on the flat would prepare the horse for jumping. In general, it can be said that all horses of pre-Caprilli days approached and jumped obstacles badly, and to riders of those days the possibility of being criticized because of a slightly late take-off, or because of a stiff jump, or because of the horse star-gazing on the apex of the jump would have seemed preposterous.

The English at least did not bother with all these details of technique; they put the emphasis on something else:

There is no denying that our friend is a capital horseman, and bold as need be. "The King of the Golden Mines," with a workman on his back, can hardly be defeated by any obstacle that the power and spring of a quadruped ought to surmount. He has tremendous stride, and no less courage than his master, so fence after fence is thrown behind the happy pair with a sensation like flying that seems equally gratifying to both. (*Riding Recollections*, by G. J. Whyte-Melville, London, 1878.)

I introduced Fillis' thoughts on jumping as an example of how ignorant the 19th century was in this matter, for Fillis after all was probably the best among many other manege riders of the period who tried to adapt classical riding to purposes other than High School. These half-reformers were quite unable efficiently to solve the problem of jumping and fast cross-country riding; these types of riding, since they had little or nothing in common with manege riding, had to be developed on an entirely different basis. As you know, the problem was ingeniously solved in Italy, by Captain Federico Caprilli.

Captain Caprilli was born in 1868 and died only thirty-nine years later. He began to work on his completely new method of riding for the cavalry in about 1897. After several years' struggle with the old-fashioned army brass, Caprilli finally won out, and from 1904 on he was teaching and experimenting in the Italian Cavalry School at Pinerolo. A year or so later his method was adopted by the Italian cavalry.

Because his theories were based on the natural mechanics of the horse's movements, he obviously had to spend a great deal of time observing free horses in motion, and he found many different ways to do this. For instance:

His most original combination of duty and play was the fitting to the back of his favorite mare—his inseparable companion in experiments—of a straw-stuffed dummy of the kind used in all armies for sabre or bayonet practice. Left to her own devices in the Tor di Quinto stable yard with his life-size puppet on her back, the mare entered wholeheartedly into the spirit of a game of tag with the captain's troopers, while Caprilli studied her movements in her efforts to escape the encircling soldiers, and the mannikin's reaction thereto. (*The Forward Impulse*, by Captain Piero Santini, originally published in 1936. Quotations are from Country Life, Ltd. edition, 1951, London.)

Caprilli, furthermore, was an even greater student of the horse's psychology, as is evident throughout the few pages he wrote.

Caprilli's biographers usually intimate that he was a gay blade but a poor student in school. The latter evidently indicated an aversion for the printed word because, unfortunately for us, he wrote very little—a few articles which total only seventeen single-spaced typewritten pages. These were published in 1901 in the cavalry journal, the *Rivista di Cavalleria*, under the title, "Principi di Equitazione di Campagna," "Principles of Cross-country Equitation."

In substance these articles combine a presentation of the fundamental principles of his method with arguments against the existing army method. They are not well constructed, but are rambling, repetitious and much too brief. All that Caprilli said was to be said much better and more profoundly later on; yet these writings comprise an historical document of great importance. I shall quote the paragraphs which seem to me to be the most significant. They may not bring you any new ideas; you may have heard them all before; and many of you probably have never ridden in any other way than that herein recommended—perhaps without knowing where and how it all started. This, however, is the first tentative formulation of Forward Riding:

The military horse must be essentially accustomed to the field, since it is here that the cavalry must perform in war —uneven and varying terrain should be as familiar to the rider as it is to the horse. . . .

I call a field horse a horse that is of good disposition, calm and confident in the rider, fast and strong, accustomed to galloping for long periods over any kind of terrain, calm and alert in difficulty. . . .

Long years of practice and of continual observation have convinced me that the horse acquires these qualities without effort provided that the rider subjects him to rational and uninterrupted training, throughout which he tries to make his own actions the least disturbing that he can to the horse, and tries not to impede him in the natural development of his aptitudes and energies. . . . By this I do not mean to say that one should let the horse do as he pleases; one should, instead, if necessary persuade him with firmness and energy to do the rider's will, while leaving him full liberty to avail himself of and to use as best it suits him his balance and his strength. From this fundamental and unchanging principle stem all the practical rules of equitation with which I shall deal. . . .

. . . the first rule of good riding is that of reducing, simplifying and sometimes, if possible, even eliminating the action of the rider. If the hands are used to turn and check a horse, and the legs to make him move forward and to give him resolution and decisiveness this is enough. . . .

If natural work is required of a horse [field work] and not artificial [manege work] he will be better able to make use of his impulses, instincts and his natural balance. . . .

. . . the horse who has rational exercise, during which he is allowed to balance himself as he pleases, not being punished with needless suffering, develops in the most efficient fashion, with great advantage to his way of carrying himself, and becomes docile and submissive to the wishes of the rider.

. . . in order to accustom horses to the field without ruining them and making them bad-tempered, one must always profit by the natural instincts of the animal substantiating his movements and way of going, and one must give him the least possible discomfort in the mouth, loins and ribs. One must abolish the forced position of balance, and any action of the horse's legs beyond that which is essential to move him forward.

In consequence, we shall have no more riders who ruin horses by trying to undertake work that they are not fit to ask of a horse, and that, even if well done and properly asked, not only is of no advantage but is actually harmful to the true work the horse should perform.

In his treatment of jumping Caprilli was the first to appreciate the horse's natural physical efforts and the importance of not interfering with them. He also realized that a horse who is not apprehensive of his rider over the jump will be in a much better frame of mind for doing the job. All in all, in the following few paragraphs Caprilli said more pertinent things about jumping than had all the horsemen of the past put together.

The jump . . . is the one action of a horse in which he changes his balance and his attitude most markedly, and many times in the space of a few seconds. One should therefore require of the rider a certain tact and firmness in the saddle in order to second the horse and not disturb him with the hands and weight of the body.

It is necessary that a horse approaching the obstacle should learn not to fear the action of the rider and that he should be persuaded that the rider will always give him the freedom to jump and will not interfere or hurt him to no purpose. Under contrary circumstances the horse, instead of paying attention to doing his work well, will concentrate on avoiding pain.

In order that the horse may acquire a habit of confidence in his rider and not fear his actions, it is preferable to exercise the horse mounted rather than on a lunge, that is if one is sure of riding properly.

... the rider will try above all to develop the eye; by eye I mean the ability of the horse to choose with precision and assurance the moment of the take-off. This, to me, is the most important quality one can require of a jumper and a quality partly natural and partly acquired. The horse acquires

The Progress of the Forward Seat.

Left top shows Caprilli during his first experiments with the Forward Seat. *(From* Modern Horsemanship, *by Col. Paul Rodzianko, Seeley Service & Co. Ltd., London, n.d.)*

Left bottom shows his pupil demonstrating an already more evolved form of it. *(From the* Russian Cavalry Messenger, *1906.)*

Both pictures were taken before 1906.

Above taken a score or so of years later, shows an Italian officer exhibiting the final perfected form of the forward position. *(From* Riding Reflections *by Capt. Piero Santini, The Derrydale Press, New York, 1932.)*

it, indeed, with long practice over obstacles gradually raised, but never too high, in which the rider leaves him free and completely on his own, approaching the obstacle at a moderate pace. . . .

To assist the horse, as some riders would like to do, on the jump is a very difficult thing to do at the proper time, and even if it is properly timed, it still produces, to my way of thinking, a bad result. It may indeed happen that the horse, in fear of this help, will rush the last stride and seriously endanger the performance. The good jumper does not want help at the jump, because he already knows, looking at the obstacle, how much strength he will need to negotiate it without the exertion of any superfluous pressure: mediocre and inexperienced jumpers can be improved by means of rational and continued practice, and not by the use of help or other forcible methods. Sometimes, in exceptional cases, help may be useful during the last two or three seconds of the gallop and at the moment when the horse is about to take off, if he shows signs of holding back his strength by a moment of hesitation. However, one must always be very careful and use the aids only in an opportune manner.

In order to clarify the order of historical events, I shall quote a few paragraphs in which Caprilli criticizes the Italian army method of the period preceding his reform. This is, I think, necessary, because there are those who claim that Caprilli's work was begun by Cesare Paderno, one of Caprilli's predecessors in the cavalry school. Paderno, by education a High School rider, was evidently, like Fillis, aware of the importance of cross-country riding for the army. And, judging from the following remarks of Caprilli, he persuaded the Italian cavalry of the necessity of training in open country. But he obviously did not offer anything radically new, beyond those simplifications of manege principles usual in the period.

I readily admit that in recent times a strong current in a new direction is to be noticed in our army, but the means used to implement it remain insufficient and conflicting.

I marvel that with this goal understood and admitted, i.e., that field riding should be the ultimate aim of the cavalry, they continue to want to teach a soldier a type of equitation whose principles are diametrically opposed to those of that which must be called the school of field riding itself, and while they consider the latter a necessary corollary, they still consider it *no more* than a necessary corollary to manege equitation.

It seems to me that our rules do not present with sufficient clarity the ideas and principles that I have just pointed out; wishing to conserve too many precepts of a refined and by now antiquated equitation, they do not give enough of what, since it is more consistent with actual needs, I would call modern equitation. What follows is therefore an inevitable mixture of old and new, with a prevalence of the former over the latter.

Things cannot go on in this manner. In fact manege riding presents such difficulties and so many demands, such fine tact in practice that it is impossible that a soldier, considering the brevity of his enlistment and the variety of his other instruction, should succeed in learning its principles and applying them properly.

. . . a horse "in hand" in the manege is not a horse "in hand" in the field; instead he will often be out of hand precisely in those places where the soldier must be complete master of his horse.

On the basis of the principles quoted above, Caprilli constructed a *complete* method of riding—that is, a method consisting of three integral parts: schooling, controlling, and sitting a horse. Many people today fail to appreciate this, and believe that all Caprilli did was to invent the Forward Seat. The seat is really only a part of the method, which is dedicated primarily to schooling and controlling the horse on the basis of his natural balance and his natural way of going; the Forward Seat merely unites the rider with a horse that moves naturally. However, since the seat is a relatively mechanical conception, it is easily understood in our mechanical age, while the nature of the horse, both physical and psychological, is much less obvious to anyone but a person who has lived with horses.

Although Caprilli evidently taught the Forward Seat very efficiently, he did not in 1901 describe it precisely. The fact that he knew how to teach it is evident, for instance, from the two following paragraphs that he wrote against the standard exercise of manege teaching—riding without stirrups.

> The field rider strengthens his position by practice in the open, because it is there that he learns how he can best regulate his balance for security during various movements and attitudes of the horse; he does not, as generally believed, strengthen it by long exercise without stirrups.
>
> ... Furthermore, the balance of a rider without stirrups is completely different from that which he must have with stirrups; in the end the rider must thoroughly learn the proper use of stirrups, so that he will not periodically bang the back of his horse and so that he can make himself light.

Caprilli's notes touched upon all aspects of cross-country riding and I say again that it is a pity that he never wrote later in life, after he had had a chance to experiment with his method on a large scale. Much of his teaching had to be handed down by word of mouth by his pupils, some of whom, in their turn, instructed at the Italian Cavalry School. The absence of a complete and final version of his method *in writing* led, of course, to various interpretations of his system abroad.

How much of Caprilli's thinking was completely original and

how much was borrowed from writings and examples of other horsemen is hard to say. As you will remember, the idea of developing the natural way of going of a horse had already been expressed in the second half of the 18th century by a French cavalry officer, the Baron de Bohan. And many separate points of the Forward Seat had been described one hundred years before Caprilli, by an English riding teacher, John Adams. The great American jockey, Tod Sloan, was riding a version of the Forward Seat shortly before the advent of the Italian method. And we should not forget that Russian Cossacks, well-known in Europe, and various other horse-raising peoples of the Eurasian steppes had ridden forward for centuries. The English foxhunter also, although he usually sat badly, at least tried to ride on the principle of free going. None evolved, however, a rounded, *educated* method of riding across country. There is no question but that this honor belongs to Caprilli and to the Italian Cavalry School of ninety years ago.

A Russian cavalry officer, P. Krassnoff, who paid a week-long visit to Pinerolo a few months before Caprilli's death, described the experience in three articles in the 1907 *Russian Cavalry Messenger*. Krassnoff, with the easy pen with which he later wrote *From the Double Eagle to the Red Flag*, vividly depicted life in the school, portrayed the officers, the soldiers, etc. From all this rich material I shall quote only the parts that are pertinent to our subject, particularly the descriptions of a lesson in the ring and in the training field and of a cross-country ride.

Krassnoff wrote about a class of non-commissioned officers schooling young horses in a large covered ring:

> ... all the horses were on snaffles. All the riders worked very softly with the reins, never attempting to collect their horses, but following the movements of the horses' heads with the reins. ... they rode individually in separate directions, avoiding sharp turns, making no circles at a trot; later

they worked at a canter. The riders aimed—as was obvious from the corrections of the officer—at keeping all the horses moving at the same medium-speed canter . . . and they did not pay any attention to the lead, but looked only for calmness and evenness . . . the gait was not beautiful, but it was wonderfully soft and even, and completely relaxed in the whole class. In the meantime a short log was laid on the ground and the horses individually (not in a class) began to jump over it. After this the class walked, and one of the attendants brought a small basket of oats and each of the riders in turn approached it and gave their horses a fistful or two of oats. . . .

Krassnoff described the open schooling field a couple of miles away from the school stables:

This field was about three miles in circumference. All of it was thickly overgrown with nut-trees and acacia; among these, three intersecting avenues were cut—up to 600' wide; along these were placed obstacles. . . . When I trotted to the green clearing with Captain Count Fe d'Ostiani . . . about ten non-commissioned officers were riding there with a young officer. . . . they quietly galloped over the field, jumping the various obstacles. The unusual softness of their hands was striking, as well as the complete yielding of the reins to the point of letting them slide between the fingers. This was refined, sensible riding. Horses were controlled but never interfered with. The refinements of riding could be clearly seen when they jumped in rows of four always perfectly lined up and preserving accurate intervals between the horses.

Krassnoff could hardly forget the time when he was given a horse, and in the company of Italian officers, rode across country:

"Imagine," Lieutenant Starita said to me, "that we represent a scouting party, that the enemy is all around us, and

. . . .

all the roads are occupied by him. From that hill," Starita
pointed to a high, rocky hill overgrown with thick woods,
"we would be able to see all of the surrounding country, and
to count every one of the enemy's men. And it would not
occur to anyone that there, on the summit, there could be a
mounted man. But we can get there only if unobserved. Let
us try it."

We plunged into a fresh thicket of acacia and at a soft,
calm trot crossed the copse, disregarding the prickly branches
that struck us. The cover led to a stony stream bed below.
This channel could hide us well. "Head your horse straight
across" another officer, Acerba, who rode at my side said,
"and drop the reins, the mare knows what to do." We stood
at the granite facing of the brook which was some eight feet
high, descending at a 65 degree angle into the swift water of
the stream. "This is the way to do it." And turning his horse
straight at the drop, Acerba squeezed with his legs; his horse
lined up its front legs and began quickly to slide down. . . .
My Gorilla, left to herself, did the same. . . . Stringing along
single file, we rode into the water among the huge boulders
of the stream.

Later, Krassnoff tells how in the course of this ride they

were galloping fast for a while across a field. At the end of
the field we approached a hill overgrown with trees. Up the
hill led a path, which I ascended with great difficulties later
when dismounted, helping myself by catching hold of
branches and grass. Along this path, like goats, large thoroughbreds and halfbreds were now moving. Only when the
path would make a too risky turn above the precipice, Acerba,
riding ahead, would shout to me—"drop the reins, be quiet."
But I already trusted the good animal. Holding her head low,
with hurried, but sure steps, breathing easily, Gorilla climbed
the mountain. . . .

"And now let us assume," said Starita, "that we are observed. We must get away." Frankly . . . I thought that we
would be looking for another path winding around this rock.
But not so. The same "drop the reins"—and we are descending through the scrub with a slow but sure walk. But soon
the bushes are behind. In front of us drops a 60 degree slope
at least 1800' long, which ends in a perpendicular wall, about
1½' high, separating us from the road. "Keep your horse
straight" shout the officers, and, one after another, we roll
down . . . small stones, jumping and hopping, fly ahead of
us—here is the stone wall—my horse jumps and we are on
the road.

There were other similar situations during this ride which I
omit for fear of being repetitious. This ride Krassnoff called the
"Italian High School."

Krassnoff thus summarized the teaching at Pinerolo:

All the riding is done entirely on a snaffle. Only in cases
of particularly difficult horses is it permitted to use a mild
curb, and then for a short time only.

Particular attention is paid by all the teachers to the hand
and reins. The hand must follow the reins, the reins should
follow the horse's mouth. . . .

The horses are always worked mounted and never in class
formation. The lunge is used in jumping in exceptional cases
only—and jumping in a corral is permitted solely in cases of
unable horses. If the rider does not interfere with the horse,
say the Italians, he will jump as well under the rider as
without him.

They begin a young horse's work in the ring, but do not
force him into corners, avoiding turns and any kind of bending in the ribs; they work on almost loose reins.

Jumping is begun in the ring over low but solid obstacles
. . . at the height of the season every horse jumps forty ob-

stacles during a lesson. As the horse progresses he is worked
more and more often in the field.

It all ends with swimming.

In July examinations are held ... the schooling exami-
nation consists of work in the ring, work in the training field
and, finally, in a cross-country ride similar to the one that I
described.

Thus 20th century riding for sport began on the basis of a
method conceived originally for the army.

Judging by the fact that only a handful of officers of other
countries came to study in Italy before the First World War,
the new method was not enthusiastically received by many armies. Between 1906 and 1914 (the beginning of the First World
War) only five foreign cavalrymen took the year-long course in
Pinerolo, while fourteen others went to Tor di Quinto (the
finishing branch of the cavalry school) for the winter season of
cross-country riding, foxhunting and steeplechasing. The largest
number of officers (six) was detailed by Bulgaria, while from
Spain and Roumania each came three. The major European
powers, France, Germany and Austria did not have any representatives, while Russia had one, who came on his own I
believe, as a sportsman, with the consent of the army of course.
This, significantly, points out that large armies, with a correspondingly large number of conservatively minded generals,
steeped in tradition and the bureaucratic attitude of large organizations, would naturally strongly oppose new ideas.

I do not know what was happening at the time within other
European armies, but in Russia an uneven struggle soon began
between the young officers and their commanders. While the
army was liberal enough to permit the printing of some pro-
Italian articles in the *Russian Cavalry Messenger*, the opposition
to new ideas on occasion took forms which would be considered
inadmissible among sportsmen. For instance, in 1913 at the
Moscow horse show in what we would call an open jumping

class, a regimental friend of mine made clean rounds on two horses. He had to jump off against three other horses, but was barred from this by the General (the commander of the district) who had donated the money prize ($250.00) for the event. The reason: "the monkey seat."

Since the army opposed the new method, it naturally did not provide any courses in it. This absence of instruction, combined with the lack of sufficiently complete literature on the subject, resulted in the fact that most of us, who imagined ourselves "Italians," really knew very little about Caprilli's method. I actually learned it much later.

The popularity of the Italian Cavalry School in foreign lands greatly increased, however, during the twenties and thirties, in the course of which decades about a hundred foreign students from all over the world studied there. I believe that the great increase in interest in competitive jumping at the time had a lot to do with it, and I suspect that many students then went to the Italian Cavalry School as sportsmen rather than as army officers. But more armies were now interested in changing their methods of riding than ever before; the experience of the Great War had taught many that the old method of manege riding was quite impractical for actual warfare. Furthermore, there were now several new armies.

Europe emerged from the First World War with many changes in her map as well as in the social structure of various countries. Austria was split up, and Germany no longer an empire; Russia was fighting a civil war, and losing many of its border territories to newly formed states. The new small countries created by revolutions and peace treaties, such as Poland, Finland, Czechoslovakia, Lithuania and Hungary, were beginning their lives anew; they all sent officers to Italy. It was easier for them to do this, since the organizing of their new armies was not in the hands of a long-established and consistently conservative high command.

This, by the way, is perhaps the explanation why the Italian army accepted Caprilli's proposed method so comparatively easily. Only some forty years before his time in the cavalry school, Italy still consisted of several separate states, and its north was in Austrian hands. It is quite possible that we would never have heard of Caprilli had he been born in one of the old militaristic countries, with a large cavalry and long-established equestrian traditions.

It seems quite right and fitting that the country that gave birth to the first system of manege equitation should also have produced modern methods of jumping and cross-country riding. On the surface it may appear paradoxical that the two forms of educated riding we know should have been fathered by a land that is basically not horse country at all—in the sense of using or breeding horses widely.

On second glance, however, the paradox tends to disappear. The first manifestation in the Renaissance may be attributed to the fact that the Italians were the first modern Europeans to *think* much about anything, and to the number of small luxurious courts there that were the very settings to foster manege riding. As for the ease with which Caprilli's method was accepted at the beginning of this century, that may have been due not only to the circumstances in the army already mentioned, but also to the fact itself that Italy was not a horse country. She did not have, even among civilian riders, the strong traditions and prejudices that are apt to obtain in any large body of sportsmen. The Italian character is, moreover, flexible and accommodating, and would have had less difficulty in yielding to innovation than some more dogged, Northern natures.

THE DEMOCRATIC PERIOD

CHAPTER 12

Since Caprilli

. . . .

IN a way, it should be very easy for me to describe what has happened in riding during our century—I know it so well. On the other hand, it may be difficult to take a large and unprejudiced view of events which are so recent, and in which one has been so deeply involved. Although confident that I shall be able to present the current development of riding purely factually, I am afraid that, while trying hard to be objective, personal feelings may sometimes color my appraisal of events.

The theme of this book hardly calls for a detailed description of the complex of social and historical differences that distinguished this century from the preceding ones. It might, however, be appropriate to mention a few of those that have strongly influenced present equestrian sport.

The two largest wars in history, several revolutions, the reduction of empires, the emergence of new nations, the increasingly rapid development of technology, and the resultant general dwindling of the 19th century social structure have altered the thinking, the ideals, and the mode of living of large sections of the world's population.

In the Western world, the aristocracy has practically ceased to play any important role, while the old wealthy bourgeoisie has also lost much of its prestige. Armies, while larger than ever today, no longer possess a horse cavalry. Their influence is waning, although it continues because of the active participation of some former cavalry officers in contemporary civilian riding. All this means that those categories of people that practiced and developed the educated riding of the past have ceased or will soon cease to influence it.

The aristocratic High School of the 17th and 18th centuries has no real *practical* place in life anymore; today it may interest only those few who have the time, money, and tenacious temperament to practice it as a pure art—with an occasional competition to enliven the academic monotony. The 19th century argument over the manner in which armies should ride is now, since mounted cavalries no longer exist, a matter belonging to history. New ways of life and new people, with a new outlook on practically everything, have changed the forms and ideals of riding, turning every branch of equitation into competitive sport.

At the beginning of this book I stated that the 20th century made a new contribution to riding—competitive jumping—and while today different kinds of riding are practiced simultaneously in the United States, jumping is the one that is growing the fastest. Jumping in different forms now knows no regional boundaries and is practiced all over the country. It is the form of riding most discussed and most written about. I know many people to whom the most interesting part of foxhunting is jumping. I also know some who suffer through the Dressage phase of "Horse Trials," or the program ride of a "Complete Test for Hunters," merely for the opportunity to compete over obstacles in the other phases. This holds true not only in this country. A friend of mine, a former French cavalry officer who teaches riding in France and who knows the French equestrian scene very well, has complained to me that young people there don't care about learning good riding on the flat; all they want to do is to jump, jump, jump. I have heard the same recently from several other French and English horsemen, and I heard it long ago from an instructor in Tor di Quinto. A glance at the pages of European equestrian magazines will convince you of this.

The usual explanation of this phenomenon is that in a fast-moving century of strenuous sports in general, only a fast and venturesome type of riding can capture the imagination of young people. This is unquestionably so. But certainly the Italian method, which has at once simplified and improved jumping for both men and horses, has had something to do with it.

Although I have already said somewhere that more people today have more time for riding, and in another place that no one has as much time to devote to it as formerly, this is not really as contradictory as it sounds. It is true that shorter working hours and labor-saving devices of all kinds, from dish-washing machines to frozen blue-plate suppers, have given the majority of people more leisure than ever before. At the same time a host of opportunities, distractions, and obligations have rushed in to eat up that leisure. With an automobile at the door it is harder to get out of going to P.T.A. and committee meetings, or helping with charity drives; there is no excuse for not taking the children to the beach when a fine day comes along, and less than there used to be for not dining with friends thirty miles away. Children take all sorts of extra lessons and go to many parties to which they have to be driven. Parents take on civic duties, garden clubs, and half a dozen different sports. Thus, although more people have more time, there are more demands on it; and the few people who always had time find the time that they once could spend quietly at home, or in the saddle, broken up by dozens of different calls on it. The fact that it requires less time to be good at jumping than at Dressage of corresponding quality has unquestionably helped to promote the popularity of the former.

Another characteristic of modern life—the stress on simplicity and informality in the home, in clothing and in manners, and on efficiency in general—has led us far away in every respect from the elaborate living and riding of the past. We want everything we do to possess these modern virtues. The idea of efficiency has even created a certain concept of beauty. Today to most of us a beautiful horse is the one that is a good machine. Performance, a word once associated almost exclusively with the stage, has now come to mean what a machine can accomplish for you and how well it can do it. We talk about the performance of a car. Just so, the "performance" of a horse today means his ability to cover a course or to follow hounds efficiently. With the workmanlike replacing the elaborate our ideals of beauty have changed.

No competitive riding of today could take the simple empirical forms that satisfied the old English sportsman. Our approach to all sports has become analytical and technical. Better education in general, the premium on education in every field of human activity, and the rise of "physical education" have conditioned minds and influenced sports as well. This process, you will remember, was already beginning in the second half of the 19th century, but was given great impetus by the rapid progress of practical science in our times. So quite naturally the mechanics of the horse's movements and of his balance continued to be analyzed in this century. By the thirties, we at last had sufficient knowledge of the horse's efforts in jumping to begin, on the basis of physiology, to construct a method of schooling and of riding a jumper.

In the new techniques, for the first time, a *humane approach to the horse* played a significant role. Earlier forcible means of making the horse jump, without suitable preparation on the flat, upset the animal and could obtain good results only in rare cases. A horse can jump his best only when he is frightened of neither the obstacle nor his rider. A horse must be in a calm frame of mind if he is to be physically alert without being tense. Calmness in a jumping horse has been achieved by the new method of schooling on the flat and over obstacles. While you may remember that many of the outstanding masters of the past recommended gentleness and persuasion as opposed to force,

200

. . . .

Caprilli was the first to base his method exclusively on consideration of the animal. In his case even the rider's position was conceived for the comfort of the horse. This considerate attitude which, it may be observed, is still not as widespread or as consistent as it might be, is relatively new on the part of the general public and has been brought about by several factors.

The work of the humane societies over the past hundred years has, of course, made people more aware of animal suffering; the fact that the horse, being no longer a necessity, is more of a pet than a utilitarian article has led to a less cold-blooded approach to him; and we are no longer in the habit of generally using strong coercive measures. After all, in those times not so long ago, when school masters and parents still birched children or locked them up on bread and water for minor disobediences, when men sometimes beat their wives and their servants, and when soldiers were punished by flogging to within an inch of their lives, consideration was not a part of man's attitude towards his "inferiors," human or animal. This, unfortunately, does not mean that many horses still do not suffer as a result of callousness, neglect, or even wanton cruelty—or from the perhaps even more common abuse due to horse owners' and riders' ignorance of what may cause suffering in an organism so differently made from themselves.

The striking results achieved by better riders with a combination of scientific techniques and a humane approach to riding have turned jumping into an art *as great in its way as High School ever was*. And for the first time in the history of equitation the representatives of a new form of riding do not claim that it may be helpful in other equestrian sports. This is, of course, because we live in a century of specialization, and it is quite natural for us to specialize. If all horsemen have not yet fully embraced this point of view, it is simply because riding, with its traditional conservatism, has always lagged somewhat behind the times.

Another factor has contributed to the rapid improvement in jumping achieved in the course of this century: the better horse-flesh we have at our service today. The cumulative effects of selective breeding are now enabling more people than ever before to have good horses. The better the horse (when properly selected for the task), the simpler and shorter the schooling, in most cases. This has proved to be of great importance in a century when few of us have enough free time for the long and complicated routine of schooling practiced in former days. Also the fact that training for jumping may be relatively simple undoubtedly partly accounts for the popularity of this sport. Obstacles can be negotiated quite acceptably and efficiently, up to a certain standard, by an amateur who works on the basis of making the most of the horse's natural abilities, with relatively little schooling added, in comparison with the preparatory work required for manege riding of comparable competence in former days.

The slow-motion-picture camera has played an important role in our better understanding of the mechanics of the horse's movements in general, and of the horse's efforts in jumping in particular. Much of what Caprilli guessed at we now know. Photography has contributed to better riding in other ways: today, with the help of the Polaroid camera, an instructor is able to show his pupils during the lesson itself how they look in the saddle or how their horses perform. It is much easier to judge oneself by quietly studying a photograph than by trying to watch oneself in a mirror while moving around a ring—the only means once available. Today we are so accustomed to books on riding illustrated by photographs and to "visual education" that it seems rather strange to read the subtitle of a book published in 1889, *An Original Method of Teaching the Art by Means of Pictures from the Life*.

Photographs (moving or still) of the horse one is schooling are also a great help: only a really experienced trainer can judge his horse's movement accurately from the saddle. These photographs also form a record by which to measure progress.

Press photography has both helped and hindered good riding. While it has enabled people all over the country to observe the form of famous riders or of merely successful amateurs (and an ideal to copy is one of the strongest factors in moulding taste) it has too often chosen unfortunate or awkward moments over a jump. Occasionally it has encouraged riders to emulate some talented but erratic and sensational showman with far from "perfect form," and frequently abusive riding.

Photography in the form of "Westerns" on the screen and on television has romanticized the horse and made many young people "horse crazy." The fast and risky riding shown in these pictures (although far from the sober actuality) combined with a violent plot, present life around the horse in a way that is a far cry from the gentility of the last century. No youngster today would be satisfied by walking around and around the ring merely improving the flexions of the horse's mouth. Even educated riding was bound to be affected by the accelerated tempo of life.

Another product of technology, the automobile, and the immense network of roads built for it, have made more shows possible, increased the size of some, brought mounts and riders from a very wide area together, and enabled riders to compete in literally ten times as many shows as they once could. And the horse show has played an extremely important role in developing better riding.

Against this background has grown up a new era in equitation. In shaping it the Italian method of the beginning of the century exerted greater influence than any other school of thought, although the spread and development of Caprilli's ideas were retarded by two world wars and by the depression of the later twenties and the early thirties. It was only in the late forties and the fifties that 20th century riding acquired distinctive forms that were really widely practiced.

These forms resulted from a combination of our riding inheritance from previous centuries, of modern thinking on the subject, and of the influence of the new circumstances of contemporary life. It is largely due to the latter that the Italian principles were differently interpreted in different countries.

The motion picture camera has revealed the split-second phases of the different gaits of the horse that were invisible to the naked eyes of our grandfathers. It has thus presented modern horsemanship with a truly sound basis on which to build theory. Countless points of *practical* value to a horseman can be easily observed when studying printed film strips. For instance, in view of the fact that some people still talk about collecting their horses during the approach to a jump, it is interesting to note that in this series of pictures the horse stretches his neck and head forward when nearing the obstacle and raises his hindquarters in order to engage his hindlegs. Both points are contradictory to collection, and both points have good mechanical reasons.

In this series of pictures each frame represents ¹/₂₄ of a second. *(Courtesy of Miss Iris Winthrop)*

While Caprilli's teaching was nowhere accepted without alteration, every nation assimilated some of his ideas and incorporated them into its traditional riding. The United States, since it lacked the traditions of reasoned equitation, and therefore

clung much less to the past, could more easily than European nations think originally and change its riding radically. This is one of two reasons for switching the story now from Europe to America. My second reason is that from living here for almost

forty years I know what has happened in the American riding world since the late twenties. Following my usual pattern I shall describe the riders and the teachers, attempt to explain why riding assumed certain forms and, finally, discuss current the-

ories. Since jumping dominates the educated equestrian scene here today (and as a matter of fact in Europe as well), it will have to be the main subject.

But what preceded jumping here? Prior to about 1930 the

United States had made no contribution to educated riding. People here rode for pleasure at least as early as the beginning of the 18th century. But their riding in the hunting field and their racing merely followed English sporting traditions. Later,

While the preceding film strips illustrated a complete jump from approach to galloping away, this one merely shows an instance of breaking from a trot into a canter.

The horse in shots numbers 1 and 2 is still at a regular trot. Disassociation of the diagonal pair of legs, right front and left hind, is already obvious in shot No. 6. By the last three shots the canter is established. (*Courtesy of Mrs. Robert E. Carter, III*) in the 19th century, when other than English influences made their appearance here and cities grew large, "park riding" and "musical rides" in the covered rings of riding clubs were common under the influence of Dressage riding. The latter, however, was usually much simplified and often considerably corrupted in a provincial manner. It is rather recently that the world with the help of technology has become small, and that a large segment of the American population has become familiar with continental Europe.

Wealthy Americans of the 19th century established many hunts and successfully promoted racing, steeplechasing and selective horse breeding, but they failed to become profoundly interested in the truly educated equitation then prevalent in the corresponding classes of continental European society. Only an individual here and there practiced Dressage on the higher level. As a matter of fact ". . . in this country until very recently [1905] comparatively little interest was taken in riding except in some of the Southern states and in the army. . . ." (*Riding and Driving*, by Edward I. Anderson, The Macmillan Company.)

Even in 1921, Miss Lida L. Fleitmann could write in her *Comments on Hacks and Hunters*: "Over there [in England] every one, young and old, are sportsmen and horse lovers. It is part of a child's very education. To be a horseman over here stamps you as rather a freak. . . . The average American is not a horseman. . . ." (Charles Scribner's Sons.)

Educated riding has taken hold here during the last fifty years or so. When it finally did, it took quite a new form, because by then times had changed. Today at least a claim can be made that in cross-country riding and jumping our juniors not only perform better and in a more uniform and elegant style than their European counterparts, but that they have been taught to think more clearly on the subject. Here is how it happened.

One of the characteristics of today's life in the United States that has played a very important role in shaping equestrian sport has been the general increase in income, which has not only bettered standards of living, but has also changed people's attitudes towards life. With the help of the new security, plus Madison Avenue, the former habit of saving for old age has been replaced by maximum spending to enjoy life; everyone has taken a bigger bite of everything. Everywhere today where pleasure is to be had—in golf or yacht clubs, on Florida beaches, on luxury liners—are to be seen people whose 19th century ancestors would never have dreamt of such extravagance. This new attitude towards life has also manifested itself in offering children many new opportunities, both for education and for entertainment. Today more young people go to college, and more children than ever before take art or dancing or riding or skiing lessons, or go to summer camps.

This process, which was already noticeable after the First World War, really snowballed after the second one. It is due primarily to this change in the forms of ordinary life that the number of people who participate in pleasure riding has increased so much since the Second World War. This is true not only of the United States; on a different scale, the same thing is taking place in Europe.

These new people on our equestrian scene have not merely increased the number of riders, they have also been instrumental in bettering riding techniques for the average.

When I began teaching riding in America in the late twenties, I constantly met people who, since they belonged to families that had owned horses for two or three generations and had consequently ridden from childhood, believed that all that was necessary to be a good rider was to have a strong body, a bold character and a lot of experience (all undoubtedly valuable assets). If one had to have a few pointers at the beginning, the old family groom was the best person to give them. In those days, the distinction between a riding teacher and a riding groom was rather obscure.

The new people, on the other hand, entering an unfamiliar

field realized that they would have to learn the game. Many of them had succeeded in life because of education, and there was nothing upsetting to them in *learning* how to do something; their children were brought up in the same spirit. Those who had gotten places on sheer ability often appreciated the value of education for their children, and were ambitious enough to offer them what they had missed themselves.

Learning a sport leads usually to the desire to match one's skill with that of others—in this case to participation in horse shows. It is easy not to be in sympathy with the over-competitive spirit that keeps many of our juniors indefinitely on the stage, and that has turned some of them into little "professionals" at the age of sixteen. This is very different indeed from the 19th century, when the precept obtained that a lady's name should appear only three times on the pages of a newspaper: at birth, marriage and death. On the other hand, competition is directly responsible for the rise of standards in riding.

Their pupils' desire to win has obliged many riding teachers to learn more about riding and schooling. For instance, more than two hundred teachers alone have come to me in the course of years; some of these, in their turn, have taught other riding instructors. In many communities today a riding school that cannot produce winners will never reach the top. Thus the ball began rolling.

Better performances, particularly in jumping, resulting in stiffer competition, called for more difficult conditions, and "twice around the ring" over four identical post-and-rail fences was replaced by courses of varied obstacles. Later on, these were influenced by international courses. These in turn required still better riding and better schooled horses. The ball kept on rolling.

The combination of knowledgeable teachers and knowledgeable exhibitors improved the judging considerably—both because of the efforts of at least some of the old judges to keep pace with the times, and because the better educated younger generation was gradually joining the ranks of the judges. Better judging made the importance of learning more about riding even more obvious.

Gradually the desire to ride better, primarily to win, influenced even uncompetitive country riding. Many riders who started out as exhibitors, perhaps as early as the age of ten, eventually took to foxhunting. The superior cross-country riding of some of these gradually exerted its beneficial influence on at least the juniors in this sport. Or vice versa, many of those children who started riding in the hunting field sooner or later fell under the spell of showing, and were forced to better their riding, as well as the performance of their horses, in order to

A recent development in the riding field is children's caring for their horses. Although largely the result of the rising cost of labor, children have undoubtedly gained more than lost from this dismounted association with the animal, which teaches them much about a horse that helps them when they are back in the saddle. *(This picture was taken at the Junior Equitation School, Vienna, Virginia, and used by courtesy of Mrs. William Dillon, director of the school.)*

practice it successfully. Foxhunting alone has produced many competent riders, and it has always had its share of talented ones, but in former days it never aimed to develop fine techniques in the saddle. It is only recently that some hunts, promoting "Horse Trials," and many more establishing Pony Clubs, with their rallies, have begun to sponsor certain standards in riding and schooling. Here again, competition has done it.

A significant question arises here: why have our junior competitions taken such artistic forms in the fifties and sixties? Why have they all, except junior open jumping, aimed at beauty, rather than spectacular achievements? Why were the horse's calmness, natural way of going, and his flowing performance such factors in winning a class? A long list of answers could be given to these questions. For instance, the ideal way of going

There are many excellent junior riders in the horse show and hunting field today, and many of them are well mounted. *(Photo by Allen, Middleburg, Virginia, and used by courtesy of Mrs. William Dillon.)*

of a true working hunter certainly had something to do with it, as well as the assimilation of at least some Italian ideas and, of course, the spread of educated techniques. But I believe that the participation of girls and women on a large scale has played a very important role. On the basis of experience I may say that in general, overlooking exceptions both ways, girls are more able riders than boys. There are several reasons for this.

In the first place girls have more sympathy towards animals, and consequently understand them better than boys. They are more patient with horses, are more considerate of their individual characteristics, are always ready to make allowances for a misunderstanding. The average boy who meets resistance in a horse instinctively tries to solve the problem by force; a girl in the same predicament will try to win by persuasion. This trying to avoid a headlong collision with the horse often wins the day, while a straight fight rarely does. By nature also, girls are softer in anything they do, so they have greater potentialities for acquiring good hands; they have enough strength for the sport, but not so much as to be detrimental. And finally, a larger percentage of them have aesthetic sensibilities. They more easily appreciate the good and the bad in a horse's movements and the plasticity of an athletic jump, and are less apt than boys to evaluate a round over obstacles simply by the number of fences touched or knocked down. I am certain that girls are largely responsible for the elegance of the riders' positions, and for the smoothness of the horses' going that we see today in junior and working hunter classes—at least in the better shows. I doubt whether boys alone would have set such high standards. Many boys are inclined to prefer straight open jumping, particularly at speed. Boys, since they are brought up to group sports, and are virtually required to participate in them, find such things as team jumping or polo more familiar than individual riding, and they tend to identify themselves more with their team mates than with their mounts. The fact that outstanding boys have won important horsemanship trophies now and again does not change this general picture.

I began by giving credit to girls rather than to women just because the number of the former is much larger in this sport. Many stop riding as they grow up. While the rarely reached ideal of a riding department in a girls' preparatory school is to have fifty percent of the students ride, in a girls' college twenty percent is hardly to be hoped for. And not more than five percent still ride a few years after graduation. A job, new interests, city life, marriage, children, etc., bring the percentage down. Some resume riding after their children are grown, but their riding is then apt to take merely a recreational form. The predominance of women in this sport is still obvious, however, and the quality of their riding is consistently superior to that of men of the same age. There is more to it than the usual explanation that women are apt to have more time.

If I am right that girls have played such an important role in raising the standards of riding in this country, then the question arises: where were women in the past? Why was it only recently, and so dramatically, that they began to appear on the equestrian scene?

It did not happen all at once. Women in the Middle Ages hacked, travelled on horseback, and even hunted, and they continued to do so throughout the following centuries. But women did not take part in the High School riding of early Dressage, and in the 18th century they again rode less. At the beginning of the 19th century most ladies who would have been in a position to ride were supposed rather to spend their time in the drawing room, busying themselves with embroidery, the spinet, water colors, local gossip and the latest novel. It was soon afterwards that ladies' riding began hesitantly moving towards its present position.

In 1805, John Adams, who claimed to be the first to write on "a ladies' system of riding," said that "the custom for ladies to ride becomes daily more and more prevalent ... and no longer restrained by the former prejudices of 'bold, masculine, and indelicate for ladies to ride.' " And he adds that now the ladies "may enjoy a recreation which exhilarates the spirit, invigorates the body, amuses the mind, gratifies the eye, and contributes so much to the felicity of the gentlemen who are honored with the care and attendance of our fair country-women in these salutary exercises."

But progress in women's riding was slow, and *The Lady's Equestrian Manual*, written in about the middle of the 19th century, suggests that "No lady of taste ever gallops on the road. Into this pace, the lady's horse is never urged, or permitted to break, except in the field: and not above one among a thousand of our fair readers, it may be surmised, is likely to be endowed with sufficient ambition, and boldness, to attempt the following of hounds." (Philadelphia reprint of 1854.)

By the early 20th century this percentage had substantially increased. John Masefield, in his description of a hunt in *Reynard the Fox*, mentions fifteen girls and women in a field of fifty-five. It may sound little today, but at the same time ladies did not yet participate in large numbers in competitive jumping. In the last horse shows that I remember in Russia, just before the First World War, a few ladies rode side-saddle, exhibiting conformation horses at gaits only. Jumping was at least ninety per cent military; I can remember only one woman competing over fences. At that time, in America, women also rode predominantly side-saddle, but they were beginning to change, and in 1921 Miss Lida Fleitmann wrote:

    ... There are few places where a graceful, well turned-out woman looks better, or appeals more to the masculine eye, than in a side-saddle, and there are few places where the same woman looks less graceful, less chic, or less feminine than when she is attired in breeches and boots astride of a cross-saddle. ... Why, therefore, shouldn't women be willing to submit to the few very slight inconveniences of the side-saddle in order to look graceful, feminine, and lady-like, instead of like a vulgar, badly shaped and knock-kneed man. (*Comments on Hacks and Hunters*, Charles Scribner's Sons.)

Just four years later a different attitude was taken in England by Lt. Colonel M. F. McTaggart in his book *Mount and Man* (Country Life, Ltd.):

> Personally, I hope that the time is not far distant when the side saddle will look as absurd as the crinoline, and that the only place to find one will be in the museums. . . . It seems to me that ladies possess naturally the qualities of horsemanship more than men. They pick up anything that is delicate and precise so easily. The grasp of rhythm and cadence and balance seems to come naturally to them. . . . Then, again, the delicacy of touch and the sympathy which is a necessity for good "hands" are both feminine attributes.

Now we know that women soon ceased to submit to the "slight inconveniences" of the side-saddle because as competition developed these put them at a disadvantage when competing with men mounted astride. Though feminine charm today may have assumed a different aspect, it is still undoubtedly with us.

The rise of women's colleges during the second quarter of this century and the growth of physical education departments in them have also done much to increase women's participation in most sports, riding not least.

In developing jumping to the status of an art, teachers, particularly those who were serious enough to study new ideas and bold enough to preach and write about them, have played a big role.

At the beginning of the century there were comparatively few riding teachers in the United States who had had an equestrian education. In those days the usual riding instructor was a man who had started life as a stable boy, later becoming a riding groom or a professional rider for a commercial stable of one kind or another, eventually opening a combination of a boarding stable and riding academy of his own. If, besides ambition, he had common sense and was blessed with an engaging personality, he stood a good chance of gradually establishing his reputation as a good instructor. Substituting experience for knowledge, and adding brains, some of these teachers succeeded in obtaining good practical results with their pupils. The most talented and ambitious of them studied the subject and became knowledgeable horsemen. The less able ones, however, never sought to better themselves and continued their primitive and often simply bad teaching, while perhaps doing a good business on the basis of charm and of public ignorance in equestrian matters. Such teachers of course retarded, and are still retarding, progress in raising the standards of riding, at least in their own communities.

In the early twenties the ranks of professional riding teachers were joined by refugees from the Russian Revolution; these were former cavalry officers. Only one of this group of about forty men was really familiar with the Italian method, while the rest of us were the product of Fillis' teaching, with the addition of a smattering of the Forward Seat. Around the same time a few former cavalry officers of other nations also were teaching riding here.

I arrived in the United States knowing only "yes" and "no" in English, and started my American life as an ordinary laborer. Then in 1927, when I could speak some English, two other Russian cavalry officers, Colonel Prince Kader A. Guirey and Captain Sergei N. Kournakoff, and I, with the help of a financial partner, opened the Boots and Saddles Riding School in New York City.

I do not think we were very good teachers during the first two or three years; it was hard in the beginning both to forget the old indoctrination and to adjust ourselves to the needs of civilian amateurs. From the very first, however, we were blessed with success. Probably the main reason for this was the fact that we offered something rather new then in America—a *well-organized presentation* of riding on an educated basis. I am certain now that our young pupils did not know what we were talking about, but their parents and our adult students were fascinated by this different approach. And then, of course, the fact that we were willing to discard fond memories of our army days and to try hard to adapt our teaching to the very different conditions of life here, and to think independently about riding, helped to create a lively atmosphere in the school. There was nothing stagnant about Boots and Saddles.

In the mid-thirties we were beginning to give lessons to young riding teachers, practically all of them educated young women, many of whom were college graduates. This was a rather new type of riding instructor, who was destined to play an important role later on. In 1947 a group of these women who taught riding in women's colleges and girls' preparatory schools, at last organized the establishment of riding standards for the National Section on Women's Athletics (today The Affiliated National Riding Commission) of the American Association for Health, Physical Education, Recreation and Dance (a department of the National Education Association). This organization also inaugurated Centres for teaching riding instructors and for rating those who passed examinations. Today the ANRC holds some four Centres yearly, in different parts of the country. Some outstanding professionals have come out of this group, and, what is perhaps more important, the Centres have enabled many beginners to get started on the right track.

After the Second World War, a new group of European refugees appeared on the American equestrian scene; again many of them were former cavalry officers. A few of those who joined the profession and who are teaching jumping and cross-country riding today have a modern approach to these sports, while others teach merely an improved version of what previous refugees taught years earlier—that is, the familiar army mixture of old and new. But the new part is by now more coherent than it was in my days. Considering that for a number of years American amateur riding has been developing along its own more efficient lines, some of the newcomers, in the opinion of many people, have interfered with the process rather than helped it. On the other hand, horsemen who believe that some of the old type of manege schooling is helpful in making jumpers and field horses have welcomed their arrival.

The picture of educational possibilities in this country is further complicated by the fact that many amateurs, of various beliefs or none, are teaching. There are also those amateurs disguised as professionals, who represent neither the horse sense of uneducated but experienced, born-in-the-trade horsemen, nor any educated school. Probably many of these will learn eventually or will drop out. Finally, there is the type of riding instructor who, whether educated or ignorant, is not going to struggle for any ideal and who will teach whatever is in demand at the moment.

These various teachers are the products of such different backgrounds and methods that teaching in this country is necessarily far from standardized. One could probably find someone to teach any method of cross-country riding or jumping that has obtained anywhere at any time in this century. This makes for both confusion and controversy. The former is harmful, the latter often stimulating and productive.

There has also been that impersonal teacher—the Horse Show. Since the monkey element still functions in us effectively, many children have learned a great deal from simply hanging over the rail at shows long enough and observing attentively enough. To be sure, the ones who have learned by this method had to possess natural aptitude to begin with; and they frequently still cannot tell you why they do something, although they may do it correctly—the latter because they have, naturally, imitated the winners in Horsemanship classes. Today, the American riding scene is very complex indeed.

The parts of this chapter which deal with the progress of educated riding may give the impression that all is beautiful in the riding world in the United States today. Actually, the broad picture is not uniform. While some of the new people who entered this sport brought with them what was necessary to improve riding, others did not contribute much beyond vulgarity and a new type of cruelty which was often the result of the latter. For the sake of winning trophies, by hook or by crook, they resorted to painful or sometimes simply absurd bits and gadgets, and to any manner of riding they thought might make the horse clear a course of obstacles. In order to collect ribbons, horses today are made to jump so much and so high that among consistent winners really sound animals are in the minority. Although some of these, with the help of iron constitutions and veterinary science, continue to appear in the show ring year after year, a disturbingly large number of horses are turned into nervous wrecks or are buried in their prime. Essentially there is nothing new in this picture; only its forms have changed. Good riders and considerate ones have always been outnumbered by poor or rough ones, and in the past horses were as much abused by forcible and unintelligent Dressage riding as they are today by jumping. None of this should be forgotten when rejoicing in the achievements of educated riding.

Of the many negative elements present in American riding today one in particular should be discussed at some length— this is the reluctance of the average horseman to study the theoretical side of riding.

This apathy toward thinking deeply about riding is quite a serious fault, for it not only limits the riding potential of the individual but has an adverse effect on those policies which try to promote better riding on a national scale.

The majority of our horsemen who are interested in jumping

and who have accepted the Forward Seat and other Italian practices connected with control and schooling have not studied the theoretical basis for them. Nor have they ever been curious to find out what Forward Riding replaced, and why.

Since the modern method was especially devised for field riding and jumping, it worked well even when approached superficially and purely practically. It enabled our juniors to

With the substitution of the Forward Seat for an old-fashioned one on advertisements, and finally even on postage stamps, its popular acceptance was evident.

ride better over fences than their European counterparts; but their reluctance to study theory has left them without any convictions. On the other hand, the majority of continental Europeans, old-fashioned as many of them are, have a traditionally scholastic approach to riding. Although their devotion to the past may impede their progress in riding over obstacles, they usually can give reasons for what they are doing. While these reasons may be basically incorrect, they possess, just the same, a certain logic. Europeans, being well-educated in traditional schools of equestrian thought, know how to argue in defence of their doctrines, while Americans on the whole are unable either to attack European logic or to defend their own. Thus, rather naturally, they have acquired an inferiority complex on the subject of theoretical equitation, and are easily led astray.

America has always had a group of people who copied Europe. But in the past this set confined itself to a superficial imitation of the English hunting squire—and no theories were attached to his kind of riding. Today many Americans would like to imitate continental European manege riding for the purpose of schooling hunters or jumpers, and some of those who have the money, time and energy endeavor to promote it beyond their own use. Among the latter there are quite a few who do this through no educated conviction that the Dressage type of schooling is best even for a hunter or a jumper but merely because conformity with the trends of prestige-holding groups is prevalent among us today. Many people talk Dressage without truly understanding it, for the simple reason that such a policy is imperative in some communities in order to be in the swing of social activities.

Continental Europe, as mentioned before, has on the whole accepted fewer Italian ideas than we. So the attempts to imitate it may be regarded as conservative ones. Thus, instead, of advancing equitation, they really retard it. This movement, however, could have been of considerable educational value if our

American horsemen had been in the habit of approaching riding on a theoretical basis. For in that case this reactionary attitude could at least serve as a basis for interesting theoretical disputes, which might widen our horizons. Nothing of the sort has taken place, however, and no theoretical reasons lie behind the opposition to Dressage, but simply the fact that many people who have tried it have messed up their horses. The latter is hardly a sound reason, since most of them upset their horses not because they practiced Dressage but because they practiced it without sufficient theoretical and practical preparation.

While many riders have not accepted Dressage simply because they find it too unfamiliar or too complicated (not sufficient reasons for an ambitious horseman), others have welcomed it simply in hopes that it might prove to be a panacea for all ills, or because they could not resist an extra chance to compete, or simply as a matter of following a new fad. These riders usually plunged into Dressage without first studying its theory, and they seldom practiced this difficult form of schooling methodically enough to make sense in it. The term *elementary* Dressage is used now to cover every sin against this ancient and scholastic type of riding. Much of what is practiced today under the name of Dressage is counterfeit and, as such, is in bad taste. Here again the lack of a habit of thinking about riding and studying it theoretically or practicing it assiduously is responsible for this unfortunate state of affairs.

This typical American attitude is alone sufficient to preclude the wide-spread success of any complicated method. And, true enough, the general picture of riding in this country indicates that the comparatively simple Forward Riding has contributed more towards raising standards in jumping and riding to hounds and towards lessening the abuse of horses than any other method practiced so far. It should be noted that it is more in conformity with the old, sound, and purely American ideal of a *working hunter* than any European system.

226

CHAPTER 13

The 20th Century in Print in America

. . . .

IT is often said among riding teachers that it is easy to teach such mechanical things as a good position, but hard to make pupils think as horsemen. The interests of a beginner quite naturally do not go beyond his immediate needs and, because the majority of those who attempt to ride remain beginners for the rest of their lives, thinking about riding is not very widespread in the equestrian world. If these people ever read anything, it is invariably something very simple, which merely gives a little practical advice that they can immediately put to use. It is quite different in the comparatively limited sphere of educated riding, which by the way, has always been small. Among horsemen at this level there is curiosity which goes beyond the mere expediency of the moment. They are interested in books as a means of getting acquainted with the opinions of other horsemen, and hence with different theories on how and why one method may be better than another.

It is very pleasant to be able to report that this small group of riders has lately grown and consequently it may be said that books have played a role in bettering and advancing riding. This statement, however, should be qualified—only some books have been helpful in raising the standards of riding, while many have been useless; others have merely created confusion. Only a few books have been written by horsemen who not only possessed the necessary knowledge, but appreciated the requirements of the times, who were able to present their theories in a manner palatable to the amateur, and who had something new to offer. Many books have been slapped together for purely commercial reasons, and others written by people who had just discovered something new to them but actually as old as the hills, and who felt an irresistible urge to share it with everyone.

All the important books on equitation published in the United States have appeared during the last thirty years. They all deal with the Forward Seat and jumping, and schooling hunters and jumpers. Because of the demands of the market there have also been unoriginal books which in different words treat the same theme—some of these, however, in an attractive enough manner to sell. There are also books on Dressage sold in this country today. I shall discuss these in Chapter 15, when describing the present conservative movement against Italian principles. Here it should merely be pointed out that practically all the latter books have added the Forward Seat (often of a peculiar variety) to their repertory. This addition represents the influence of our century on the ancient art of manege riding. One cannot get away from the fact that jumping is the game of the century.

On the other hand, as recently as 1922 Count Baretto de Souza could publish his *Principles of Equitation* (E. P. Dutton & Co., New York) which, since it was about elementary riding, was intended for everyone, but still contained no chapter on jumping at all. Perhaps today, when the word *Dressage* (often completely misunderstood) is in vogue, a book about riding on the flat only, or even on pure High School, could again sell, but this could hardly have happened until recently.

The comparison between de Souza's book for beginners and recent books addressed to the same audience has additional interest, not merely because of the difference in the forms of riding but also because of the difference in spirit. De Souza's book conspicuously belongs to another era; it is still Victorian in character, with all the gentility of the period pervading the text. This gentility leads to apprehension, and hence the dangers of riding are stressed. A few disconnected quotations will illustrate this:

> . . . just as no "gentleman"—and still more no "lady"—will, or ought to, associate in daily life with people of disreputable character, and degraded morals, except in doing missionary work, so no such refined person should associate with any vicious, disreputable or roguish horse. . . .
>
> Even when there are *excellent* medical reasons for doing so, e.g.: a prompt reduction of flesh, *a rider should never feel tired-out on dismounting.*
>
> But it is a difficult thing, especially for a novice, to stop a horse; sometimes even a good rider of the usual sort finds difficulty in doing it. In a few cases it requires the intervention of a third party—usually a mounted policeman [in a city park] and in fortunately rare cases it involves broken bones, or possibly still more serious consequences.

Principles of Equitation is a well-constructed and well-written book. It was obviously conceived by an experienced instructor who knew how much to water down the Dressage type of riding in order to make it practical for the majority of his pupils who rode in covered rings and city parks. It contains much common-sense advice—mostly, of course, from the Victorian point of view. Very characteristic of the period are the reasons given for riding. Competitiveness in equestrian sport had not yet penetrated the mass of riders and, instead, health was regarded as the primary reason for learning to ride:

> Nearly all diseases are caused, and a number of others are aggravated, by unhealthy conditions of the digestive tract—

especially the intestinal portion of it—in proof of which the first care of a visiting physician is to enquire about his patient's digestive functions. This essentially undesirable condition can be combatted without resort to medicine *only* by equestrian exercise. . . .

In the late twenties, when already partly retired, de Souza sometimes rented the ring and horses of the Boots and Saddles Riding School for his private lessons. From our many conversations one of his phrases, which sums up his general attitude, has stuck in my mind: "any fool can make a horse go; it takes a rider to stop him."

In the present discussion of books of the 20th century, I shall continue my general policy in this volume of quoting or mentioning only those which either played an outstanding role in the advancement of educated riding or are interesting because they throw light on the character of the period. Thus in previous chapters I have overlooked scores of excellent books and many more insignificant ones. In this chapter you may miss some books that you have on your shelves.

The 19th and the early 20th century books printed in this country were primarily unoriginal. Even in the foreword of *A Manual of Equitation* published by the United States Cavalry School in pre-Chamberlin days (sometime in the twenties) it is frankly stated that:

"No claim is made to originality. . . . It presents no new principles, and is thus directly or indirectly indebted to the vast field of allied literature that precedes it. . . ."

The Manual of Equitation of the French Army, 1912, heads the list of sources for this book.

Then there were books printed in America during the past hundred years (particularly during the 19th century) that were conspicuously provincial. Among these were books written by primitive horse-breakers who called themselves "professors," and who were on a par with fair barkers selling patent medicine. One of these, in 1878, wrote a book entitled *Prof. Williams' New System*. It says, in a chapter called "The First-Step to be Taken with a Wild Colt":

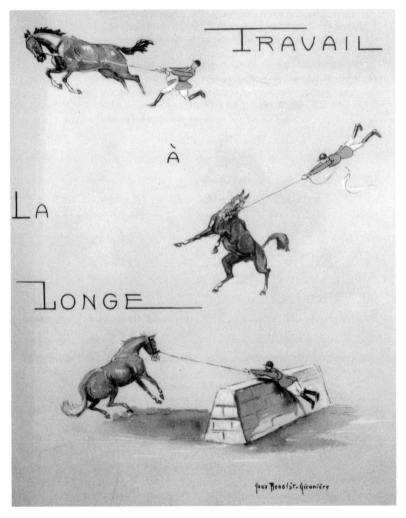

An illustration which enlivens a serious book on various types of dismounted work. These few witty water-colors among the numerous purely instructive drawings are characteristic of those touches of Gallic humor which make French works so easy to take. See pages 271 and 276. *(From* Croquis Hippiques, *by Commandant Yves Benoist-Gironière, published by Librairie des Champs-Elysées, Paris, 1953.)*

Get your colt into some enclosure—small barnyard or barn floor. . . . Prepare yourself with a good spring-top whip, step into the enclosure . . . stand quietly for a few moments and then give your whip a sharp crack . . . now gently approach him . . . if he attempts to turn to run from you, give him a sharp crack with your whip around the hind legs and under the flank. . . . After applying your whip in this way until he will stand quiet with his head towards you . . . gently approach him saying Ho! boy; but in approaching him, if he should turn and run from you, apply the whip smartly to his hind legs. . . . In a very few moments he does not turn his quarters towards you, but will stand and face you, and allow you to place your hand upon his neck, pat and caress him. In so doing, you gain his confidence, and awaken two qualities of his nature, fear and love; he loves to be with you and he fears to leave you. . . . The next step is to teach him that his strength, compared with yours, amounts to nothing. . . . This is best accomplished by the use of our surcingle . . . gently raise the left forward foot, and place it in the surcingle by the use of the strap attached to the surcingle. . . . Your horse is now upon three legs. . . . He finds that he is fast and in trouble, and as you have taught him to come to you for protection, he instantly comes to you for help . . . be ever ready and willing to assist him. By so doing, you awaken his love and gratitude. As you approach, gently pat and caress him, and relieve his foot. After caressing him for a short time, step to the other side and place the right foot in the surcingle. . . .

And finally, almost all American books published prior to the thirties were very superficial and in this respect close to the English tradition. They are full of such slip-shod statements as:

The seat about to be described was that of the earliest riders, represented by Phidias, described by Xenophon [still

. . . .

without a saddle] employed by the Bedouins and other Eastern horsemen. . . .

When the animal alights, [in jumping] it must find some support from the bit, so that in case of a peck or of a stumble the forehand can rise until a bearer comes under the center of gravity and saves a fall. The bending back of the rider's body as the forehand reaches the ground is, of course, of great assistance in recovering from a misstep. (*Riding and Driving*, by Edward I. Anderson, 1905.)

Probably the two most serious books of the period written on American soil were de Souza's *Advanced Equitation* and a book by de Bussigny, a Frenchman who taught in Boston; both were about Dressage, of course. It was only in the thirties that some very interesting books on modern riding were published here. They were not, however, the first on the subject.

Probably the first book to describe the Italian method was written by a Russian cavalry officer, Colonel Paul Rodzianko, who studied in Pinerolo in 1906. This book was published before the First World War, but was never translated into other languages, and hence is unknown outside Russia. The same thing happened to a little pamphlet of the same period by another Russian cavalryman. And you will remember the articles by Krassnoff, from which I quoted previously. All this material was unfortunately not complete enough for serious study. Perhaps various articles and booklets on the subject were written in other less familiar languages, but in the English-speaking world the credit for being the first to write about the Forward Seat is usually given to an English cavalry officer, Lt. Colonel M. F. McTaggart. In his book, *Mount and Man*, published in 1925, by Country Life Ltd., Colonel McTaggart included a chapter entitled "The Forward Seat," and thus became the pioneer in a popular Anglo-Saxon misrepresentation of Caprilli's teaching. All the English writers of the time took the Forward Seat out of the context of the method, often partially corrupting it, combining it with a few old military Dressage principles, and adding a dash of traditional foxhunting practices.

As a matter of fact, the thinking of most horsemen of other nations at the time was equally confused on the subject. Few of them understood that the Italian method consisted of three parts, logically combined: *schooling, control* and *seat*. All these authors missed the point that these three parts were organically related to each other, and that together they constituted a homogeneous and completely original method. It was evidently hard for many to see that Caprilli's innovations went beyond giving the rider a novel position. It obviously was equally hard for them to forget what they had learned in their youth about schooling and control. This mixture of the old and the new was very prevalent until the early thirties. From then on Italian ideas begin gradually to predominate in the more important books on jumping and cross-country riding. Lately, however, we are witnessing a revival of the old mixture; I shall discuss this movement in later chapters.

McTaggart was probably also the first to call the Forward Seat the Balanced Seat in print and, while naming it correctly, to open the way for every kind of misinterpretation of a good forward position. Any good seat is obviously a balanced one. A cowboy seat may be as well balanced in its own way as the Dressage seat or the Forward one is in its way. There are several ways of balancing oneself when mounted in order to achieve unity with a horse in motion. For example, in the Dressage seat the rider's balance is based in the saddle (the best balance for uniting the rider with a horse moving at collected gaits), while in the case of the Forward Seat the rider is balanced primarily in the stirrups (the best for fast galloping and jumping or merely riding a freely going horse). So the adjective *balanced* does not describe a particular seat, while *forward* does. The ambiguity of the term *balanced seat* left every rider free to interpret it in his own way, and thus to combine it with any other type of riding.

I am bold enough to be so critical of others for corrupting the Italian method and for mixing the Italian seat with the practices of manege riding, since I must confess that at one time I was guilty of the same crime. It is rather ironic to realize that the mixture of elementary Dressage (diluted Fillis in my case) and the Forward Seat that I taught in the thirties enjoys a minor revival in the United States today, under the guise of the latest word in European equitation.

Two horsemen-writers, Major Piero Santini of the Italian cavalry, and General H. D. Chamberlin of the United States cavalry, played particularly important roles in, so to say, modernizing many of us horsemen in America.

Major Piero Santini (1881–1960), wrote three books in English. His first, *Riding Reflections*, originally published in New York in 1932 by The Derrydale Press, was the book that particularly clarified many points in my mind. As the first authentic presentation by an Italian of the principles of the Italian method and of its seat, the book was read by thousands of horsemen, and undoubtedly had a wide-spread influence, at least as far as the seat goes.

This masterfully written book combines a lucid presentation of the subject with a caustic wit and with poetic descriptions of foxhunting and country riding. The search for perfection which fills its pages is evidence that the author made no concessions to the popular market. This perhaps accounts for its being as fresh today as when it was first printed.

Unfortunately, the scope of *Riding Reflections* is not large; it discusses primarily the Forward Seat—the reasons for it, its "geometry," and its application—mostly in the hunting field. But this was precisely what I needed in those days. Perhaps the fact that on several occasions I had an opportunity to discuss riding with Major Santini, both at about the time the book was published, and again much later, makes this work particularly vivid to me.

A second book, *The Forward Impulse* (Huntington Press,

1936), is largely a recapitulation of *Riding Reflections*, with some important additions. It is distinctly worthwhile to study both, rather than merely one.

Major Santini did some teaching on this continent and in England. He taught as he wrote—in perfect English, authoritatively, often sarcastically, always trying to achieve perfection, and with the accent on the rider's position. His teaching made a strong impression.

Major Santini, following Caprilli's fundamental principles, presents the Forward Seat as something essential first of all for the horse. (The following quotations are from *Riding Reflections*):

> The verb "to sit" should be eliminated from our vocabulary where riding is concerned. . . . he (the rider) should be well forward in the saddle, with loins bent inwards, and fork close to the pommel, thereby reducing to the least possible fraction contact between buttocks and saddle. If this position is adopted we are immediately struck by the impression that a horse can comfortably carry much more than his usual burden, and for obvious reasons: he has the bulk of the rider's weight where he feels it the least, i.e. on the forehand, his propelling apparatus—loins and quarters—free of encumbrance. . . .

This is a true horseman's approach to riding and very different from that of "mounted pedestrians" whose thinking begins and ends with consideration of the rider alone. The latter attitude is particularly irritating to me when encountered among outstanding riders.

But the rider was also taken into consideration by Santini who, always very much of a stylist in everything he did, wrote and taught that "nothing gives a greater impression of lack of style and *chic* in a horseman than using the saddle as he would the family armchair." It is hard to argue with Major Santini about the armchair, but I know from experience that in many cases an excellent, *chic* Forward Seat can be obtained only at the expense of stiffening the rider, and consequently diminishing the efficiency of his control. Some people are built to sit stylishly, while to others this presents real difficulty; an instructor should have a practiced eye to recognize how far he can go in every individual case in striving towards the ideal. I always aim primarily at a "workmanlike" Forward Seat, which will benefit both the horse and the rider and then, in cases where it comes easily, it is very pleasant to have a pupil look chic as well. A good position is not merely an elegant one, but one that enables the rider to control his horse efficiently.

Santini knew how to underline the attractions of country riding:

> The centuries-old association between man and horse had its origin in the chase; the more we keep this basic idea in mind the purer our diversions will be; the farther we wander from it the more artificial will they grow. In this mechanical age we should cling more than ever for the good of our bodies and souls—to the few simple things that are left us, and not allow arc lights, grand-stands and applause to encroach on or get confused in our minds with the sky, green and brown fields, hedge and ditch and timber and the often unshared and purely personal and intimate satisfaction of finding one's way over a difficult country—far from white ties and hand clappings. There is contradiction in the very terms "sportsman and showman."

Unfortunately opportunities to pursue the type of riding so engagingly presented by Santini are becoming rarer and rarer as suburbia extends its networks and encroaches almost everywhere on "good hunting country."

As you may gather, Santini did not like horse shows; here are some things he has to say on the subject.

> If the public knew what sometimes goes on behind the scenes, and what crocks and "bad actors" in private do brilliantly in public, their unreasoning admiration for the sleek animals that go back to their boxes adorned with all the colors of the rainbow would receive a rude shock. . . .
>
> In jumping events, which particularly lend themselves to dramatization, the acrobatics which thrill the ignorant are totally unnecessary, and are the result of the histrionic spirit we all possess to a greater or lesser degree, and which is encouraged by the presence of spectators. . . .
>
> The only real use of horse shows lies in *the improvement of horsemanship by observation and fastidious criticism*, and this is the attitude of mind which should be encouraged in the public, or at least such portion of it as are themselves actively interested in riding as a sport. This class of spectator should frequent the show ring in much the same spirit as that in which a painter looks at a picture gallery or a musician listens to other musicians—for the improvement of his own art by absorption, study and criticism of fellow-craftsman's methods.

There is no question that open jumping classes do not necessarily contribute to better horsemanship. However, the forms which our horsemanship and hunter classes have taken since *Riding Reflections* was written have definitely played the leading role in raising the standards of riding and in spreading better riding all over the country. At the time Major Santini was working on his book it was hard to foresee to what extent horse shows would grow. In 1961, during the month of May over one hundred and thirty shows were held in the British Isles and over one hundred and forty in the United States. In May 1990, the number of shows were eight hundred and sixty-five and two hundred and fifty-seven respectively. But it is not only that the number of shows has grown to a fantastic figure; the quality of performance in them has improved immensely since the middle thirties. Major Santini's advice to observe the techniques of the contestants is very much followed today, and very carefully, I may add, by the participants themselves. For many juniors the horse show is their most effective teacher.

Unfortunately, neither *Riding Reflections* nor Santini's second book *The Forward Impulse*, take up schooling. In this respect Colonel Harry D. Chamberlin's books, *Riding and Schooling Horses* (Derrydale Press, 1933) and *Training Hunters, Jumpers and Hacks* (Derrydale Press, 1937) substantially widened my horizons on an important subject.

Colonel H. D. Chamberlin (who died a General, in 1944) is well remembered for his winning and stylistically brilliant performances and for those of the United States Army Team that was trained by him. These exerted an enormous influence in spreading a modern educated method of riding over obstacles.

Colonel Chamberlin's second book is the one that particularly dispelled all my uncertainties about the course I should take in schooling. It taught me much that was new to me. It also supported me in many things that I was already teaching but for which I often encountered such strong criticism that on occasion doubts would assail me.

Colonel Chamberlin studied both at Saumur and at Tor di Quinto; he was at the latter school in 1923. In the prefaces to his books he modestly says that "for the Seat advocated, the writer is principally indebted to the Italian Cavalry School," while the "credit for the system of training enunciated herein is due to the French Cavalry School." He modified both seat and schooling, however, and his second book in particular represents neither the French nor the Italian school in its purity, but is his sound, original contribution to the cause of educated riding.

Those ideas of Chamberlin which resulted from his studies in Italy were the ones which were the most influential in helping

240

me to form my own techniques, since some of the Italian reasoning was still new to me, while I was already familiar with the French school of manege riding. The following quotations, which represent fundamental points of the new type of riding, are taken from different parts of the book:

Photographs of Col. H. D. Chamberlin illustrating the Forward Seat.
(Left top) At a trot—"Since the seat is out of the saddle much of the time [when posting], the rider is necessarily riding during those periods in the stirrups."
(Left bottom) At a slow canter—"Even when fully seated at the gallop, no effort is made to keep the seat glued tight against the saddle . . . a large part [of the rider's weight] slips through the relaxed knee and ankle joints into the heels."
(Above) At a fast canter or gallop—"The rider is actually standing in the stirrups."
Compare the above basic points of the Forward Seat quoted from Chamberlin's book with those of the German interpretation of it described in Chapter 15. *(From* Riding and Schooling Horses, *by Harry D. Chamberlin, The Derrydale Press, New York, 1933.)*

> At the walk ... the strides, when studied from the side, should be long, free and close to the ground ... the hind leg moves freely with little perceptible flexion at the hock. ...
>
> The trot, though springy, should be low, with feet moving close to the ground as a result of minimum flexion of knees and hocks.
>
> A good galloper's feet travel close to the ground with little knee and hock action. ...

These key phrases clearly indicate that collected gaits were not a part of the Chamberlin method.

"Jumping and cross-country work over varied terrain both on a loose rein and with the normal contact, improve balance and agility. ..."

Loose-rein work, particularly at the beginning of schooling, has since become a very important and successful part of my teaching.

> Balance can be immeasurably improved by special gymnastic exercises. However, the artificial form of collection acquired through high-schooling is not suitable to improving the balance of these horses [hunters and jumpers]. In high-school collection the hocks are flexed, the croup lowered, the neck raised and the face brought in to an almost vertical plane ... such horses ... are unable to handle themselves cleverly when given their heads and left to their own devices and so are practically worthless for cross-country work. ...

Absurd as it may seem today, this paragraph made me ponder a long time. I knew that the advanced forms of High School collection should not be used in field riding, but I had been brought up on the idea that a lower degree of collection should be a part of the training of every horse, no matter what his job. It was rather difficult to abandon this notion, which had been drilled into me, and to replace it with the conception of what

Chamberlin calls "natural collection," that is the ability of the horse to gather himself for a few seconds here and there when a sudden change in terrain, an abrupt slowing down of the gait, or an abrupt halt calls for it. There is a tremendous difference between the horse gathering himself under these circumstances or moving *forward* at collected gaits. By the term "natural collection," which Chamberlin unfortunately never precisely defined, he also obviously meant that at gaits the horse should be united; today, I often use the term a "connected horse."

But to resume quoting Chamberlin:

Keeping the horse's head turned inward while working on the circle is occasionally beneficial as a gymnastic and disciplinary exercise but should not be insisted on normally. . . . It is unnatural, impedes the inside shoulder, shortens the stride and instigates resistance. . . .

The pernicious custom, frequently seen in high-schooling and elsewhere, of striving to hold the horse's body on an absolutely straight line while at the gallop, and the even more ruinous one of habitually bending the spine and neck outwards to conform to the curve being travelled, shorten the stride, cramp and annoy the horse. These faulty methods are to be carefully shunned in the practical training of outdoor horses. . . .

I must confess that it was hard for me to relinquish the belief once taught me that the horse should be bent to correspond to the curve of the line along which he moves. I had preserved this tenet of Dressage longer than any other. Evidently it is equally hard for many other horsemen to abandon this idea, and even today some of them, by requiring small circles, induce that bending of the horse which according to Chamberlin is a "ruinous" procedure.

"Cantering false—i.e. leading with the left leg when curving or circling to the right, or vice versa—lengthens and lowers the stride; supples the spine; lowers the head and neck; puts the horse on the bit; and improves balance and agility."

This exercise eventually became one of the very fundamental ones of my method. I teach it to a green horse when he still does not know the leads and is too awkward to make changes by himself. Consequently, in the early stages of schooling in a ring, I never insist on the inside lead; this results in a certain amount of accidental cantering on the wrong lead and thus the false canter develops by itself, and brings with it all the benefits enumerated by Chamberlin.

If you compare these fundamental principles of Chamberlin with those of Caprilli you will find that they have a great deal in common. Much of what Caprilli taught and Krassnoff described, Chamberlin wrote. The same belief in free gaits, in absence of real collection, in not bending the horse in the sides and neck when making a turn, in disregarding the lead (that is, cantering false) and in riding either on loose reins or on soft contact, is there. If I were not afraid of being tiresome I could make a still longer list of Italian elements in Chamberlin's teaching. On second thought, I would like to include here one more of his paragraphs, about flexions of the mouth and the poll. You will remember that these flexions always were predominantly important in Dressage schooling and were taught dismounted, in hand. On this subject Chamberlin wrote:

Suppling of the jaw while dismounted, still practiced by some high-school experts, is entirely unnecessary for the average riding horse. These flexions were perhaps essential when few horsemen owned thoroughbred horses, or those close to the blood. For the most part, saddle horses of those days were coarse, thick-necked, and poorly bred. Moreover, they were continuously held to slow gaits suitable to the airs of the high-school, for there were no equestrian sports requiring great speed. The slow, collected gaits, and training of former times are unsuitable for modern riding.

Not surprisingly, nearly all Chamberlin's ideas on jumping proper are of Italian origin. Thus his fundamental principle is non-interference with the horse's own calculation of the take-off:

> The main and most difficult task of the trainer when riding over an obstacle is to "let the horse alone." Simple though this sounds, in practice it requires cool nerve and great co-ordination. . . .
>
> . . . The idea that one can "place" his horse for each jump over a course of big and imposing obstacles is erroneous. Many really brilliant riders have tried it, but without complete success. The horse must do the jumping, and the less he is bothered, except to encourage and rate him, the better he will do. . . .

Unquestionably Chamberlin's method (which I have used as a guide for the last twenty-five years) brings the best results with the great majority of riders and horses when courses are not higher than 4'6" and obstacles are not crowded. With better horses and riders the fences may even be raised somewhat. In recent international competitions, however, the fences have become so high and the courses so complicated that it is doubtful if a horse can function almost on his own. These courses and some of the more complicated ones at the national level are possible because there exist some riders in both fields with such an outstanding sense of timing that they are usually able to place their horses accurately. When the same thing is attempted by riders and horses with less natural talent and less developed techniques, then what Colonel Chamberlin said is quite true. After all, it is foolish for any but a talented and experienced rider who plans to enter advanced competitions to try to practice this type of control.

The last paragraph of the book is also written in Caprilli's spirit:

If one has a good cross-country horse, the author deems it inadvisable to teach extreme collection or the delicately balanced airs of the high-school. Riding the horse on the bit with a *normal* head carriage, improving his natural balance through the simple exercises detailed heretofore, *and thereafter allowing him, as a rule, to go in the manner most comfortable to himself, is the safest and surest road to success and pleasure for the practical horseman.* (The italics are mine.)

To this I would like to add that if an experienced trainer should beware of High School movements when schooling a hunter and a jumper, a typical amateur rider should avoid even the simple forms of Dressage. Even these, in the hands of such a rider, are apt to make the horse nervous, spoil his perhaps naturally good free gaits, and warp his natural jumping abilities. In my clinics I meet such cases all the time; the number of horses who have lately been ruined by complicated schooling is prodigious.

As to the French influences on Chamberlin—I find so few traces of them in his book that I wonder why he so emphatically gave credit to Saumur and to the French horsemen of the 18th and the 19th centuries; he specifically mentions such men as de la Guérinière, Baucher, d'Aure, etc. Here is what remains from the old manege riding in *Training Hunters, Jumpers and Hacks.*

1) *Placing the head (Ramener)*, you may remember, is one of the basic points of Dressage, and I quoted Gerhardt and Fillis on the subject. Chamberlin considerably curtails its use by finding it advantageous only at very slow gaits, in the abrupt decreasing of gaits, and at abrupt halts. He says:

When the horse is at fast speeds, the bend at the poll decreases and the face becomes more nearly horizontal as the neck and head are extended and lowered. . . . On the other hand, when slow speeds cause a short base of support, the horse raises and retracts his balancer. In this latter position the face normally approaches an angle of forty-five degrees with the vertical and becomes almost perpendicular when the pace is quickly decreased or a sudden halt required.

Chamberlin hopes that the horse will acquire this ability to change the attitude of the neck and head, depending on the speed of the gait, by himself, naturally, and not through the coercion of the rider's hands and legs:

"... when a graceful placing of the head does not result from the intelligent selection and use of various training exercises, great caution ought to be exercised before attempting to force the horse to flex his poll greatly or change his natural head carriage. If the ramener obviously causes discomfort and nervousness it should be abandoned. ..."

Again this is very different from French 19th century Dressage, in which ramener was taught rather forcibly in hand during the first schooling lessons; and it may be remarked that ramener still is one of the early lessons in the High School of today.

2) *Shoulder-in and Appuyer* or *shoulder-in while moving obliquely* are, of course, typical Dressage movements. To the same group belongs the *half turn* (half circle) during which the horse is required to move obliquely even while making the turn. The *two tracks* also belongs to the category of manege exercises not to be found in the Italian schooling of a cross-country horse. In the past I taught all of these except the shoulder-in, but little by little I discarded them, as practical evidence proved that they contributed little or nothing to the improvement of the performance of a hunter or jumper, particularly when practiced by amateur riders, even good ones. Two tracks, however, may be a useful exercise for developing an advanced rider, because it emphasizes coordination of the aids, and I continued to teach it for this purpose.

I have devoted so much space to *Training Hunters, Jumpers and Hacks* because I believe that it is, in its field, the greatest book of the century, not only in the United States but in the world. I know of nothing comparable produced abroad. The book was well received, because Colonel Chamberlin's success in showing gave him fame; but I doubt whether it had the influence it deserved. I have known many people who bought the book, but only rarely do I come across someone sufficiently familiar with its contents to be able to discuss it. The reason lies in the simple fact that the book was not written for amateurs, and most of them find it hard going.

A popular interpretation of modern educated riding was obviously needed, and I was one of those who attempted to provide it. I succeeded best, I think, with my last two books, *Common Sense Horsemanship* (D. Van Nostrand Co., 1951) and *Schooling Your Horse* (D. Van Nostrand Co., 1956). Based on Caprilli's ideas, they represent an adaptation of the original Italian method to the necessities of the contemporary American amateur; even the Italians themselves have altered some of the details of Caprilli's teaching of sixty years ago. As a matter of fact, the whole history of equitation is nothing else but a continuous chain of inventions and adaptations inspired by the current exigencies of life. It seems to me that it may be said that, while I changed some minor techniques of Caprilli's method to advance it with the times, I preserved its spirit intact.

In 1934 the Boots and Saddles Riding School privately published *The Defense of the Forward Seat*, written by my former associate, the late Captain Sergei Kournakoff and myself. Because only sixty-two subscription copies and two hundred and fifty ordinary copies were printed, the book is little known, hence I would like to say a few words about it now.

It all started by Captain Kournakoff's and my wishing to prove to ourselves *scientifically* that the Forward Seat was really helpful to the horse in jumping. To achieve this we felt we should analyze the horse's jumping efforts in at least three different ways, and then compare the results obtained. One way was obvious and, although unoriginal, of great importance—that was photography. Kournakoff, who had a good mathematical education, took upon himself the analysis of the case from the standpoint of the laws of ballistics—and then we thought of a third way, never before used for this purpose. This consisted of attaching a small but very bright electric bulb to one or another part of the horse's body, with a dry battery feeding it secured to the saddle. A camera was placed exactly on the line of the jump, which was installed in an artificially lighted ring. Shortly before the horse started for the jump, the shutter of the camera was opened and was left open until the jump was completed. The result was that the fast-moving body of the horse would hardly leave a blur (due to poor lighting conditions), while the light of the bulb would trace a clear-cut line on the plate. Thus the trajectory of the jump ceased to be imaginary and its variations, depending on the seat used, were convincing factors in our research.

We began our experiments with the camera and the electric bulb in 1932, using upwards of thirty horses as models. The results of our work were first published in a series of articles in *The Rider and Driver* beginning in January 1933; a year later they were printed in book form. Reviewing it *The Sportsman* wrote:

"It is probably the most scientific work on equitation ever written. . . . they [the authors] have taken riding out of the arts . . . and placed horsemanship among the sciences, where it belongs. . . . to the mind that seeks to grasp the why and the wherefore it is a banquet. . . ."

The hundred and forty-two pages of this book are concerned only with the jump itself; that is, a fleeting moment of about two seconds' duration. Today, with thirty more years of practical work behind me, I could easily double the volume's size without padding it. But incomplete as the book may seem at present, at the time it was written it was an original contribution to educated riding, and for the writing of it Kournakoff deserved more credit than I did.

Out of the considerable number of popular books published in the course of the last twenty-five years, one definitely deserves to be mentioned here—and not because the author is a good friend and former pupil of mine, but for its own merits. It is *School for Young Riders*, written by Jane Marshall Dillon (D. Van Nostrand Co., 1958). Addressed to junior riders, it presents modern riding in a technically sound, practical, simple and very appealing way. The book unquestionably has a healthy, widespread influence today. Such books, combining simplicity of language and informality of presentation with a sound scholastic basis, have begun to appear only during the current century, and successfully only in this country. Although the English have often attempted such things and have frequently produced entertaining reading, their basic approach has usually been too superficial. German books, on the other hand, suffer from their thorough-going exhaustiveness and heavy presentation, and the few French books written in this vein are too sophisticated for beginners.

International Competitions in the 20th Century

· · · · · · · · · · · · · · · ·

THE most conspicuous development in riding in Europe during the past forty years has been the spectacular growth of the competitive spirit. Even the English amateur, in the past so happily relaxed, has recently become highly competitive. And the modern Olympic Games, founded in 1894 (the first Games were held in 1896) on the principle that "the main thing is not winning, but taking part, for the essential thing in life is not so much conquering as fighting well," has today become an arena for the strongest nationalistic rivalries.

With this new spirit as the motivating power, the youth of all European countries has enthusiastically welcomed a novel theme in equitation—jumping. At the advanced levels of show riding, jumping in Europe has taken a form similar to that known in America as "open jumping" (though with different rules); and because of the geographical proximity of nations, international open jumping has developed fast. This competition between the best horses and the best riders of various nations has been the cause of a rapid increase in the difficulty of the courses. It is particularly since the Second World War that severe international courses have begun to pose new problems in the selection, schooling, and riding of jumpers.

These new problems have induced some horsemen to re-evaluate Caprilli's method. There is a certain irony in this, since it was Caprilli's system that enabled horses and riders to jump consistently well over higher and more complicated courses than those prevalent in his days, and to continue to do so for almost a generation afterwards. But there then occurred in riding what has often happened before in other human activities—man's ambition to attain the barely attainable took over jumping; it forced many international horsemen to drop Caprilli's method and to search for other, more forcible means of making horses negotiate almost impossible combinations of obstacles. Today many of these horsemen will rightly tell you that Caprilli's basic tenet, that "there is little in common between ring riding and cross-country riding" could be altered to—"there is little in common between cross-country riding and international show jumping." Show jumping has become a narrow specialty. Consequently, one of the medalists of the jumping competition in the London Games of 1948, a Frenchman, the Chevalier d'Orgeix, could write, "I am not a specialist in cross-country riding . . ." and add that he neither practiced nor studied the latter.

Artificial jumping problems, and the correspondingly artificial means of solving them, have placed such jumping just around the corner from the tanbark of the circus. Just as in former days our ancestors admired the particularly artificial feats of High School, so today many of us enjoy a new type of circus—unnaturally high obstacles assembled in tricky combinations. And the more spills there are and the more crashing of timber, the more thrills some people get.

Here are some data to illustrate how difficult the international courses of today are in comparison with those at the beginning of the century.

In the Olympic Games of 1912 in Stockholm (the first Games to include equestrian events), the maximum height of the obstacles was 1.40 metres—that is, about 4'6" (one metre equalling about 3'3"). Several obstacles were only 1.10 metres (about 3'7") and 1.15 metres. In the Olympic Games of 1960 in Rome, the highest obstacles were 1.60 metres (about 5'3"), while the majority measured between 1.40 and 1.50 metres (about 4'6" and 4'10"); and there was only one obstacle of 1.30 metres in the individual competition, and one of 1.35 metres (about 4'3") in the team competition. In other words, the lowest obstacle in Rome was only about three inches lower than the highest in Stockholm. But the main difference in the difficulties between the old and the new type of course lies in the spacing of the combinations, particularly in the treble ones, and in the breadth of some of the obstacles which form the combinations.

The actual result of all this in the Prix des Nations of the Olympic Games of 1960 was as follows: out of eighteen teams that started, nine were eliminated in the first round, and another three in the second round. The winning team (German) had a total of 46½ faults; the winners of the silver medal (U.S.A.) had 66 faults; and the team in the third place (Italian) had 80½ faults. The three remaining teams had respectively 135½, 164¾ and 168 faults. These figures mean that a good many fences were knocked down that day.

Something similar happened on another day, during the individual jumping competition over fourteen obstacles which constituted a total of seventeen jumps. The course consisted of big fences, many with very wide spreads, and a trappy treble combination made up of a wall about 4'9" high, followed twenty-four feet later by a triple bar over brush fences, about 4'11" high with 6' spread, followed twenty-nine feet later by parallel bars about 4'11" with 6' spread. In the first round, thirty-five horses failed at this combination, another six refused, two fell, and two were eliminated; only eleven jumped clean. In the second round, sixteen horses cleared this combination.

All in all, in this extremely arduous competition, out of the sixty horses that started, fourteen were eliminated in the first round, while only one horse made a clean performance. In the afternoon round another ten horses elected not to start, two more were eliminated, and the two best horses had two knock-downs each. Only thirty-four horses (a little better than half of the number that started) finished the two rounds. The winners of the medals had respectively 12, 16 and 23 faults. These scores, under the circumstances, were very low; the majority of scores lay between 28 and 65 faults. During this day, more than three hundred obstacles were knocked down.

Such unfortunate spectacles as the two jumping competitions of the 1960 Olympic Games make a feeling horseman pity the animals, and they spoil his enjoyment of the sport. Another reaction of many of us is that much of the performance is simply ugly—often as ugly as that of many of our domestic open jumpers. Thus the question arises whether some cases can be classified as an exhibition of educated riding and schooling. All this does not, of course, prevent us from acknowledging the skill involved in getting a horse over this kind of course, as well as the great natural abilities of many of the horses. But there is a difference between simply recognizing skill and talent or thoroughly enjoying a beautiful performance.

Obviously the sport is up a blind alley. We cannot return to the easier courses of former days, and international jumping is bound to continue on its steep and narrow path, separating itself more and more from amateur riding, and becoming a game in which only a professional can participate. As a matter of fact, all international riders are virtual professionals already. Not professionals in the usual meaning of the term—men who earn their living by riding; but professionals in a special sense—that is, horsemen who, having independent means, are able to devote more time to riding than to earning a living by other work.

But there is another factor which separates the chosen few from other horsemen even more than merely ways of making money. This is an exceptional and very special inborn talent which is essential to these riders (and, it may be added, to the horses which compete in modern international shows) if they are to win. No riding teacher or trainer has ever made international winners out of merely able men and horses. All the great international riders and international horses were made in heaven; the teachers and trainers they may have had helped merely to develop their gifts. Only a handful of men and horses can play this extremely difficult game, which today for ninety-nine per cent of horsemen must be a spectator sport.

The story of advanced Dressage in Europe during the 20th century has been a mixed one. There was a decline in popularity in the middle of the century at the same time as progress in refinement. The latter was particularly evident at the level of High School. This had been stripped of all its highly artificial movements such as cantering to the rear, cantering on three legs, airs above the ground, etc. Olympic Dressage now culminated with the Passage and the Piaffe. At this level, although the program is simpler, it seems likely that the movements that remain may be executed with greater refinement than in the past.

In 1990 pure Dressage—that is, an art *per se*—aiming at High School and practiced without any utilitarian purpose—is largely confined to Olympic and other international competitions. The small, elegant circuses, with their aficionados, which still fostered Dressage in the early part of this century, have long disappeared. In the new, modern circuses, with their appeal to a different public, including many children, there would be little reason to spend money on a highly skilled rider whose refined performance would be recognized by only a few patrons. On the other hand, today the increased number of high-level equestrian competitions, the explications in programs and by loudspeaker and the generally much increased television audience has made many non-participants more familiar with the sight of Dressage—some perhaps even with its finer points.

Where well-staged spectacles of horses performing in a group are still still to be seen today are in the Spanish Riding School of Vienna or at Saumur when the Cadre Noir performs. These may appeal even to modern audiences totally ignorant of the history or of the refinements of technique and schooling required to produce such performances. Many of the spectators in such audiences, however, would soon become bored if required to sit and watch a series of individual horses executing very precise but much less spectacular movements.

The European continent, of course, is probably where there is the most intelligent and knowledgeable interest in Dressage —even among those who do not practice it. In Germany in particular, there is a keen interest. In the United States, where a superficial acquaintance with a subject often seems to be enough, one may find people talking glibly about Dressage. The Spanish Riding School of Vienna, with its white horses and its columned hall, is a favorite sight with American tourists, many of whom are impressed by the spectacle, although they may not even know how a horse should walk. This sort of interest has, of course, little to do with equitation. The fact that the United States now has a number of riders of Olympic caliber has still not educated our general public.

It may be interesting and instructive to compare the present situation with a description of that obtaining in the early 1960s, when this book was written. Dressage on the level of the Grand Prix of the Olympic Games was then the goal of very few people indeed.

In the Games in Rome, for instance, France (of all countries!) did not have any entries in the Dressage competition, and only seventeen horses in all, representing ten nations, participated (the number of horses was limited to two from each country, and three countries had only one entry each). Germany in this respect is an exception, probably due to the fact that disciplining, training, dominating, and working pedantically are German characteristics.

Although not so long ago most European High School riders had been army officers, their thinning ranks were often being filled by women. This is quite understandable, for this sport could be practiced successfully by individuals chiefly with wealth and leisure; and it was most likely to be a woman who had both. Professionals, of course, were a special case. In Switzerland and Sweden, the two countries not involved in wars during this century or disturbed by revolutions, the major representatives of High School were still members of the army. Swedish officers had won more Olympic medals in the Grand Prix de Dressage—and more of them gold ones—than any other country; five gold medals against Germany's two, and France's, Switzerland's, and Russia's one each. Medals won in the Olympic Games, however, do not indicate the condition of amateur riding in a country. Neither did the perennially victorious d'Inzeo brothers prove that Italy is a riding country with much excellent jumping; nor does Filatoff's gold medal in Rome mean that all Russians are connoisseurs of High School.

The high standards of the competition for a few, rather than the number of people involved in the game, were what had been responsible for bettering the performance of Dressage. The *exhibitions* of High School riding in former days did not call for the perfection of detail that today's *competition* demands. It is very possible that James Fillis himself, with all his genius and artistry, might not win in modern Olympic contests, simple as the program might appear to him. It is also possible that he would be bored by the tedious mechanical details that modern competition has made imperative.

The progress of manege riding up to the 1960s is best illustrated by the changes in the program of Dressage in successive Olympic Games.

In 1912 in Stockholm, the then so-called *Individual Dressage* did not include such movements as Passage, Piaffe, Pirouette, or a specified number of flying changes of leads in a given number of strides. It required only such things as a collected and extended trot and canter, backing, turns on the haunches, only four arbitrary flying changes of leads on a straight line, small circles, a figure eight at a canter, with and without change of leads, and so forth. Five small jumps and an obedience test were added to this program. The latter consisted in making the horse pass objects from which he had previously shied.

Obviously the program was conceived for a cavalry officer who actually served in the ranks, and who consequently did not have as much time to devote to sport as the people who take part in international competitions today. In those days army teams consisting of officers who were taken out of regular duty and given a special job (and paid for it) to school for international competitions and ride in them, had not yet come into being.

The Dressage program of the Olympic Games in Antwerp in 1920, Paris 1924, and Amsterdam in 1928 were quite similar to each other, differing only in detail. On the whole they were simple, although more difficult than the test of 1912. For example, they included two-tracks both at a trot and at a canter, and a specified number of flying changes of lead, every 4th, 3rd, 2nd, and every stride.

In 1932 in Los Angeles, the Passage and Piaffe were introduced for the first time. Unfortunately I lack information on when the Pirouette at a canter was added to the program; it was, however, a part of it in Berlin in 1936, when the test included all the High School movements mentioned and was considerably longer than the test in Stockholm: 17 minutes against 10.

In 1948 in London the test was shorter again (13 minutes) and the Passage and Piaffe were omitted. This was due to the fact that there had not been sufficient time to prepare horses during the rather short interval since the end of the war. The programs in the next three Olympic Games, Helsinki in 1952, Stockholm in 1956, and Rome in 1960, although differing somewhat from one another, were all at least of the standard of the Berlin test.

Every Olympic Games' Dressage competition is followed by

heated arguments about the correctness of the judging. These start on the spot and are often continued later on in the press and during special Dressage conferences. This does not necessarily mean that judges are unfair. It merely emphasizes the fact that High School, as any art, is a matter of taste—in this case, national rather than personal taste. This taste, like national temperament, is largely the product of economic and geographic conditions and historical factors; no two nations can see quite alike. Thus, for instance, the two major Dressage schools of today, the French and the German, are bound to appreciate different things, and therefore to strive for different results. The average German horse usually performs rather mechanically and stiffly, requiring strong aids, but it performs with great precision; these horses have been compared to wooden soldiers. On the other hand, the French horse of the same calibre performs very lightly and elegantly, although it may make technical mistakes here and there; it has frequently been likened to a ballerina. But besides differing in the fundamental temperamental approach, the schools differ in many technical points, the source of many of which may again be traced to basic national characteristics. These technical points, as a matter of fact, naturally limit the size of an intelligently appreciative audience, for most of them are Greek to even good riders in other fields. Unfortunately one has to know a lot to be able to differentiate between good and bad High School.

Another competition of the Olympic Games, the "Complete Test of Equitation," popularly known as the "Three-Day Event," originated around the turn of the century as a test for officers' chargers. As such it was included in the first equestrian Olympic Games under the name of "Military." Since then it has been gradually changing hands from military to civilian, and today is simply a versatility test.

The conditions of the "Complete Test of Equitation" changed with the years, and by 1936 the eighteen obstacles of the 1920 cross-country phase had already increased to thirty-five. This was their number in Rome. The obstacles today are also considerably more difficult than they were in 1912, while speed is at a premium in the steeplechase and the cross-country, and is rewarded by bonuses.

After Rome there were two popular criticisms of the present form of this competition. The first was that the second-day phase is much too difficult (in Rome only six teams out of eighteen finished) and often results in the death of horses (three died in Rome). The second criticism was that the Dressage phase did not represent the type of schooling that leads to better jumping or fast cross-country riding. This is underlined by the fact that of the twenty horses who had been most successful in Dressage in Rome, eleven were eliminated during the cross-country phase and six others were heavily penalized.

This is already an old argument, and it is resumed after each Olympic Games. Once even, in the Games of 1920, the Dressage Test was abolished. The Italians, quite naturally, are always against it in its actual form; but many horsemen of other nations, also quite naturally, are firmly for preserving it in its present spirit of the old manege riding.

Here it is interesting to note that in the century of specialization, some horsemen are against this competition in general, as a hodge-podge for horses who are jacks-of-all-trades. In the thirties in Europe it was occasionally said that the competing horses were mostly those that were not good enough at Dressage to compete in the Grand Prix de Dressage, that could run, but did not possess the speed for regular racing, and that could jump, but not high enough to take part in international open-jumping competitions. All their critics, however, admit that these horses have to possess at least two extremely valuable qualities—endurance and boldness. But admitting this, they say that the competition, in order to be brought up-to-date, should be stripped of the Dressage, Steeplechase and Arena Jumping phases and should consist only of Endurance and Cross-country

·   ·   ·   ·   ·   ·   ·   ·   ·   ·   ·   ·   ·   ·   ·   ·   ·

tests, thus becoming a specialty in its own right. Obviously such a point of view had little chance of winning, at least at that time; I merely mention it here as one of various current ideas.

Many signs point to the fact that this kind of competition (in various abridged forms) may soon become a rather well-liked sport with amateurs. However, due to the obvious difficulties of holding such events they will never be able to compete in popularity with the horse show.

Today when, in all countries, the ambition of practically every young rider is not only to jump but eventually to compete in jumping competitions of one kind or another, consistent winners in international jumping exert (with the help of the press) considerable influence. They are understandably admired and their practices studied, and many ordinary riders try naively to imitate them. I say "naively," for it is not so much these practices by themselves that lead to success as that their often inimitable application by a rider of outstanding talent makes them work efficiently. I can think of several great riders during my lifetime who, although they rode quite differently, in the end obtained the same results. Nor should the horses be forgotten. Every top international jumper was born with a physique particularly suitable for this form of athletics, with a talent for judging obstacles, with ambition to clear fences, and with unfailing boldness and willingness. A method suitable for schooling and riding such horses may not work at all with the average horse. Besides this, many horses, outstanding or ordinary, present individual problems.

All jumping techniques fundamentally aim at the same thing. They all are based on the tenet that the horse must arrive at the take-off area in proper balance, at an advantageous speed, and with a sufficient reserve of energy. Then, in the cases of very high and complicated courses, it is often up to the rider to indicate to the horse the best distance from the obstacle at which to take off and to give him the extra impetus to clear it.

The conceptions of proper balance, speed and reserve energy

when nearing an obstacle remain the same, no matter what the school, although every one of these points can be, and often is, differently interpreted. In Forward Riding these points are not too difficult to learn. On the other hand, neither Caprilli, nor Chamberlin, as you may remember, subscribed to the placing and the extra urging—for which a rider needs special talent. But I wonder whether they would not change their minds if faced with modern international courses. They might be forced to, because the complexity of the latter is such that the horse's mind is not quick enough to cope with the new and extremely difficult situations which constantly arise. The riders, at least, can walk and memorize the course; they know what to expect and can decide ahead of time on the best way of negotiating it.

Stephanie Steck winning the AHSA Hunter Seat Championship at Madison Square Garden in 1963.

The forcible riding over obstacles practiced by 19th century riders, simply because they knew no better, is almost inevitable again today in international shows because of the quite artificial mathematical problems in vogue at the moment. Artificial problems breed artificial riding. But then, of course, there are degrees in every method, and forcible riding today is practiced on the basis of both more knowledge and more experience than obtained in former days.

Today it is generally recognized in Europe that the riders and horses of the United States Equestrian (jumping) Team perform in a particularly homogeneous and pleasant style, which is at least reminiscent of Italian doctrines. To be sure, their performances are not based on the principle that the horse does the job, with the rider merely indicating what to do and helping only here and there. Our riders definitely dominate their horses, as do the other international riders. But here the matter of degree enters, and it is supported by refined techniques, which conceal much of the actual forcibleness. The fact that in most instances the controlling efforts of the members of our team are less evident than those of many other international riders (and of our domestic open jumpers), speaks highly for their horses' schooling and for their technique as riders. This is particularly interesting in view of the fact that our team is largely under the influence of German theories, and several outstanding German winners have ridden quite roughly. I saw the Germans only in Madison Square Garden in 1958 but, since my impressions have been confirmed by many Europeans who see them frequently, I feel justified in making this statement.

There was no beauty in the performance of the Germans at the time that I saw them. Their horses often galloped between fences in a choppy, uneven fashion, pulling, with necks frequently arched and chins in; while the riders, in the struggle for an efficient take-off, exhibited positions ranging from rather good to completely grotesque. Hans Winkler, on his famous

Halla, was the most attractive rider of the German team, particularly at the beginning of a round, when Halla would come back softly and the rider had no trouble in placing her; in the latter part of the round, when Halla would begin to pull, the original softness was often replaced by yanking and everything that goes with it. It was only during the jump itself that the Germans and their horses often looked well, because at that moment the riders changed very acrobatically from their nondescript positions to a Forward Seat, and gave sufficient freedom to their horses' necks and heads. In justification one may add —what our open jumpers have said all along—that their business is not to demonstrate beautiful riding, but to win. This goal the German riders pursue very successfully, and they are great artists in aiming and shooting at obstacles. In this respect their exceptionally talented horses often assist them by correcting an occasional mistake of the rider in placing them and by jumping clean in spite of it. In view of the great talent of the German horses, the failure of the contemporary German Dressage method to make them perform more smoothly between obstacles and without the need of very conspicuous aids is remarkable.

I should add that I have also seen Germans who performed in excellent style but, unfortunately, these were not top winners. All this illustrates the fact that beautiful riding and winning do not necessarily go together.

It must be quite obvious from what I have said that I personally admire an inconspicuous control of the horse; however, because it is undramatic, it leaves many people cold. And there is another factor: while many people today like to ride on the basis of a partnership with the horse, just as many love to dominate the animal and to feel that he is merely an animated instrument in their hands. This category of rider will always prefer a method based on pushing and pulling, which gives the sensation of dominion. When talented riders take this road the results may not be too bad, but when every Tom, Dick and Harry attempts it, the level of average riding goes downhill, and upset and unhappy horses become a common sight. Fortunately there is no question that in following hounds, showing hunters, and competing in horsemanship classes, the dictator's attitude is not only unnecessary but even detrimental in most instances. Nothing is more beautiful than a performance which looks easy and natural. There are many people, however, who will not agree with me; and those who are apt to be impressed by ribbons rather than by a fine performance will always be ready to accept any grotesque technique as long as they associate it with winning.

As the military have gradually been replaced by civilians in international competitions, many ambitious amateurs have begun to fancy themselves or their children as potential representatives of their country. Even in their simple daily riding they have begun to imitate the practices of the international arena. This has led to some unsound notions. There is, for instance, the belief that an amateur in his hunting or jumping should try to follow the earlier principles of military riding with its basis of dressage. This belief can only originate from a quite unrealistic approach to the actual needs and the potentialities of the majority of today's horsemen. Unfortunately the old 19th century cavalry attitude is still with us among many teachers and promoters of riding. In this country two of the strongest factors creating such a point of view have been the influence of our own United States Equestrian Team and of England through some of our Pony Clubs. It seems, however, that England, which embraced this belief somewhat earlier than we did, has already had its share of disappointments, and perhaps is about ready to take a different road. For example, Lt. Colonel C. R. G. Hope, the editor of the magazine *Light Horse*, was writing in the 1960s:

ABOUT DRESSAGE

The majority of horsemen and women in these islands get their riding out hunting, following a doctrine—if you can call it such—that has changed little in the last hundred years, perhaps longer. Most of them are none the worse for that, and their horses appear far more comfortable than those on whom dressage is so assiduously practiced. . . .

Now let us consider the three-day event from the horse's point of view. First of all, the first two phases—dressage and endurance—are becoming more and more contradictory. The dressage test has become too long and too formal, with less and less relation to the main requirements of the event. It is more and more noticeable that horses who have done bad dressage tests go superlatively well across country. It is the exception rather than the rule for a horse to be top at both.

ABOUT PONY CLUBS

Our instruction of youth, in the Pony Club and elsewhere, is based on a hangover from Weedon and Saugor. I do not decry them; I owe much to them myself; but while they existed they were truly alive, doctrine was ever developing and marching—slowly perhaps—with the times. When they were closed down the doctrine was frozen, was practiced and taught unchanged by their alumni, who are instructors and examiners for the British Horse Society, and so passed on to the riders of today. The riders of tomorrow need something else. . . .

The Pony Club . . . have introduced a new universal saddle for Pony Club members. . . . It is unfortunate that, with its comparatively straight front flap . . . it perpetuates that outdated fallacy of the "general purpose" seat, which is probably responsible for so much of the bad jumping style shown by young riders today . . .

CHAPTER 15

Modern European Literature

. . . .

THE majority of serious books on equitation published in Europe in the course of the current century have still been written by cavalry officers.

It is to be expected that most of the books written by cavalrymen, or by well-educated civilian professionals brought up in the spirit of former military riding or of the yet older High School, would reflect the past rather than anticipate the future. There is, however, one big difference between the books of the early part of the century and those written lately.

At the time of Fillis it was sufficient to describe jumping in one short chapter; today as much as a third of a book may be devoted to jumping, or it may even be the main subject. Jumping itself is now usually described in Italian terms; some interpretation of the Forward Seat is included, and is more or less awkwardly combined with manege riding on the flat. The latter is still preserved in many books as "basic" training—in itself an old-fashioned idea in our century of specialization. Moreover, a substantial part of the European literature on riding during the second quarter of this century has been concerned with the elements of international competitions; books have been published on High School, Jumping, the Three-Day Event, and on the construction of obstacles and courses. During the first quarter of the century, military riding was still a common subject, and throughout the two periods popular books for civilian beginners (often written by other beginners) have come off the press in great numbers. This is a rather modern development, which started in the late 19th century, and to which were added, in the 20th, many books for juniors. A few scientific books on the horse's locomotion continued too to be printed.

From the many books on Dressage that have appeared, I would like to single out one particularly—*Dressage*, by the late Colonel André Jousseaume, a French cavalry officer, winner or runner-up in several International Dressage competitions. This book was published in Paris, in 1950, by Fer à Cheval, and has been issued in English by D. Van Nostrand Co.

Jousseaume's book is the only modern work on High School I know of that presents the subject in a form anyone can understand. Starting with some thirty pages of *débourrage* (breaking), the book divides Dressage proper into six periods, each of which is in turn divided into several lessons. The book contains no arguments and no abstract theories; it is a simple, matter-of-fact presentation of the routine of schooling. (In many books this subject is treated as black magic.) While jumping is not discussed in the course of these lessons, the clean-cut impression produced by an exclusive concentration on one type of schooling is marred in the short Conclusion of the book by Jousseaume's statement that it would be perfectly possible to school the horse over obstacles simultaneously with his Dressage and that it is even to be recommended.

There are some details in Jousseaume's method that make his book particularly sympathetic to me. For instance, he says that while the shoulder-in may be a helpful exercise, it should not be considered a "universal panacea," and that it is not sufficient by itself to make a finished horse. Furthermore, he points out that there is a serious disadvantage in giving the horse a false position in early lessons.

Horses that move crookedly are so common that I myself am

indeed loath to sanction their being made crooked for any purpose whatsoever. The shoulder-in (as many other manege exercises), may once upon a time have been necessary in order to supple clumsily made horses for the execution of artificial movements. I fail to see any necessity for it in training today's thoroughbreds for such natural activities as field riding and jumping. De la Guérinière, by the way, is usually credited with the invention of the shoulder-in, and there is no question but that he fully developed this exercise; Newcastle, however, some seventy years earlier, described a movement that was certainly its forerunner.

Another point of interest in the book is Jousseaume's recommending, for application at least at the beginning of schooling, Baucher's principle of "legs without hands and hands without legs." Jousseaume believes that this practice prevents a green horse from becoming confused, as he might be if simultaneously driven forward with the legs and restrained by the hands. Many amateur trainers who have only glanced through a book or two on Dressage often teach a young horse to rein back by the combined use of legs and hands.

Just recently I was helping a pupil to buy a green horse. The colt was shown well by his trainer, and was moving on the bit after only six weeks of schooling. But I was surprised at his choppy gaits, which were not indicated in his conformation. During the second schooling lesson under his new owner the horse's gaits became normally good. This was the result simply of riding on loose reins (checking here and there to keep an even pace) while using the legs to maintain the impulsion— "legs without hands." About three weeks later the colt moved just as well on light contact. His former owner had obviously insisted on this contact too soon. Since he is an experienced horseman he would unquestionably have remedied the situation eventually, but an ordinary rider working on this principle can spoil a horse's gaits, perhaps forever.

Lightness of hands is particularly stressed in Jousseaume's

book. And because of it, the author can talk about the lightness of the legs. He even quotes General l'Hotte's saying that a horse should be "obedient to the breath of the boot."

It is interesting to recall this expression of the great 19th century French High School rider today, when the German Dressage riders seem to find that the total force of the legs is insufficient to drive the horse forward, and that the braced back must be brought into action in order that the seat may assist the legs in creating impulsion. Fundamentally, there is nothing new in the German Dressage seat; only some of its elaborations are modern. In Russian cavalry text books published during the 19th century a very similar seat was described. And I have little doubt that the braced back is helpful in achieving the German High School aim of having the horse's center of gravity pushed further to the rear than is required by the French school.

But here in the United States, the idea of the "braced back" and of "pushing with the seat bones" has been acclaimed by some riders as a great, present-day discovery, and is being applied to jumping. The strong use of the legs, which may be necessary when facing *extremely* difficult obstacles, is definitely harmful when applied in a routine manner to ordinary jumping. The majority of riders will have better success at the latter if they approach the fence normally in a galloping position, and sit for the last strides *only* if they feel that the horse is losing impulsion, and that they cannot apply their legs strongly enough when their seat is out of the saddle. There is no question but that the rider can use his legs more effectively from a sitting position; but it is easy to school a good horse to go boldly at most jumps almost on his own, most of the time; in my experience (working chiefly with thoroughbreds) the problem is often just the opposite— that is, how to control the horse's excess of natural impulse.

Some Germans, however, carry the point of sitting with a braced back a bit further and imply that the *seat bones alone* can, by their pressure, "influence" the muscles of the horse's back:

270

". . . the pressure of the seat bones from back to front that is exerted when we push our pelvis forward also exerts a forward thrust upon the horse's back." (*Horsemanship*, by Waldemar Seunig, Doubleday & Company, New York, 1956.)

The many pages of extremely learned discussions in German books do not convince me that a rider can exert any real pressure through a saddle purely with the seat bones—that is, at least as long as the laws of physics on this planet are in practical effect.

The same writer even goes so far as to stipulate the proper rider's conformation for this purpose and explains that a fleshy seat interferes with the forward action of the buttocks which "can act as an impelling force without the assistance of other parts of the seat only if the rider's weight acts upon the dorsal processes of the horse's spinal column (which are vertical in this region) at an angle that is at least 90 degrees." And adds that:

"The principle that only an extended surface of contact affords stability, plus breathing and swinging in time with the mechanism of the horse, is satisfied by a thigh that is flat on its inner surface. . . ." A rider who is not naturally blessed with this fortunate shape will be obliged "to spend years massaging the disturbing, round fleshy muscles to the rear. . . ."

Understanding how to school a horse so that it would collect itself on comparatively soft hands, Jousseaume did not need extremely strong leg aids; he could consequently ride with stirrups at hunting length and with the torso easily erect, without bracing his back, often even inclining slightly forward, as several of the illustrations in his book show.

Many other books on Dressage have been published in France in the course of our century, and of various types too. Very different from Jousseaume's book is the much more theoretical *Equitation Académique* by General Decarpentry, published in 1949 by Editions Henri, Paris. It required many generations of cultivated horsemen to permit General Decarpentry to write his sophisticated text in an elegent and beautifully logical manner.

This work is not for a beginner, but it is a delight to the educated horseman.

While most French books describe the schooling of a jumper in terms of more or less simplified Dressage, jumping itself is sometimes treated in a very modern manner. As an example I shall quote from one of the several books written by Commandant Yves Benoist-Gironière, who at one time competed in international jumping. The following paragraphs are from his book entitled *Epitres aux Amateurs d'Obstacles*, published in 1956, by Les Éditions de Neuilly:

> ...There are two diametrically opposed theories on the subject of schooling [over obstacles]: one which would let the horse work by himself without direction from the rider; the other which, on the contrary, would leave all initiative to the rider, the horse having but to obey his command. . . . believe me, let us keep to the first formula; leave the horse to correct himself. He will take more or less time, according to his temperament, but when the result is obtained it will be for good. . . . our directive would be to let the horse learn his work by himself, the rider only guaranteeing the proper acceleration, maintaining impulsion if it becomes too feeble. . . .
>
> Our first preoccupation as riders over jumps is to obtain from our horse the greatest possible extension of his neck and head. The absolute certainty that the neck and head in their function of "balancer" are the foundation for a correct jump should not leave our mind for an instant. . . .
>
> In the show ring we desire the strong balancing gestures, the long strides: we should have long reins. . . .
>
> The snaffle should be your favorite bit, it corresponds entirely to our ideas, which are liberty for the balancing movements of the neck and head. . . .
>
> Don't risk a jerk on the mouth. Your pride shouldn't make you ashamed to hold the mane . . . [advice to beginners].

.   .   .   .

Do not simply assume the jumping position at the moment of negotiating the obstacle, but long before approaching it. It is a fundamental mistake to change position at the moment of the jump, because the equilibrium of the horse is upset by it. . . .

The books on military riding require no comment, since they no longer have any bearing on actual equitation—except in the Versatility Test. Among the French books on the mechanics of the horse's locomotion, *The Gaits, The Horseman* should be cited. It was originally published in France in 1918, and in an English translation in 1930 by the United States Cavalry School. It was written by Captain de Beauregard, under the pseudonym of L. de Sévy. The book was an important influence in my life, since from it I learned in detail the role the neck and head of the horse play as balancer during the jump. I made wide use of the contents of this book in my own research on the horse's efforts in jumping.

Another quite remarkable book on the subject, *Mécanique Equestre*, was written in 1950 by a French veterinarian, André, and published by the Imprimerie Artistique, Lavour, Tarn, France.

You may remember that at the beginning of this book I said that I would use the term Dressage in the present popular interpretation of the word; this seemed necessary in order to make the book read more easily. Here, I think, before we leave French equestrian literature, is the appropriate place to discuss how the French use this by now American word, *Dressage*. It is not for the first time that it is used in the English-speaking world. The few 17th century English horsemen, like the Duke of Newcastle, who were influenced by continental riding, employed the term in the form of "dressing horses." It later went out of use, but has come back into the English language again, when horsemen of the English-speaking nations have once more come under the sway of the continent in matters of equitation.

Accepting this term in a superficial manner, both the English and we have missed the fact that the French themselves, advancing with the times, have come to distinguish between *Dressage de manège* (ring schooling), which eventually may lead to High School (*Dressage académique*), and *Dressage sportif* (for sport) which is schooling for horses destined for cross-country riding or for jumping. The latter Dressage is conceived under the Italian influence but, its method being still formulated, it more often than not preserves some practices from the past.

One often hears that the French word *dressage* merely means schooling. This is correct. But do those people who prefer the French word *dressage* to the English word *schooling* use the first in referring to a cowboy's schooling of a cutting horse, or to schooling a gaited horse, or to the early-morning, last-minute schooling over the outside course on the show grounds? Why not be consistent? A Frenchman would use the word *dressage* in all cases cited; as a matter of fact, *dressage d'obstacles*—that is schooling over fences—is a standard French expression. Those English-speaking people who insist that the French word *dressage* is equivalent to the English word *schooling* do not seem to practice what they preach.

But another factor has influenced our use of the word: in the days before Caprilli, when there was only one basic system of schooling (manege schooling), the word *dressage* signified this and nothing else. At that time, variations were limited to individual interpretations of what was fundamentally the same method. But today, with two systems existing side by side, the logical French, who like to express themselves very accurately, define which kind of Dressage they mean by adding either the word *manège* or the word *sportif* to it. Today in France the word *dressage* is used without a modifying adjective only in reference to manege Dressage, and this is why both competitions of the Olympic Games, the Dressage phase of the Three-Day-

Event and the Grand Prix de Dressage—are so termed. Both of these competitions represent fundamentally the same type of riding, but they are on two very different levels. What is it that relates them? Collection, of course. You will remember that all educated riding in the past was based on collection (more or less of it), while the first thing Caprilli's revolution did was to abandon it. Today, in English, the word *dressage* really refers to a specific type of schooling on the flat, based on collection. If one insists on using the same word *dressage* to designate schooling of Caprilli's type, the adjective "sporting" should be added. Whether it is called this, or *Forward Schooling* or *Natural Schooling*, or by some entirely new name, does not matter; but the user of the term should know what he is talking about and make it clear to his listeners.

Elementary Dressage, of which we hear so much today—that is the elementary level of ring Dressage—is considered by some people to be practical basic training for hunters and jumpers. This is an inheritance from the days of the military horse, and if one's hunter or jumper was expected to be as versatile as the old-fashioned military horse, some schooling of this type might be necessary. In an age of little time on the one hand and on the other hand of that narrow specialization which leads to high standards in competitions, the only really practical training is that directed toward the special end one has in view for a horse.

Even the elementary level of ring Dressage is based on collection, on *giving the horse a central balance*. This means *moving* with central balance, neck high and chin in; it is not only of little use to the hunter or jumper, but it will delay if not actually impede his acquisition of a good *forward balance* with stretched neck and long flat strides—the balance at which he will ultimately be required to function. Efficient elementary schooling for any type of horse must be based on the *type of balance at which he will be expected to perform*.

Some people who watch me teach movements like the half-turn on the haunches say with surprise, "So you teach Dressage!"

275

Actually, the superficial similarity between Dressage and Forward Schooling is even greater than that—both schools, for instance, make their horses walk, trot and canter! The difference between Dressage and Forward Schooling is not so much in the movements the horse is required to execute as in the manner and balance in which he executes them.

After French scholastic equestrian literature, German is unquestionably the second in importance. To the Teutonic mind it is probably superior to any, but many educated European horsemen of various nations will disagree with this. As national tastes in High School differ, so the literature of each country possesses its own flavor. A glance at one typical page of a book often suffices to indicate the nationality of the author. This is particularly evident in the case of German, French, and English works.

I have read German books in translation only—which means that I have not read many—five, to be honest; and one of these was not properly German, although it belonged to the Germanic school. But because the three that I shall discuss are recommended in print by members of our international jumping team, I have good reason to believe that they are among the best.

Suspecting that the cumbersomeness of the style in two of these books (*Horsemanship*, by W. Seunig, and *Give Your Horse a Chance*, by A. L. d'Endrödy) may be the fault of the translator, I am prepared to believe that the originals read more easily, and shall criticize only the substance of the text. In this respect I am fully aware that a perfect book has never been written, that every work contains errors, or is at least obscure in places—my own books, unfortunately, illustrate this.

In the first place, to me these German books lack the brilliant logic of the French, which is so characteristic of the latter culture in general. I also miss in these books the attraction of a cultivated presentation of the subject, and of that Gallic lightness and elegance which make even profound passages pleasantly palatable. In comparison with the French books the German texts are often quite naive in their earnestness and are pretentiously ponderous. Since they attempt to be pedantically exhaustive, they are apt to be overcrowded with details. Many of the latter, even of the simplest kind, are often described in a complicated scholastic manner which should be reserved only for those instances when there is no other way of presenting some abstruse point. Because of this the average reader soon ceases to see the woods for the trees. These turbid tomes illustrate the saying of Ruskin which Piero Santini so aptly quoted at the beginning of his own refreshingly lucid book, "It is far more difficult to be simple than to be complicated."

Surprisingly the thinking behind these involved sentences is not consistently sound. An educated horseman will soon find many loopholes. While errors in nonchalantly written passages may be excusable, one naturally objects to them when they are presented in a serious and weighty manner. The uneducated horseman, however, is invariably impressed by the whole performance, and especially so because he is unable to make head or tail of it. But after a certain amount of struggle with the printed word he lays the book aside forever. I know, from talking to hundreds of American amateurs about these books, that instead of promoting the desire to read other books, they are apt to discourage them with equestrian literature for quite a long while.

There is a type of American, however, who although definitely in the minority, loves to be complicated in anything he undertakes; it is he who bravely reads these books through. But many riders of this type, lacking the guidance of well-informed riding teachers, misinterpret much of the text and accordingly mess up their horses. Such books, as any technical book on riding, can of course be useful as a supplement to lessons, but cannot teach by themselves. The more complicated the book, the more this applies.

The educated horseman's manner of reading is quite different. An accomplished High School rider, for instance, will read a new book on his subject, not in order to learn how to ride or how to school his horse, but to acquaint himself with the point of view of another horseman, which eventually may change his own approach toward a certain schooling procedure, or may substantiate his position on a debatable matter. To many readers of this calibre the German books mentioned are disappointing, because instead of containing new ideas they are on the whole quite unoriginal, and may be of interest only because of the meticulous description of details, some of which perhaps were never before so fully described.

One would expect the horsemen of a country long dominated by a militaristic tradition to cling tenaciously to the formulae of the former cavalry. And, true enough, the old simplifications of manege riding for use in the ranks are now adapted to jumping and civilian cross-country riding. While refusing to accept the Italian method, which is based on obtaining the horse's cooperation rather than on dominating him, the Germans have, as everyone else, adopted the Forward Seat, but, taken out of a logical system, it is in this case artificially and without consistency added to another method. Many Germans, among them Waldemar Seunig, (*Horsemanship*, Doubleday & Company, New York, 1956) still think that the Italian method of schooling cannot produce a "correctly moving cavalry or saddle horse," and that such horses cannot stay in service for a "long time." Yet we all have seen hundreds of dependable and easily controllable hunters and jumpers still useful at the age of twenty years, made by methods closer to the Italian than to the old manege system.

Seunig also fails to recognize the fact that the Forward Seat and the Dressage Seat (he calls the latter the Normal Seat) have little in common, because the balance of the first is primarily based in the stirrups and that of the latter in the saddle. Obviously not realizing this, he believes that the "forward seat is developed organically from the normal seat." He also believes that it is impossible to maintain the Forward Seat "by balance alone"—which is precisely what beginners learning the Forward Seat are required to do by many American riding teachers. The Germans, who have apparently never discovered how easy this is when properly taught, make a strong point of the fixed knee, and teach that the rider should raise himself above the saddle not from the stirrups but "from the knees." Although I know a few excellent riders who ride with pinched knees, such a seat used by the majority would be quite disastrous, both from the point of view of security and that of softness.

One error leads to another, and Seunig wrongly claims that the fixed knees become "a shock absorber." The shocks of locomotion cannot be effectively absorbed if the knees are fixed, and this is why:

In order to absorb these shocks the rider's body must be springy. A straight, erect body has no springs in it. In order to be springy on the ground or in the saddle, a man must first of all acquire an angular position, with semi-relaxed joints forming three angles—in the ankles, knees and hips. But sitting in a chair in an angular position without his feet touching the ground, a man has no springs in his body. In order to obtain springiness he must stand on his feet, raising himself slightly above the chair, body inclined forward—in balance on his feet. It is a law of nature that we can deliver a spring only from our feet. When in the saddle the stirrups are the substitute for the ground; the impetus can come only from them. Pinching with the knees disconnects the torso from the feet and thus removes an essential element of the spring system. True enough, one can post at a trot without stirrups, from gripping knees, but this opening and closing of the angles of the knees should not be confused with spring. This is not a book on the techniques of riding, so I shall not go into a discussion of how a strong grip with the lower thighs, knees, and the upper calves may interfere with springiness, or when one is preferable to the other, and how and when compromises should be made. Here I merely wish to point out one of the numerous instances of error common to even the best German books. I have chosen the seat simply because it is the easiest to illustrate; when it comes to schooling a jumper or cross-country horse the errors, in my opinion, are many and large.

Books written by Eastern Europeans often bear the marks of German influence. For instance, a former Hungarian cavalry officer, Lt. Colonel A. L. d'Endrödy in his book, *Give Your Horse a Chance* (published in English by J. A. Allen & Co., London, 1959), also deals in a highly complicated manner with how the rider should use his seat as one of the aids in driving the horse forward and "influencing" the muscles of the horse's

By the middle thirties the Forward Seat and Forward Schooling of a hunter and jumper were already well established in this country. The rider is Chester A. Braman, shown at the Old Chatham Hunter Trials in 1934. *(Photo by Carl Klein)*

back. And he further takes the joy out of riding by including the thighs as other aids which, by pressing "on the muscles of the horses' withers," are able to "exert influence smoothly both on the back and the neck of the horse, and to affect directly even the shoulders."

As to his description of the Forward Seat—I am ready to confess that I find it completely baffling. The two following phrases, perhaps unfairly taken out of context, are nevertheless typical, not only of the description of the seat, but of much of the book:

> . . . the upper body, from the joints of the hip, exercises a pressure on the thighs which tends to keep the seat in its elevated position;
>
> The effects of the elevating function of the thighs and the pressing-down force of the upper body counteract each other and produce an elastic tension in the seat, which is thereby endowed with the necessary action-readiness and stability.

The photographs in the book illustrate the instability and awkwardness of the seat described at length by this author.

This book, however, since its ultimate objectives are the Three-Day-Event and show jumping, gives very interesting information on the schooling of a horse for these competitions. A reader gifted with powers of concentration and with the ability to select will undoubtedly find much of practical value in the text on these subjects.

These books, written by educated and serious horsemen, seem to exemplify the natural tendency of practitioners in any field to elaborate their knowledge and hedge it about with difficult language so that the layman will stand in proper awe of it, hence of them. Most riding teachers in this country or in England have not yet reached this stage of their art.

Riding Logic, by W. Müseler, the English translation of which was published by Methuen & Co., London, 1937, is another book of the same school which is, by contrast, quite readable, although the value of its content for today's riding is doubtful.

Only one of the pictures of jumping in the book (of an Italian officer) depicts good form as we understand it today. The rest of the illustrations of supposedly good form (mostly of German officers) represent riders in insecure positions, too far out of the saddle, with legs swinging rearward, and with hands on the horses' necks. The cause of the bad form may be deduced from the text, which misinterprets the Forward Seat in the standard German manner.

Müseler, who recommends a Dressage seat for moderate gaits, evidently even across country, and switching to a forward position only to catch up with the horse at a fast gallop or on the jump, describes a version of the latter based on shortened stirrups and *pinched knees*. This type of forward position almost inevitably throws the rider out of balance too far forward—a defect that is tacitly admitted by Müseler's stipulating that the rider at the same time rest his hands on the horse's neck. This, while perhaps necessary under certain circumstances, should not and need not be a part of the ideal finished position.

Because of these many misconceptions of the Forward Seat by the Germanic school, I reproduce in this book three photographs of Colonel Harry D. Chamberlin, showing the Forward Seat on the flat. The caption for one of them (at the gallop) reads—"Riding in stirrups" and, I may add, in a state of balance. They are from his book *Riding and Schooling*, first published by the Derrydale Press in 1933.

The text and illustrations that deal with Dressage are the best in Müseler's book. But in this respect it is interesting to note that Müseler's fundamentals of the rider's position for this type of riding are practically identical with those of Colonel Bobinsky's Russian text of 1836 (formulated under the German influence of the period). Bobinsky wrote:

"Lean back with the upper part of the torso and push the

belt and the stomach forward (the braced back) ... sit resting on ... the two seat bones and the crotch. These points ... form the base of the rider's position."

As to the control of the horse through the "influence" of the back, Müseler, after many pages of its description, arrives at the wise conclusion that it can exert control only in "conjunction with the legs." With the fact, long ago recognized, that the legs can act at their strongest only when the back is braced nobody will, of course, argue.

Of the many other European works, that written by the Polish G. von Romaszkan in 1940 is worth noting. Readers of the present book may consider the substance of the following quotation from Romaszkan an old story, but I thought it worthwhile to give it as an example of up-to-date European thinking on the subject of two different balances of the horse in motion, each of them determining the specialization of the horse:

The natural system of equitation stems from the idea that a horse puts himself in equilibrium, properly speaking, and does it correctly of his own accord; he does it without any action of the rider or his aids directed particularly towards this end. The rider offers the horse, in accordance with the type of movement and the character of the terrain, increasingly difficult tasks, and by this means attains his aim: that the horse acquits himself properly of these tasks, that it is to say puts himself in balance.

The rider only uses his aids as much as is necessary to keep the horse at the gaits desired, at the particular speed and in the proper direction. By much riding over appropriately varied terrain, as well as by frequent changes of gaits, speed and direction (halts and backing) the rider will obtain that engagement of the hindquarters necessary to put the horse in equilibrium for outdoor sporting equitation.

A balance obtained by this method, however, may be insufficient for the shortened gaits of manege riding, and especially for that of High School. The rider will not easily find natural means, outside the action of his aids, to force the horse into this kind of movement; although in liberty the animal will often execute similar ones of his own accord. . . . By following the system of natural equitation he [the rider] will never succeed in a higher domination of the horse, which—trained by this method—is always more individualistic and more independent. . . .

But, on the other hand, it is true that a horse schooled in this attitude, (the attitude of service) across country, on the basis of a kind of independent cooperation, is more skilful than the horse that has been trained only at collection in a manege. In this sense both horses—the cross-country horse and school horse—are in a way specialists, each in a different field of equestrian art. (From Gregor von Romaszkan's *Reiter und Pferd in Gleichgewicht*, published by Albert Müller Verlag, Ruschlikon-Zurich, Switzerland, 1940.)

Nothing of real importance or originality has been written lately by the English. They continue to write in their pleasing and often entertaining, informal manner, which makes for easy reading, but they offer the reader merely superficial and often confused technical information. A nation does not develop a logical approach to equestrian matters overnight. The void has been filled only by English reprints of good books from other countries.

For centuries the English wisely refused to use Dressage methods to school their cross-country horses. Now, ironically, that the Italians have provided the world with an ideal system for schooling hunters, the English have taken up a method which they previously firmly resisted. It was the British post-war occupation of Germany which probably inspired this remarkable about-face, by bringing many young Englishmen into personal contact with Continental riding. Although I have just belittled

German theories in comparison with French, Italian and some American, German riding is undoubtedly more educated than English, and has a much longer history of scholastic equestrian thinking. A thorough, serious, and analytical approach to the techniques of riding and schooling was a new experience for the English, and they were obviously duly impressed and intrigued. German victories in all three Olympic Games tests, as well as in international competitions in general, appeared to substantiate the superiority of the German system. Inexperienced thinking on the subject came to the simple conclusion that what is good for an international horse and rider should be good for every other horse and rider. The same logic would indicate that the difference between the schooling of a great jumper and of an ordinary hunter is merely a matter of degree. And so *elementary* Dressage became the by-word.

At the same time the English developed a strong competitive spirit themselves, and with it the desire to win in international shows and in the Olympic Games. This, of course, greatly increased English interest in continental riding, and led to considerable imitation of the types of riding and schooling practiced across the Channel. And it just so happened that some outstandingly talented English riders and horses soon began to bring home international trophies. It has been in the fashion of the day to attribute their success not to their native talents but to their Dressage. In the 1960 Olympic Games, however, the only English medalist was David Broom on Sunsalve (winner of the bronze medal in the individual jumping), and neither he nor his horse could, I am told, be suspected of any association with Dressage. Similar experience in the future may change the English point of view. Perhaps significantly, the English magazine *Light Horse* serialized the translation of Caprilli's writings in 1961.

One outgrowth of international competitions and of the shrinking of the horseman's world has been the necessity for riders of different nations to understand each other's technical terms. This need has been excellently answered by Zdzislaw Baranowski's *The International Horseman's Dictionary*, published by the Museum Press Ltd., London, 1955.

While many European books, French, German, and English have sold here, some American ones have been reprinted in England. Among these are the books by Major Piero Santini and by Colonel H. D. Chamberlin which I discussed in one of the previous chapters. Four of my own books have also been published in England and one (*Be A Better Horseman*), in an abridged form in Spain. The French have also printed some of my things—the magazine *Le Cheval*, in a series of eight articles, published chapters of my book *Common Sense Horsemanship*, while another magazine *l'Eperon*, in a series of three articles, printed my brochure, *Do Collected Gaits Have Place in Schooling Hunters and Jumpers?* I believe I am thus far the only American equestrian author whose technical works have been translated into French.

I do not think it can be said that American riding literature has so far exerted any influence on Europe; as a matter of fact, we have not even hoped for such a thing. Not really aware of what has been accomplished in this country, we are quite apologetic about our equestrian achievements; particularly today, when the trend is to copy Europe. The very fact, however, that American authors are reprinted across the ocean represents a development of the second quarter of the current century.

CHAPTER 16

The Long Arm of the Cavalry

· · · · · · · · · · · · · · · · · ·

SEVERAL new elements particularly characterize the modern equestrian scene. In the first place, what educated riding there is today is primarily for sport; in the past it had its place in the army or at court. This means that sporting riding is often being approached analytically as never before. Then, the increase in the number of people today able to participate in this game has had a democratizing effect upon it. Last but not least, the modern taste for competition has forced it to organize itself to a far greater degree than pleasure riding in the past. The forming and hunting of a pack of hounds, for instance, required organization, but this organization had almost nothing to do with actual riding.

As an example of how the sport was becoming more and more organized, in 1961 a Congrès du Cheval de Sport was held in Paris, the purpose of which was to further systematize the classification of shows, riders and horses. The approach to the latter is of particular interest.

The main purpose for the classification of horses was to prevent that abuse of young animals caused by too hasty schooling or by entering them too early in difficult jumping competitions. It was accordingly established that:

1) A four-year-old horse is considered in a period of *preparation* and *pre-selection*. The height of jumps for this category is limited to about 4', and time classes and jumping-off are both prohibited (only one class, at the end of the season, is to have a jump-off).

2) A five-year-old horse is considered in a period of *transition* and *selection*. This category will take part in jump-offs but not in speed competitions. The recommended limit to the height of obstacles is about 4'3".

3) A six-year-old is still to be excluded from participation in the *Championship of France* and *Puissance* classes. A *Grand Prix* for horses of this age will probably be organized for the end of the season.

Only after the age of six is the horse free to enter all the more difficult competitions.

Another interesting recommendation made was that of establishing a National Stud Book for the riding horse, with a special section for the *sporting horse*. Stallions and mares would be selected according to their ability to transmit to their offspring the right qualities for a *competitive horse*.

Although as early as the 16th century there were a few organized riding schools, and their number increased rapidly in the following centuries, it was only in the armies, and particularly those of the 19th century, that *educated riding* became truly organized—and, it may be added, organized on such a scale and with such uniformity that it affected even civilian riding. This was natural at a time when there was a single prevalent concept of what educated riding was, and when this was consistently taught and practiced by a large, prestige-bearing cavalry.

Today, this former role of the army has been taken over by civilian organizations, of varying degrees of influence and with differing aims, which naturally have a considerably harder time promoting their various ideals. One of their difficulties in this country results from popular differences of opinion as to the best method of riding and schooling cross-country horses and jumpers. Those who promote Italian ideas have as hard a time as those who believe in what they call *basic* Dressage training.

The rivalry between conservatives and radicals is as keen in the riding field as in most other human activities—almost as strong as in politics. At times it is hard to know who is winning, for on occasion the losing group may be the better organized, hence the more vocal. And I sometimes doubt that the complete dominance of a single point of view would produce a healthy situation. Again, as in politics, a two-party system is bound to stimulate both thought and effort.

The majority of amateurs who studied equitation in the 1960s—whether in Europe or in the United States—are juniors. This group can be particularly easily influenced, one way or another, by its teachers and by its seniors in the sport. At that time, the strongest educated conservative influence was exerted by former cavalry officers who were no longer active in their profession, either because of their age, or of the mechanization of the cavalry, or of political changes in various European countries. Many of these men had become either professional riding teachers or volunteer teachers in various riding organizations, or moving spirits in the latter. Probably the direct influence of this group of men was strongest in Europe, but it affected this country also through our imitation of European ways.

Because, up to the last, armies never accepted the Italian method for riding on the flat, the average cavalry officer of any country (except Italy) was still brought up basically on the principles of 1900, with the addition of the Forward Seat for jumping, and of some other modern details. While, unquestionably, typical military sporting riding at the time of the Second World War (during which the major reduction of horse cavalry took place) was much more modern than at the turn of the century, many old practices were still retained. Although horsemen of the United States disagree on the merits of a method based on the latter, they often take sides without either knowledge of the technical points involved or consideration of the practical problems of life. This confusion is partially the result of a common reluctance on the part of American horsemen to study the theory of equitation. No good riding can be taught or learned without knowing the logic behind the practical advice.

This unpopularity of theoretical knowledge, as long as it continues, will weaken all our efforts towards better riding. Not by being faddists, but by making our horsemen think and evaluate methods, dispute the comparative merits of different systems, and thus thoughtfully arrive at constructive conclusions can we raise the standards of equitation.

While the military period died hard, a new type of amateur civilian sportsman, with his own aims and ideals, arose. The main pleasure of this modern horseman is jumping (primarily competitive)—a form of sport which was merely taking shape at the time the cavalry schools were forming their latest tenets. The daily life of the new people in our sport—who, as I mentioned before, have come from various backgrounds, are of all ages and varying means, possessing horses differing in type and quality—is a far cry from that uniformity which was a distinguishing characteristic of former cavalries. These new people have needed a new method of riding and schooling horses, a simple and flexible method which would in the shortest possible time satisfy their comparatively simple ambitions (to hunt and compete in amateur shows). And in more and more cases they not only require a method that will do this for them, but one that will do it without abusing their mounts. Only those rather few horsemen who are in a position to combine ability with money and spare time for studying, and with continuous enthusiasm for riding, can hope to participate in international competitions; these can, and even should, approach riding in a complicated manner. But they are in such a minority that they do not need to be considered when developing a method that is practical enough to raise general standards of riding. The simple fact that raising standards in international competitions has little in common with raising them for general riding is rarely understood by the organizers of the sport on a national scale. This is hardly surprising, for only a wide and active experience of the riding scene at different levels can bring this point home.

In this book I have frequently used the term "amateur" and "average," but not in a disparaging sense. By amateur I do not imply a putterer, but simply a non-professional. And I employ the expression "average amateur" in a double sense. In one sense it refers to the rider with average aims, average time and means at his disposal, and in the other sense, of course, to his degree of ability in the saddle. As far as the latter is concerned it is from the ranks of these average riders, who can be counted in the thousands, that the hundreds of really good riders ultimately come. That the number of the latter may not grow greatly from year to year is due chiefly to the fact that a large percentage of them stop riding in their twenties. Despite this circumstance this group is, if anything, increasing rather than diminishing, which means that some riders who are average this year will have advanced considerably by next. The credit for this progress should go mainly to our riding teachers. To turn out hundreds of good riders yearly is, seriously speaking, a greater accomplishment than to give the finishing touches to a few exceptionally talented ones. Teachers should receive recognition of the same kind, too, for making horses which are pleasant to watch over 4' courses out of hundreds of ordinarily good animals. Again, to turn a few brilliant horses into outstanding jumpers is less of an achievement than this. Although it is little wonder that the superficial riding enthusiast may fail to see all this, it is regrettable, for many of our equestrian policies, both local and national, would be sounder if they were based on an appreciation of these circumstances.

While on the subject of organizations and teachers it may be worthwhile to point out that, in their natural desire to produce successful riders, they both may have a tendency to encourage a promising prospect to devote a disproportionate amount of time and energy to riding. Although some good amateurs are obviously marked for a riding career, the vast majority will find more rewarding occupations in other fields, and they should not be allowed to be carried away by youthful enthusiasm for the sport, and thus jeopardize the development of other interests which they will have more opportunity on the whole to pursue in life.

Moreover, dreams of glory come easy, and some professional teachers as well as some groups of organized amateurs would like to feel that they are helping to produce potential international riders. Because international riding was, until just lately, specifically military, and is still under the military aegis, some of these groups have welcomed former cavalry officers as teachers and advisers. Then too, as a body, cavalry officers have had a better equestrian education than civilians. Among the civilian riding enthusiasts are those who have joined and often run such organizations (or teach in them), not necessarily because of their thorough knowledge of equitation. They may do it because of their organizing and administrative abilities, because they have spare time, energy, money perhaps, and last but not least, because of a desire to play an important role in the community. These people need technical help and, with the present availability of former cavalry officers, the latter constitute an obvious choice.

The majority of cavalry officers have, of course, received an orderly equestrian education, but they are not all, necessarily gifted or imaginative horsemen; to many, the cavalry was just another kind of a military career—and talent is rare anywhere. The military world is apt to be a rigid one, and men who have been brought up in the army often find it harder to adapt themselves to changing conditions of life than do civilians. This is an occupational disability. Quite a few of the former cavalry officers teaching in this country have come here too recently to have been able to appraise more than the local segment of the riding situation with which they have come into direct contact. I know from my own case how long it took me before things fell in their proper perspective and I could see the forest for the the trees.

It is almost impossible for the former military man to begin otherwise than by trying to teach civilian pupils along the proper army lines, since he firmly believes that the theory in which he was indoctrinated is the best. It is only gradually that he begins to reflect that since his new pupils are riding for pleasure and not because a higher power requires it of them, that they need a faster-working and more flexible system than the army one. And he finally will come to the conclusion that theories usually hold good only in the circumstances for which they were evolved and can seldom be successfully applied in toto under quite different conditions. This process of assimilation sometimes is retarted by the fact that, since no uniform theory of educated modern riding obtains consistently in this country, it makes it all the easier for these teachers to acquire quite a local following, a situation that tends to confirm them in their belief in the superiority of their method.

So, although the military century proper—that is, the period when a military type of riding suited even civilians—ended around the time of the First World War, the effects of this period are still with us—just as the reactionary effects of the aristocratic era lingered on in the early military one.

However, although there were obviously conservative elements in every period, riding has continued on the whole to change with the pattern of the times, to have its forms dictated by the conditions of the life of which it is a part. It has not been and should not be static, and only by recognizing this can we make it give its most to man in any given period.

293

Bibliography

The books and periodicals listed below bear the date of the editions actually used by me—not necessarily the first ones.

Adams (John), *An Analysis of Horsemanship*, London, 1805.

Anderson (Edward I.) and Collier (P.), *Riding and Driving*, Macmillan and Co., Ltd., London, 1905.

André, Docteur-Veterinaire, *Mécanique Equestre*, Imprimerie Artistique, Lavaur, 1950.

Astley (Philip), *Astley's System of Equestrian Education*, London, c. 1800.

Aure (Cartier) Count d', *Traité d'Equitation*, 3d edition, Paris, 1847.

Baranowski (Zdzislaw), *The International Horseman's Dictionary*, Museum Press, Ltd., London, 1955.

Barroil (E.), *L'Art Equestre*, J. Rothschild, Paris, 1889.

Baucher (François), *Méthode d'Equitation*, 14th edition, Paris, 1874.

Benoist-Gironière (Yves) Commandant, *Epitres aux Amateurs d'Obstacles*, Les Editions de Neuilly, St. Germain en Laye, 1956.

Bilderling, Major General, *Ippologichesky Atlas (Hippological Atlas)*, St. Petersburg, 1889.

Blundevill (Thomas), *The Art of Riding*, London, 1609.

Bobinsky (Ivan) Colonel, *Kratkaya Ippologia i Kours Verkovoy Iezdy (A Short Hippology and Course in Horseback Riding)*, St. Petersburg, 1836.

Bohan (Loubat), Baron de, *L'Examen Critique du Militaire Français*, Genève, 1781.

Bourchier (Sir John) Lord Berners, *The Chronicle of Froissart*, London, 1901.

Broue (Solomon) de la, *Le Cavalerice François*, Paris, 1646.

Burckhardt (Jacob), *The Civilization of the Renaissance in Italy*, George Allen & Unwin Ltd., London, Edition of 1955.

Caprilli (Federico) Captain, articles in *Rivista di Cavalleria*, Italy, 1901.

Castellamonte (Amedeo) di, *La Venaria Reale*, Torino, 1674.

Cavendish (William), Duke of Newcastle, *A General System of Horsemanship*, London, 1743.

Chamberlin (Harry D.) Colonel, *Riding and Schooling Horses*, The Derrydale Press, New York, 1933.
Training Hunters, Jumpers and Hacks, The Derrydale Press, New York, 1937.

Decarpentry, General, *The Spanish Riding School in Vienna*, translated by E. Schmit-Jensen, Rennes, 1947.
Equitation Académique, Editions Henri, Paris, 1949.

Dillon (Jane Marshall), *School for Young Riders*, D. Van Nostrand Co., New York, 1958.

Dupaty de Clam (Mercier), *La Science et l'Art de l'Equitation*, Paris, 1776.

Edward, second Duke of York, *The Master of Game* (written c. 1410), Duffield & Co., New York, 1909.

Eisenberg, Baron d', *Description du Manège Moderne*, London, 1738.

Encyclopaedia Britannica, 14th edition, article on "Cavalry."

Endrödy (A. L.) d', Lt. Col., *Give Your Horse a Chance*, J. A. Allen & Co., London, 1959.

L'Eperon, a periodical, Paris, 1961.

Fiaschi (Cesare), *Trattato dell Imbrigliare*, Venice, 1613.

Fillis (James), *Principes de Dressage et d'Equitation*, Ernest Flammarion, Paris, 1890.
Breaking and Riding, 2nd edition, Hurst & Blackett, Ltd., London, 1911.
Journal de Dressage, Ernest Flammarion, Paris, 1903.
Réglement pour le Dressage du Cheval d'Armes (translation from the Russian by J. Fillis), Ernest Flammarion, Paris, 1914.

Fleitmann (Lida L.), *Comments on Hacks and Hunters*, Charles Scribner's Sons, New York, 1921.

Fouquet (Samuel) Sieur de Beaurepere, *Traitté des Emboucheures*, Paris, 1663.

Gerhardt (A.) Captain, *Dressage et la Conduite du Cheval de Guerre*, Paris, 1862.

Goubaux (Armand) and Barrier (Gustave), *The Exterior of the Horse*, J. B. Lippincott Co., Philadelphia, 1892.

Grisone (Federico), *Gli Ordini di Cavalcare*, in German translation *Kunstlicher Bericht*, 1608.

Guérinière (François), de la, *Ecole de Cavalerie*, Paris, 1733.

Hayes (M. Horace), *Among Horses in Russia*, London, 1900.

Hislop (John), *Steeplechasing*, E. P. Dutton & Co., New York, n.d.

Hope (C. R. G.) Lt. Col., editorials in the *Light Horse*, a periodical, London, 1961.

Hope (Sir William), *The Complete Horseman*, London, 1717.

Information Hippique, a periodical, Paris, 1961.

Jousseaume (André), Colonel, *Dressage*, Fer à Cheval, Paris, 1950.

Lawrence (John), *History of the Horse*, Philadelphia, 1830.

Löhneisen (Georg Engelhard) von, *Hof-Kriegs-und Reit-Schul*, Nürnberg, 1729.

Margaret, Duchess of Newcastle, *The Life of the Thrice Noble, High and Puissant Prince William Cavendish, Duke of Newcastle*, George Routledge and Sons, Ltd., London, n.d.

Masefield (John), *Reynard the Fox*, William Heinemann Ltd., London, 1932.

McTaggart (M. F.) Lt. Col., *Mount and Man*, Country Life Ltd., London, 1925.

Melfort (Drummond) Count, *Traité sur la Cavalerie*, Paris, 1776.

Mennessier de la Lance (Général), *Essai de Bibliographie Hippique*, Lucien Dorbon, Paris, 1915–1917–1921.

Müseler (W.), *Riding Logic*, Methuen & Co., London, 1937.

Muybridge (Eadweard), *Animals in Motion*, Chapman & Hall, Ltd., London, 1925.

Orgeix, The Chevalier d', *Horse in the Blood*, Nicholas Kaye, London, 1951.

Pembroke (Henry Herbert) Earl of, *A Method of Breaking Horses and Teaching Soldiers to Ride, Designed for the Use of the Army*, London, 1762.

297

Picard (L.) Capitaine, *Origines de l'Ecole de Cavalerie*, Saumur, 1890.

Pluvinel (Antoine) de, *Maneige Royal*, Paris, 1623.

Podhajsky (A.) Colonel, *The Spanish Riding Academy*, Brüder Rosen-baum, Vienna, 1947.

René, King of Anjou, *On Tournaments*, written c. 1465. *Le Livre des Tournois du Roi René*, Verve, Paris, 1946.

Ridgeway (William), *The Origin and Influence of the Thoroughbred Horse*, University Press, Cambridge, 1905.

Romaszkan (Gregor) von, *Reiter und Pferd in Gleichgewicht*, Albert Müller Verlag, Zurich, 1940.

Ruse (Lavrent), or Rusio (Lorenzo), *La Mareschalerie*, first printed c. 1486, last edition, Paris, 1610.

Russian Cavalry Messenger (Vestnic Russkoy Konnitzi), a periodical, St. Petersburg, 1906, 1907, 1908.

Santini (Piero) Captain, *Riding Reflections*, The Derrydale Press, New York, 1932.

The Forward Impulse, Huntington Press, New York, 1936.

Schmit-Jensen (E.), *Equestrian Olympic Games*, Welbecson Press, Ltd., London, 1948.

Seunig (Waldemar), *Horsemanship*, Doubleday & Company, New York, 1956.

Sévy (L.) de, *The Gaits, The Horseman*, The Cavalry School, Fort Riley, Kansas, 1930.

Sind (J. B.) Baron de, *L'Art du Manège*, Cologne, 1762.

Souza (Baretto) Count de, *Principles of Equitation*, E. P. Dutton, New York, 1922.

Swire (John), *Anglo-French Horsemanship*, Vinton & Co., London, 1920.

Trevelyan (G. M.), *Illustrated English Social History*, Longmans, Green and Co., London, 1952.

Wells (H. G.), *The Outline of History*, The Macmillan Company, New York, 1921.

Whyte-Melville (G. J.), *Riding Recollections*, London, 1878.

Williams (C. H. C.), *Professor Williams' New System*, Claremont, N. H., 1878.

Xenophon, *On Horsemanship*, written in the 4th century B.C, English Edit., 1802.

Anabasis, 4th century B.C.

Index

Adams, John, 90, 95–99, 187, 217–218
Affiliated National Riding Commission (ANRC), 221
"All-around horse," 59
Alberti, Leone Battista, 20
Amateur, 291
Anatomy of the horse, 98
Anderson, Edward I., 233
André, 273
Anshutz, Ottomar, 133, 136, 144
"Artificial" vs. "natural," 119, 120, 121, 122, 180
Astley, Philip, 100–101, 103
Aure, Count d', 93–94, 107–108, 111–113, 118–120, 122, 123, 176
"Average rider," 291

Balance of the horse, 99, 144, 145, 146, 147, 163, 164, 165, 168, 169, 171, 180, 181, 186, 242, 275, 276, 282, 283, 284
"Balanced seat," 234
Ballet (horse), 65, 66, 67, 68
Ballotade, 29, 54, 63, 81, 96
Baranowski, Zdzislaw, 286
Baroque era, 28–29, 30, 62–65, 99
Baucher, François, 22, 107, 108, 109, 110, 111, 113–118, 119, 123, 127, 163–164, 169–170

Benoist-Gironière, Commandant Yves, 272, 273
Bits (Renaissance), 54
Blundevill, Thomas, 52, 72, 73, 74
Bobinsky, Colonel Ivan, 135, 137, 282
Bohan, Baron de, 99, 187
Boisdeffre, Chevalier de, 93
Boots and Saddles Riding School, 220, 221, 230, 248
Braced back, 270, 271, 283
Broue, Solomon de la, 37, 38, 40, 76–77, 87, 88
Bussigny, de, 233

Canter (gallop) departure, 119–120
Canter on three legs, 157
Canter rearward, 159
Caprilli, Captain Federico, 10, 11, 98, 99, 119, 150, 152, 165, 174, 175–187, 193, 202, 203, 244, 245, 246, 252, 262, 285
Capriole, 10, 29, 54, 63, 81, 96, 100
Carousel, 61, 63, 65–67
Chamberlin, General H., 120, 235, 239–248, 262, 282, 286
Circles, 243
Circus, 22, 26, 100, 103, 156–157, 158, 160–161

Index

Classification of show jumpers (modern), 287, 288

Collected gaits (*see also* Rassembler), 21, 118, 119, 120, 121, 123, 145, 163, 167, 171, 242, 243, 244, 275, 276

Combined Training Test, 59

Conservatism in riding, 92, 102, 108, 129, 222, 225, 226, 267, 269, 270, 278, 289, 290, 291

Cossacks, 129, 171, 172, 173, 187

Courbette, 42, 55, 81, 95, 160, 166

Crécy and Poitiers (battles of), 56

Crescenzi, Petrus, 20

Cross-country riding, 9, 10, 180, 181, 184, 185, 187–191, 237, 246

Croupade, 29, 81, 100, 158

Cruelty to horses, 71–74, 102, 232

Decarpentry, General, 271

Dillon, Jane Marshall, 250

Dismounted work (in hand), 116, 166, 167, 244

Dressage, 9, 10, 14, 68, 76, 96, 101–102, 161, 162, 165, 167, 211, 225, 226, 233, 247, 255–260, 266, 268–270, 271, 272, 273, 274, 275, 276, 284, 285

Dupaty de Clam, Mercier, 92, 93

Edward, second duke of York, 20

Eisenberg, Baron d', 34–35

Endrödy, Lt. Col. A. L. d', 276, 280, 281

England, 22, 32, 33, 45, 68, 69, 70, 85–87, 100, 102, 119, 137–139, 140, 148, 150, 151, 177–178, 209, 211, 284–286

Equestrian vocabulary, 69

False canter, 244

Fillis, James, 8, 22, 112, 116–117, 127, 155–174, 176, 178, 257

Fleitmann, Lida L., 211, 218–219

Forward Riding, 10, 179–180, 181–191, 226, 262

Forward Schooling, 100, 112, 128, 275, 276

Forward Seat, 97–99, 173, 185–186, 187, 224, 228, 233, 234, 235, 236, 237, 241, 248–249, 267, 278, 279, 280–282

France, 38, 44, 93, 94, 108–109, 230, 256, 257, 259

Frederick the Great, 83, 89–90

Froissart, 60–61

Gallop to the rear, 159

Gerhardt, Captain A., 146, 147

Germany, 119, 148, 150, 152, 153, 256, 257, 258, 259, 263–264, 270–271, 276–282, 284, 285

Grisone, Federico, 9, 21, 25–26, 37, 38, 39, 40, 71, 72, 74–76

Guérinière, François de la, 35, 37, 44–45, 65, 77–88, 90, 91, 94, 99, 124, 134–135

Hastings, Mr., 32–33

Hayes, Captain M. Horace, 158, 160–161

High School, 16, 21, 22, 38, 54, 55, 56, 60, 61, 74, 76, 82, 83, 85, 95, 100, 102, 103, 116, 120, 152–153, 156, 158, 160–161, 163, 164, 165, 166, 170, 198, 201, 255, 256–257, 258, 270, 277–278

Hope, Lt. Colonel C. R. G., 265–266

Hope, Sir William, 31–32, 36, 38–39, 47–48

Horse shows, 6–8, 61, 212–215, 222–223, 238–239

Hotte, General A. l', 111, 149–150, 270

Humane approach to horses, 200–202

Hunting and hunters, 5, 20, 30, 31, 85–87, 96–98, 151, 214, 215, 228

Innovations in Dressage, 114
International competitions, 251–266, 267
Italy, 38–40, 61, 62, 192, 193, 256, 257

Jousseaume, Colonel André, 268–270
Jousting, 59–61
Judging shows, 213–214, 258–260
Jumping, 3, 5–9, 10, 13, 14, 22, 86, 87, 88, 96, 175–178, 181, 183–184, 188, 190–191, 198, 199, 200, 201–202, 213, 215, 219, 228, 233, 245, 252–254, 261–265, 267, 272–273
Junior riding, 199, 212–217, 289

Kikkulis, 14
Knights in armor, 50–56
Kournakoff, Captain Sergei, 220, 248, 249
Krassnoff, General P., 187–191, 233, 244

Lippizaner, 170
Littauer, V. S., 4, 11, 22, 83–84, 168, 212, 220, 239, 241, 243, 245, 246, 247–248, 273, 285, 286
Locomotion of the horse, 99, 100, 141–147, 171, 248–249
Löhneisen, E. von, 64, 66–67

Manege horses and manege riding, 89, 90, 92, 95–96, 139, 171
Manuscripts, 26, 27
Masefield, John, 218
Melfort, Count Drummond de, 91–92, 96
Mennessier de la Lance, 44, 112–113, 118
Mézair, 79–80
Middle Ages, 19–21, 38, 50–54, 59
Military riding, 21–22, 50–56, 89–95, 100, 102, 115, 118, 133–137, 158–160, 164, 165–168, 187–192, 278, 289, 292–293
Mongolia, 174
Müseler, Major W., 282–283
Muybridge, Eadweard, 100, 141–142, 144
McTaggart, Lt. Colonel M. F., 219, 233, 234

Napoleonic Wars, 21, 93–94, 124–126
"Natural" vs. "artificial," 119–122, 171, 180
Natural movements, 92, 99, 118–122, 242, 243, 244, 246
Neapolitan school, 38–40
Newcastle, Duke of, 33, 37, 45–49, 58, 99, 115
"Noble" (epithet), 49

Obstacles, 87–88, 252–253
Olympic Games, 251–260, 285
Ordinary gaits, 164–165, 242
Organization of Equestrian Sport, 287–289, 291–293
Orgeix, Chevalier d', 252

Paderno, Cesare, 184
Parade horses, 56, 92, 95
Passage, 26, 78, 79, 83, 95, 121, 160, 257, 258
Pembroke, Henry, Earl of, 90–91, 96, 116, 166
Pesade, 79, 83, 100, 160
Phillips, Edward, 63
Photography, 100, 133, 136, 141–142, 144, 202–210
Physical education, 219, 221–222
Piaffe, 79, 82, 160, 257
Picard, Captain L., 116, 123
Pillars, 41, 43, 77, 91, 170
Pinerolo (Italian Cavalry School), 178, 187, 191, 192, 233
Pirouette, 83, 160, 257

Pluvinel, Antoine de, 33, 37, 38, 40–44, 77, 115
Podhajsky, Colonel A., 44, 55
Pony Club, 215, 265, 266
Posting trot, 122–123
Professionals, 254, 257

Quintain, 61, 62

Ramener, 146, 163, 164, 165, 246–247
Rassembler (*see also* Collected gaits), 146, 163
Renaissance, 27, 28, 38, 61, 62, 68, 101, 193
René, King of Anjou, 21
Ridgeway, W., 69, 85
Riding teachers in the U.S.A., 4, 10–11, 212–215, 219–223, 289, 290, 292
Rodzianko, Colonel Paul, 233
Romaszkan, Gregor von, 283–284
Rome (ancient), 19
Rusio, Lorenzo, 20
Russia, 132–137, 154, 158, 159, 162, 167–171, 191–192, 257

Saint-Phalle, Captain, 149
Santini, Major Piero, 179, 235–239, 276–277, 286
Saumur Cavalry School, 68, 111, 112, 152, 239, 255
Scientific approach to equitation, 102, 128, 140–148, 200–202, 248–249
Seat-bones (control by the), 271, 280, 281, 283
Seunig, Waldemar, 271, 276–280
Sévy, L. de, 273
Shoulder-in, 82, 91, 92, 247, 268, 269
Side-saddle, 218, 219
Sind, Baron de, 95
Sloan, Tod, 187

Social background, 3–4, 12, 26–28, 29, 30–36, 61–68, 89, 107–109, 123–124, 129–134, 137–138, 192–193, 197–211
Souza, Count Baretto de, 228–230, 233
Spanish Riding School, 66, 67, 68, 152–153, 158, 170, 255–256
Specialization of horse's work, 58–60, 95
Steeplechase, 6
Step-and-jump, 81
Sweden, 257

Terre-à-Terre, 79
Theory of riding, 223–226, 227–228, 290
Thiroux, Charles, 44
Three-Day Event, 8, 198, 259–260, 274–275, 281
Tilt, 59, 60
Tor di Quinto (Italian Cavalry School), 178, 179, 191, 199, 239
Tournaments, 59, 60
Tsourikoff, Lt. General, 168–169

United States, 205–226, 228–250
United States Army Horse Show Team, 239
United States Cavalry School, 230, 248, 273
United States Equestrian Team, 253, 263, 265, 276

Victorianism, 229
Volte, 79, 83

Williams, "Professor," 231–232
Winkler, Hans, 263–264
Women (girls) in riding, 216–219
Working hunter, 216

Xenophon, 14–19